Content Distribution for Mobile Internet:
A Cloud-based Approach

Zhenhua Li • Yafei Dai • Guihai Chen • Yunhao Liu

Content Distribution for Mobile Internet: A Cloud-based Approach

Second Edition

 Springer

Zhenhua Li (iD)
Tsinghua University
Beijing, Beijing, China

Guihai Chen
Shanghai Jiao Tong University
Shanghai, Shanghai, China

Yafei Dai
Peking University
Beijing, Beijing, China

Yunhao Liu
Tsinghua University
Beijing, Beijing, China

ISBN 978-981-19-6984-3   ISBN 978-981-19-6982-9   (eBook)
https://doi.org/10.1007/978-981-19-6982-9

This Springer imprint is published by the registered company Springer Nature Singapore Pte Ltd.
The registered company address is: 152 Beach Road, #21-01/04 Gateway East, Singapore 189721,
Singapore

Preface

Content distribution (also known as *content delivery*) is among the most fundamental functions of the Internet, i.e., distributing *digital content* from one *node* to another node or multiple nodes. Here digital content can be in the form of a web page, an image, software, audio, video, big data, etc.; a node can be a large server cluster, a personal computer, a smartphone, a small sensor, a tiny RFID (radio frequency identification device) tag, and so on.

Typical content distribution paradigms include Client/Server (C/S) over TCP/IP connections, Content Delivery Network (CDN) like Akamai and ChinaCache, Peer-to-Peer (P2P) like BitTorrent and eMule, Super Node Relay (SNR) like KaZaa and Skype, and Peering via Internet eXchange (PIX) that is adopted by many Internet Service Providers (ISPs) to overcome the traditional Transit-Stub architecture's shortcomings. They each have specific merits and drawbacks, targeting distinct application scenarios such as file download, media streaming, real-time interaction, and AR/VR.

Since Amazon's launch of Elastic Compute Cloud (EC2) in 2006 and Apple's release of iPhone in 2007, Internet content distribution has illustrated a strong trend of *polarization*. On one hand, great fortune has been invested by those "content hypergiants" (e.g., Google and Netflix) in building heavyweight and integrated data centers across the world, in order to achieve the economies of scale and the high flexibility/efficiency of content distribution. On the other hand, end-user devices have become increasingly lightweight, mobile, and heterogeneous, thus posing rigorous and volatile requirements on the bandwidth, latency, traffic usage, energy consumption, service reliability, and security/privacy of content distribution.

Through comprehensive real-world measurements, unfortunately, we observe that existing content distribution techniques often exhibit undesirable or even poor performance under the above-described new settings. Motivated by the trend of "heavy-cloud vs. light-end," this book is dedicated to uncovering the root causes of today's mobile networking problems and designing innovative cloud-based solutions to practically address such problems, in terms of four key metrics: Speed (Part II), Cost (Part III), Reliability (Part IV), and Security (Part V).

Our work included in this book has led to not only academic papers published in prestigious conferences like SIGCOMM, NSDI, MobiCom, and MobiSys, but also actual effect on industrial systems such as Xiaomi Mobile, MIUI OS, Tencent App Store, Baidu PhoneGuard, UUTest.cn, and WiFi.com. In addition, the included work has won several academic awards, e.g., Best Student Paper Award of the ACM MMSys 2017 conference, Excellent Paper Award of the Tsinghua Science and Technology 2019 journal, Best Demo Award of the ACM MobiCom 2019 conference, and Best Student Paper Award of the ACM SIGCOMM 2021 conference (the first time Asian scholars get this award from SIGCOMM).

In this book, we provide a series of insightful measurement findings and firsthand system experiences to researchers and practitioners working on mobile Internet and cloud computing/storage. Additionally, we have released as much code and data used in our work as possible to benefit the community. Should you have any questions or suggestions, please contact the four authors (in particular the first author) via *lizhenhua1983@gmail.com*, *dyf@pku.edu.cn*, *gchen@cs.sjtu.edu.cn*, and *yunhaoliu@gmail.com*.

Finally, we sincerely appreciate the professional assistance from Celine Chang, Jingying Chen, Lenold Esithor, Christina Fehling, Ramesh Marimuthu, and Ellen Seo at Springer Press. Also, we would like to thank the following people for their contributions to this book: Sen Bai, Jian Chen, Qi Chen, Yan Chen, Fan Dang, Di Gao, Liangyi Gong, Taeho Jung, Xiangyang Li, Yang Li, Hao Lin, Zhen Lu, Kebin Liu, Wei Liu, Yao Liu, Rui Miao, Chen Qian, Feng Qian, Zhiyun Qian, Weiwei Wang, Xianlong Wang, Yinlong Wang, Christo Wilson, Ao Xiao, Xianlong Xin, Tianyin Xu, Jinyu Yang, Xinlei Yang, Ennan Zhai, Lan Zhang, Ben Zhao, and Xin Zhong. In particular, we are grateful for Yannan Zheng's helping typeset several chapters of this book.

Beijing, China   Zhenhua Li
Beijing, China   Yafei Dai
Shanghai, China   Guihai Chen
Beijing, China   Yunhao Liu
December 2021

Acknowledgments

This work is supported in part by the National Key R&D Program of China under grant 2022YFB4500703; the National Natural Science Foundation of China (NSFC) under grants 61902211 and 62202266; and Microsoft Research Asia.

Contents

About the Authors

Zhenhua Li is an associate professor at the School of Software, Tsinghua University. He obtained his PhD degree in Computer Science from Peking University in 2013. His research interests are chiefly in mobile networking, cloud computing, and big data analysis. His work focuses on understanding realistic problems in today's large-scale mobile (cellular, WiFi, and IoT) systems, and on developing innovative solutions to practically address them. His research has produced not only academic papers published in prestigious conference proceedings like SIGCOMM, NSDI, MobiCom, and MobiSys, but also concrete effects on industrial systems such as Xiaomi Mobile, MIUI OS, Tencent App Store, Baidu PhoneGuard, and WiFi.com, benefiting hundreds of millions of mobile users.

Yafei Dai is a full professor at the School of Electronics Engineering and Computer Science (EECS), Peking University. Before joining Peking University, she held positions as a full professor, associate professor, and assistant professor at the Department of Computer Science and Technology, Harbin Institution of Technology (HIT) in China starting in 1987. She obtained PhD degree, MS degree, and BE degree from HIT in 1993, 1986, and 1982, respectively. Her research interests are mainly in distributed systems, storage systems, and social networks. She has published over 100 academic papers in competitive conference proceedings and journals.

Guihai Chen is a distinguished professor at the Department of Computer Science and Engineering, Shanghai Jiao Tong University. He earned his PhD degree in Computer Science from the University of Hong Kong in 1997 and has served as a visiting professor at Kyushu Institute of Technology in Japan, the University of Queensland in Australia, and Wayne State University in the USA. He has a wide range of research interests in parallel computing, wireless networks, peer-to-peer computing, high-performance computer architecture, and so on. He has published more than 200 papers in competitive conference proceedings and journals. He has won many honors and awards, in particular the First Prize of Natural Sciences by the Ministry of Education of China.

Yunhao Liu is a Changjiang professor and dean of Global Innovation Exchange at Tsinghua University. He received his PhD degree and MS degree in Computer Science from Michigan State University in 2003 and 2004, respectively, and his BS degree from the Automation Department of Tsinghua University in 1995. His research interests include distributed systems, wireless sensor networks/RFID, Internet of Things (IoT), etc. He has published over 300 papers in prestigious conference proceedings and journals, as well as two books: "Introduction to IoT" and "Location, Localization, and Localizability." He is currently the Editor-in-Chief of ACM Transactions on Sensor Networks and Communications of China Computer Federation. He is a fellow of the ACM and IEEE.

Acronyms

ABR	Adaptive bitrate streaming
AMH	Adaptive multi-homing
AP	Access point, or WiFi home router
ARF	Acceptance-rejection function
BCCH	Broadcast control channel
BTS	Bandwidth testing service
C/S	Client/Server content distribution
CCN	Content centric networking
CDN	Content distribution (delivery) network
CIS	Crucial interval sampling
CSP	Cloud services provider
DPDK	Data plane development kit
DSS	Data-driven server selection
DTN	Delay-tolerant networking
EBP	Elastic bandwidth probing
EC2	Elastic compute cloud
GFW	Great firewall
HLS	HTTP live streaming
ICN	Information centric networking
IoT	Internet of Things
IRB	Institutional review board
ISP	Internet service provider
IXP	Internet eXchange point
LAN	Local area network
LTE	Long term evolution
MVNO	Mobile virtual network operator
NDN	Named data networking
NIC	Network interface controller
ODR	Offline downloading redirector
P2P	Peer-to-peer content distribution
P2SP	Peer-to-server and Peer content distribution

PAC	Proxy auto-config
PIX	Peering via Internet eXchange
QoS	Quality of service
RAT	Radio access technology
RDMA	Remote direct memory access
RFID	Radio frequency identification device
RSS	Received signal strength
SDN	Software-defined networking
SNR	Super node relay
SPDK	Storage performance development kit
SUR	State update report
TIMP	Time-inhomogeneous Markov process
UHD	Ultra high definition
UIO	User-space I/O framework
VNO	Virtual network operator
WAN	Wide area network
WWW	World wide web, or "world wide wait"

Part I
Get Started

Chapter 1
Background and Overview

Abstract This chapter presents the background and overview of the book. First, we introduce the basic concept, the crucial design principle, and the brief history of Internet content distribution. Next, we illustrate the "heavy-cloud versus light-end" polarization of Internet content distribution under the novel settings of cloud computing and mobile Internet. Afterward, we review various frontier techniques that attempt to address current issues of Internet content distribution. At the end, we outline the entire book structure.

Keywords Content distribution · Mobile Internet · Cloud computing

1.1 Internet Content Distribution

Content distribution (a.k.a., *content delivery*) is among the most fundamental functions of the Internet, i.e., distributing *digital content* from one *node* to another node or multiple nodes. Here digital content can be in the form of a web page, an image, software, audio, video, big data, and so forth. A node can be a giant data center, a large server cluster, a home router, a personal computer, a tablet or a smartphone, a small sensor, or even a tiny RFID tag.

Since its birth in 1969 (known as ARPANET, then comprising only four nodes), the Internet has been featured by its *best-effort* content distribution. Different from the traditional Switched Telephone Network (STN) that guarantees the Quality of Service (QoS) for content distribution through link resource reservation along an end-to-end path, the Internet scarcely ever promises bounded QoS to its upper-layer applications for content distribution. Instead, somewhat like in the case of National Highway Network (NHN), the first and the most important design principle of Internet content distribution can be stated as *achieving high utilization while maintaining moderate fairness* or simply *balancing utilization and fairness*. In essence, the Internet is designed for the general public to provide mostly acceptable (and sometimes desirable) QoS, rather than for the privileged elite to offer ideal QoS.

Z. Li et al., *Content Distribution for Mobile Internet: A Cloud-based Approach*,
https://doi.org/10.1007/978-981-19-6982-9_1

3

Fig. 1.1 Client/Server (C/S)
content distribution through
TCP/IP connections

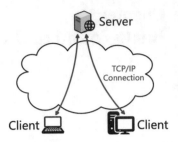

C/S and TCP/IP The commercial tidal wave of the Internet first rose at the Silicon Valley of the USA in 1990s, represented by several pioneering companies like Yahoo! and Netscape. At that time, digital content distributed over the Internet is mainly composed of web pages, images, documents, and emails. Because this content is limited in terms of type, quantity, and capacity (size), using the simplest Client/Server (C/S) paradigm, as illustrated in Fig. 1.1, to directly deliver content through TCP/IP connections can usually meet the requirements of Internet users.

The TCP/IP communication protocol is foundational to Internet content distribution, not only C/S but also the subsequent more advanced paradigms. While its concrete design is quite sophisticated (and thus we would not elaborate here), TCP/IP bears a fairly simple philosophy: achieving reliable, error-free transport-layer (a.k.a., flow-level) communication on top of the unreliable, best-effort IP layer (a.k.a., network-level) communication. Of course, this is at the cost of efficiency: TCP can hardly make full use of the available network transfer capacity, no matter in a Local Area Network (LAN) or a Wide Area Network (WAN). Notably, a major developer of TCP/IP is Vinton Cerf, known as one of the "Fathers of the Internet," the ACM Turing Award winner in 2004, and the vice president of Google since 2005.

CDN As the Internet became more ubiquitous and popular, its delivered digital content began to include large-size multimedia content, particularly videos. Meanwhile, the quantity of content underwent an exponential growth. Both issues led to severe congestions on the Internet when the most content was distributed in the abovementioned C/S manner. As a consequence, World Wide Web (WWW) gradually deteriorated into "World Wide Wait." Hence in 1995, Tim Berners-Lee, the inventor of WWW and the ACM Turing Award winner in 2016, posed a challenging question to his colleagues at the Massachusetts Institute of Technology: "Can we invent a fundamentally new and better way to deliver Internet content?"

Interestingly, the man who gave the first answer was just his office neighbor, Prof. Tom Leighton. Leighton's research team proposed the idea of Content Delivery Network (CDN) and founded the first CDN company called Akamai in 1998. CDN optimizes the performance of Internet content distribution by strategically deploying *edge servers* at multiple locations (often across multiple ISP networks), as depicted in Fig. 1.2. These edge servers cooperate with each other by replicating or migrating content according to content popularity and server load. An end user usually obtains

Fig. 1.2 Content Delivery Network (CDN) strategically deploys edge servers at multiple locations to accelerate the content delivery and reduce the original content server's burden

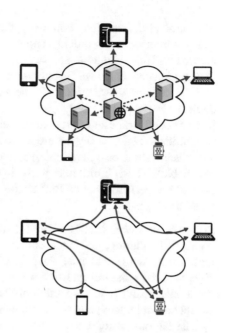

Fig. 1.3 Peer-to-Peer (P2P) data swarm directly delivers shared content among interested peers, i.e., end user devices that are interested in the same content

a copy of content from a nearby edge server, so that the content delivery speed is greatly enhanced and the load on the original data source is effectively reduced.

To date, CDN has been a widely used paradigm for accelerating Internet content distribution. Besides Akamai, representative CDN service providers include Limelight (founded in 2001), Level3 (founded in 1998), ChinaCache (founded in 1998), ChinaNetCenter (founded in 2000), and so on. Given the many choices, a content provider can simultaneously leverage multiple CDNs to mitigate the limitations of a single one. Here a representative case is Hulu's making use of three CDNs: Akamai, Limelight, and Level3 [1].

P2P Although CDN is widely used across the Internet, it is subject to both economical and technical limitations. CDN is a charged facility that only serves the content providers who have paid (typically popular websites like Apple and Netflix), rather than a public utility of the Internet. Moreover, even for those content providers who have paid, CDN is not able to accelerate the distribution of all their content, since the bandwidth, storage, and coverage of a CDN are constrained. Then the question is: can we simply leverage the resources of content receivers to accelerate Internet content distribution? More specifically, now that every end user device possesses a certain amount of bandwidth, storage, and coverage, can we organize the numerous end user devices into Peer-to-Peer (P2P) data swarms in which shared content is directly delivered among interested peers (as demonstrated in Fig. 1.3)?

In 1999, the Napster music sharing system offered a splendid answer to the above question—50 million users joined Napster in 6 months. Although Napster was then shut down soon for copyright reasons, it started the prosperity of

P2P content distribution. Following the step of Napster, a series of well-known P2P solutions/systems quickly appeared, such as BitTorrent (abbreviated as BT), eDonkey/eMule, Gnutella, and PPLive. They confirmed the huge power of content distribution concealed within end users.

P2P content distribution also bears its intrinsic limitations. First, end user devices do not work stably (i.e., highly dynamic)—they can go offline at any time. Second, end user devices are diverse in bandwidth, storage, and computation capabilities (i.e., highly heterogeneous). Third, the users and content in peer swarms are short of reputation assessment and quality authentication (i.e., highly unreliable). These limitations make it substantially more difficult to predict and control the performance of P2P content distribution, as compared to the C/S and CDN paradigms.

Super Node Relay (SNR) From the above we can clearly figure that for Internet content distribution, dedicated content servers are stable but relatively expensive and scarce, while end user devices ("peers") are unstable but inexpensive and abundant. So a natural question arises: is it possible to inherit the merits of both while addressing their respective limitations? If yes, Internet content distribution would be stable, inexpensive, and democratic.

The famous entrepreneur, Niklas Zennstrom, answered the question by rolling out two systems: KaZaa and Skype. Although they target different scenarios (KaZaa for file sharing while Skype for audio/video telephony), they share the same content distribution paradigm termed Super Node Relay (SNR) which attempts to attain a moderate balance between C/S and P2P. Specifically, SNR strives to find and utilize those relatively stable peers as "super nodes" to constitute the "backbone" for P2P content distribution; the remaining peers (called "ordinary nodes") connect to designated super nodes in a C/S-like manner. In this way, end user devices are better organized to enhance the QoS of P2P and meanwhile avoid the high expense of C/S.

Peering via Internet eXchange (PIX) Apart from the intrinsic dynamics and heterogeneities as described above, Internet content distribution suffers greatly from the "tromboning" phenomenon: as illustrated in Fig. 1.4, traffic on a network (Stub 1) destined to another network (Stub 3) in the same city can be routed to a different, remote city entirely (through Transit 1 and Transit 2 networks). Obviously, content distribution would then be slower and more expensive along the resulting circuitous path. This shortcoming stems from the traditional Transit-Stub [2] architecture of the Internet, where the vast majority of stub networks rely on the relatively few transit networks for inter-network content distribution.

In order to overcome the shortcoming, many stub networks make use of Peering via Internet eXchange (PIX), which aims to keep network traffic as local as possible by creating or leveraging Internet eXchange Points (IXPs). An IXP is the physical location and infrastructure where multiple networks directly exchange traffic without resorting to transit networks. With IXPs, circuitous routing can be effectively averted, and thus PIX provides faster connections between networks.

Fig. 1.4 Peering via Internet eXchange (PIX) has been widely adopted by many ISPs and content providers to overcome the traditional Transit-Stub architecture's shortcomings. Its improvement is usually larger than Multi-Homing in terms of both efficiency and cost

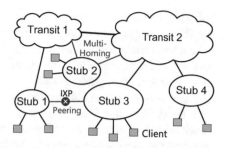

In this sense, IXPs are often considered the "glue" that attaches the Internet more closely [3].

The major drawback of PIX lies in its "heavy weight." If you (as a network operator) want to "peer" with another network, typically, you have to contact certain ISPs or the operators of another network for complicated and tedious peering negotiations, with regard to both technical and non-technical issues [4]. Besides, it is worth noting that Internet Peering is not a transitive relationship (in Fig. 1.4, if Stub 1 peers with Stub 3 and Stub 3 peers with Stub 4, we cannot say Stub 1 peers with Stub 4), but Internet Transit is.

1.2 Cloud Computing and Mobile Internet

Since Amazon's launch of Elastic Compute Cloud (EC2) in 2006 and Apple's release of iPhone in 2007 (as well as Google's release of Android in 2007), Internet content distribution has demonstrated a strong trend of *polarization*.

On the one hand, great fortune has been invested by "content hypergiants" (e.g., Google, Facebook, and Netflix) in building heavyweight and integrated data centers ("heavy-cloud") all over the world. Recent years have witnessed great successes of cloud computing (e.g., Amazon EC2, Google Cloud, Microsoft Azure, Apple iCloud, Aliyun, and OpenStack), cloud storage (e.g., Amazon S3, Dropbox, Google Drive, Microsoft OneDrive, and iCloud Drive), virtualization (e.g., VMware, VirtualBox, Xen, KVM, and Docker), big data processing (e.g., Apache Hadoop, Cassandra, and Spark), and so forth.

Based on these cloud platforms, today's content distribution systems can reliably host a huge amount of content, purchase the desired amount of ISP and CDN (peak) bandwidth, and adaptively migrate content and schedule bandwidth on demand, in order to achieve the economies of scale and the high flexibility/efficiency of content distribution. More recently, some cloud platforms provide lightweight Internet Peering services like Google Cloud Peering and Pexip Direct Peering, which we will elaborate in the next section.

On the other hand, end user devices have been growing more lightweight and mobile ("light-end"), as well as highly heterogeneous in terms of hardware, software, and network environments. The release of iPhone and iPad, together with the flourishing of Android Open Handset Alliance, has substantially extended the functions of mobile devices from traditional voice calls and text messages to almost all kinds of Internet applications. Besides, growth in mobile devices greatly outpaces that of personal computers (PCs).

Nevertheless, as revealed by our comprehensive real-world measurements (which will be described in the remaining parts of this book), most existing content distribution techniques are still geared for PCs at the moment [5, 6]; when applied to mobile scenarios, they often exhibit unsatisfactory or even poor performance. Actually, mobile devices have diverse sizes and resolutions of screens, support different formats of content and applications, and are quite limited in traffic quotas (when working with cellular connections), processing capabilities, and battery capacities. Thus, they pose rigorous and volatile requirements on the bandwidth, latency, traffic usage, energy consumption, service reliability, and security/privacy of content distribution.

Although "heavy-cloud" seems to lie on the other side of "light-end," it is not on the opposite of "light-end." In essence, the evolution of "heavy-cloud" is motivated in part by the requirements of "light-end," i.e., only with more heavy back-end clouds can front-end user devices become lighter. A representative case is that every new generation of iPhone is lighter, thinner, and yet more powerful than its predecessors, while relying more on iCloud services. In the era of cloud computing and mobile Internet, cloud platforms have to collaborate more tightly with end user devices, and thus the gap between Internet content and mobile devices can be better filled. As a result, in this book we wish to explore, investigate, and practice a variety of content distribution techniques for mobile Internet in a cloud-based approach.

1.3 Frontier Techniques

In recent years, various frontier techniques for Internet content distribution have emerged in both academia and industry. Below we first review the representative ones briefly and then discuss their relationships with our focus in this book, i.e., cloud-based content distribution for mobile Internet.

BBR Congestion Control TCP is crucial to Internet content distribution, while congestion control is crucial to TCP. Congestion control algorithms determine how fast to send data for every networked device, so that the transmission capacity of the Internet can be highly utilized without causing traffic congestion, i.e., to balance efficiency and fairness. Since the late 1980s, the Internet has been using loss-based congestion control algorithms (e.g., CUBIC [7]) which take packet loss as the major indicator of traffic congestion and sharply decrease (e.g., halve) the data sending rate upon packet loss. This worked well for low-bandwidth networks (e.g., the Internet in its early stage) whose switches and routers have "shallow" buffers, because shallow buffers would discard excess packets when data were being sent too fast.

Nevertheless, loss-based congestion control algorithms are not suited to today's diverse networks. As for networked devices that have deep buffers, such algorithms are rather lagging because traffic congestion happens before packet loss, thus leading to the notorious "bufferbloat" phenomenon. In contrast, as for networked devices that have shallow buffers, such algorithms are overly sensitive because packet loss often stems from transient traffic bursts (even when the network is mostly idle), thus leading to significant under-utilization of the network capacity.

To address these problems, Google developed the novel BBR (Bottleneck Bandwidth and Round-trip propagation time) congestion control algorithm [8], which strives to accurately identify and rapidly respond to actual network congestions. For a given network connection, BBR constantly measures its data delivery rate and round-trip time to probe its (almost) real-time available capacity. Thereby, BBR can properly control how fast to send data (termed "pacing"). Google reported considerable throughput and latency improvements by applying BBR to Google.com and YouTube network.

Detour Routing   Apart from traffic congestion, Internet content distribution also suffers from the pervasive *triangular inequality violation* phenomenon. As depicted in Fig. 1.5, suppose we want to deliver a file f from node A to node B over the Internet, and the shortest hop path from A to B is *path1*. Theoretically, delivering f along *path1* should be the fastest. But in practice, because today's Internet is complicated by many artificial factors (e.g., the ISP barriers demonstrated in Fig. 1.4), it may be faster if we select an appropriate intermediate node C to forward f from node A (along *path2*) to node B (along *path3*). This is referred to as "detour routing," where the sum of two sides (*path2* + *path3*) of a triangle is smaller than the third (*path1*) in terms of routing latency. Representative implementations include "offline downloading" [9] and quality improving for online gaming [10].

MultiPath TCP (MPTCP)   While judicious congestion control can make good use of a given network connection and detour routing can yield a better network connection, sometimes we need multiple network connections to guarantee or substantially enhance the end-to-end performance. Among such efforts, MPTCP is a practical representative that has been implemented in the Linux kernel, FreeBSD, iOS, and macOS. In March 2020, the Internet Engineering Task Force (IETF) released MPTCP specification v1.0 in its Request For Comments (RFCs) document 8684.

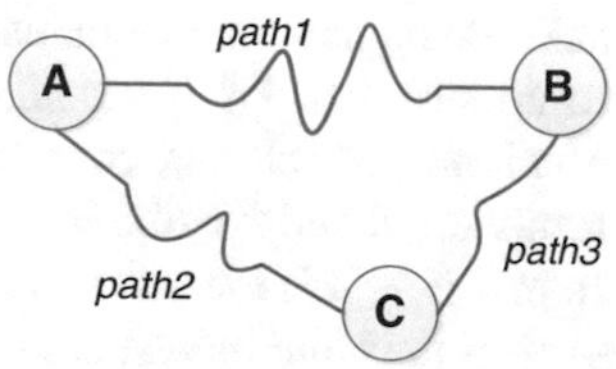

Fig. 1.5 Triangle inequality violation on the Internet, i.e., *path2* + *path3* < *path1* in terms of routing latency

MPTCP is very helpful in the context of mobile and wireless networks, particularly cellular networks with high mobility. This is quite understandable: IP connections (termed "subflows") can be flexibly set up or terminated as the user device moves in or out of certain wireless coverage, without disrupting the end-to-end TCP connection as a whole. Besides, MPTCP is designed to be backward compatible with regular TCP, so in theory it can support any upper-layer applications transparently.

Inevitably, MPTCP brings several side effects to Internet content distribution. First, it is more complex than regular TCP and requires OS support from end user devices. Second, it incurs more network and computation overhead, thus aggravating traffic congestion. Third, some special upper-layer applications do not work (well) on top of MPTCP, such as SSL decryption and malware scanning, because of the cross-path data fragmentation caused by multipath routing.

SPDY and HTTP/2 For bandwidth-sensitive applications like video telephony, using MPTCP is an intuitive optimization for higher throughput at the cost of more network and computation overhead. In contrast, for latency-sensitive applications like small-size web page loading, it is wiser to go in the reverse direction, i.e., to integrate multiple TCP connections (with the same origin and destination) into a single connection. Oftentimes, this can not only accelerate web content distribution by avoiding the repeated procedures of TCP connection setup but also save the traffic usage by compressing, multiplexing, and prioritizing the transfer of web page resources. In practice, this was fulfilled by Google's SPDY (pronounced as "speedy") session protocol, which additionally enforced the use of SSL/TLS encryption and supported web servers' actively pushing content to clients. As a result, SPDY manifested significant improvements over the traditional HTTP/1.x protocols.

HTTP/1.x is known to bear a variety of shortcomings especially for the modern Internet. Based on SPDY's comprehensive explorations and solid evaluations, the HTTP Working Group (also known as httpbis, where "bis" means twice) at the IETF developed HTTP/2, which inherited the major merits of SPDY and added several new features like request pipelining and fixed Huffman code-based header compression. After HTTP/2's standardization, SPDY was deprecated in favor of HTTP/2; as of 2021, no modern web browser still supports SPDY.

QUIC and HTTP/3 The aforementioned frontier techniques, including BBR congestion control, MPTCP, SPDY and HTTP/2, each improve the performance of Internet content distribution, but all work on top of TCP which is subject to threefold intrinsic limitations: (1) time-consuming process for connection setup, i.e., three-way handshaking, (2) trading throughput for reliability via a simplistic acknowledgement mechanism, and (3) OS kernel-layer implementation opaque to upper-layer applications. Consequently, in order to fundamentally enhance the efficiency of Internet content distribution, one needs to replace TCP with a more lightweight and flexible transport protocol, where UDP seems to be the only choice. In practice, this idea was implemented by Google's QUIC (pronounced as "quick") project [11] and then standardized by the QUIC Working Group at the IETF.

QUIC is a user-space, encrypted transport protocol working on top of UDP. It is designed to provide most functions of TCP, TLS, and HTTP/2 and meanwhile outperform them in terms of efficiency and flexibility. The user-space implementation of QUIC gives application developers the freedom to customize and improve QUIC according to their specific requirements and environments. Most importantly, QUIC devises a cryptographic connection setup mechanism which requires only one-way or (in most times) zero-way handshake, thus substantially reducing the setup delay. It has been globally deployed by Google to enhance the QoS of Chrome and YouTube and will become the basis of HTTP/3 in the future.

DASH and ABR Despite the continuous improvement on HTTP(S) by Google and the IETF, HTTP(S) was originally designed for serving small-size web page loads rather than media streaming. However, due to its enormous popularity and convenience, it has been used for video/audio streaming in practice. To make HTTP(S) more suitable for media streaming, the Moving Picture Experts Group (MPEG) developed the Dynamic Adaptive Streaming over HTTP (DASH)[1] technique to enable web-based adaptive bitrate (ABR) streaming. Hence, DASH is also known as MPEG-DASH.

At the server side, DASH splits the media content into a sequence of small segments, each containing a short interval (typically tens to hundreds of seconds) of playback time for the content. Moreover, the content is encoded at a series of different bit rates (e.g., QCIF, CIF, VGA, and HD) to fit different network environments. Accordingly, the DASH client (e.g., dash.js) adaptively selects the segment that has an as high bit rate as possible and meanwhile can be downloaded in time for smooth playback, i.e., without causing stall or re-buffering events during the playback.

Private/Bundling BT and P2SP No matter how complicated and powerful, all the above-described frontier techniques basically conform to the centralized C/S paradigm (refer to Sect. 1.1). With regard to the decentralized P2P paradigm (also refer to Sect. 1.1), in recent years there have also emerged several innovative techniques. Below we introduce three of them.

It is known that P2P content distribution suffers from the high dynamics and heterogeneities of the participant peers [12]. To mitigate this, there came two beneficial extensions to the classical BitTorrent protocol: Private BitTorrent [13] and Bundling BitTorrent [14]. The former restricts BitTorrent's working within a more narrow, more homogeneous, and more active user group, e.g., the students in the same campus. By trading the user group coverage for the authentication of users and shared content, private BitTorrent can remarkably enhance the engagement of users, the quality of shared content, and the performance of content distribution. By bundling a number of related files into a single file, the latter motivates BitTorrent users to stay longer online and share more data with others. Hence, the whole

---

[1] DASH is called HTTP Live Streaming (HLS) by Apple and Smooth Streaming by Microsoft, respectively.

BitTorrent ecosystem can be boosted to a more healthy and prosperous status. Typically, bundling BitTorrent combines a number of episodes of a TV series into a single, large file. This simple yet useful idea has been adopted by numerous BitTorrent (and even eMule) websites.

The third innovation, termed Peer-to-Server & Peer (P2SP), is more generic and pervasive. It allows and directs users to retrieve data from both peer swarms and (relatively stable) content servers, so it is in fact the integration of P2P and C/S. Till now, P2SP has been adopted by plenty of media streaming systems, such as Spotify, PPLive, PPStream, UUSee, and Funshion. Of course, the implementation complexity of P2SP is higher than that of P2P or C/S; if not properly designed, P2SP can generate even worse performance with higher overhead. Furthermore, P2SP can be extended to Open-P2SP [15], which outperforms P2SP by enabling users to retrieve data across heterogeneous protocols and content providers. For example, a user can simultaneously download from a BitTorrent swarm, an eMule swarm, an HTTP server, and an RTSP server. Representative examples of Open-P2SP include Xunlei, QQXuanfeng, FlashGet, Orbit, and QVoD. Naturally, Open-P2SP is very complicated and difficult to implement, since it involves not only technical problems but also business/copyright issues.

WebRTC   The above three innovative P2P techniques generally work well for file sharing and on-demand media streaming, but not for live streaming or real-time communication due to the extremely high requirements on interaction latency. To address this problem in a pervasive and user-friendly manner, Google developed the Web Real-Time Communication (WebRTC) protocol/API based on the initial efforts of Global IP Solutions, an online video conferencing software company. WebRTC enables interactive audio/video streaming to work within web browsers and mobile apps through peer-to-peer communication and does not require the users to install web browser plugins or additional apps. To date, it has been supported by almost all the mainstream web browsers and a lot of mobile apps, and it has been standardized by the World Wide Web Consortium (W3C) and the IETF.

A widely known open-source implementation of WebRTC is available at webrtc.org, which includes the necessary or useful JavaScript components required for RTC, such as audio/video codecs (i.e., coding and decoding software), signal processing functions (e.g., bandwidth testing, noise suppression, and echo cancellation), connection management, communication security, and media transfer [16]. Media flows between WebRTC peers are usually transported via the unreliable UDP connection, so WebRTC app developers need to tradeoff between latency and QoS. Fortunately, as the emergence of QUIC, the use of WebRTC is expected to be simpler and more efficient.

Cloud or Direct Peering   In Sect. 1.1 we have mentioned that Internet Peering can provide faster connections between networks but is rather heavyweight due to the involved technical and non-technical issues. Consequently, it is usually limited to ISPs and Internet Hypergiants, not benefiting common companies and organizations which cannot invest a great deal in network optimization. To address this limitation, in the past few years, some cloud platforms have started to provide lightweight

Internet Peering services, such as Google Cloud Peering, Pexip Direct Peering, Everstream Direct Peering, AWS Direct Connect, and Azure ExpressRoute. It is not hard to infer that Internet Hypergiants implement such services by renting part of their Internet Peering capabilities to their customers.

As a matter of fact, cloud computing is largely reshaping today's Internet content distribution (especially in mobile scenarios) by not only direct peering but also cloud-based downloading, transcoding, graphics rendering, data deduplication, advertisement blocking, security checking, and so forth. This is the basic starting point of our research presented in this book.

1.4   Overview of the Book Structure

Motivated by the trend of "heavy-cloud vs. light-end," this book is dedicated to uncovering the root causes of today's mobile networking problems and designing innovative cloud-based solutions to practically address such problems. Besides theoretical and algorithmic contributions, our research pays special attention to its *real-world effect*. Our research stands on industrial production systems such as Xiaomi Mobile, MIUI OS, Tencent App Store, Baidu PhoneGuard, UUTest.cn, and WiFi.com. A series of useful takeaways and easy-to-follow experiences are provided to the researchers and developers working on mobile Internet and cloud computing/storage.

The remainder of this book is organized in five parts, which are further made up of nine chapters. Below we briefly overview each part and chapter.

In Part II *Metric 1 Speed: Bandwidth Is The First Concern* (including Chaps. 2 and 3), we discuss bandwidth, typically the first concern during Internet content distribution. We first investigate how to measure bandwidth for mobile Internet in a fast and lightweight manner [17] and then describe how to achieve high-bandwidth content delivery by means of "offline downloading" [9], in particular the cloud-based offline downloading [18, 19].

In Part III *Metric 2 Cost: Never Waste on Traffic Usage* (including Chaps. 4 and 5), we strive to make good use of cellular traffic for Android apps (and base carriers) with a cloud-based mobile proxy [6], as well as for virtual carriers (also known as Mobile Virtual Network Operators) who work on top of base carriers' infrastructures while offering cheaper or more flexible data plans [20, 21].

In Part IV *Metric 3 Reliability: Stay Connected At All Times* (including Chaps. 6 and 7), we make long-term efforts to maintain reliable Internet connections between mobile devices and base stations, as well as between "censored" users and legitimate services. First, we measure the nationwide cellular data connection failures in China and describe how we address them effectively [22]. Second, we provide an insider's view of China's Internet censorship and develop a legal avenue for accessing those blocked services [23].

In Part V *Metric 4 Security: Do Not Relax Our Vigilance* (including Chaps. 8 and 9), we concentrate on the security and privacy issues with regard to WiFi and

IoT (Internet of Things) devices. We not only unravel a wide variety of real-world WiFi security threats for numerous WiFi access points [24] but also recognize different kinds of realistic attacks on Linux-based commodity IoT devices with software honeypots deployed within public clouds [25].

In Part VI *Last Thoughts* (also the last chapter), we make the concluding remarks by discussing important emerging techniques and envisaging the possible future work.

References

1. Adhikari V, Guo Y, Hao F, Hilt V, Zhang ZL (2012) A tale of three CDNs: an active measurement study of Hulu and its CDNs. In: Proceedings of the 15th IEEE global internet symposium, pp 7–12
2. Zegura EW, Calvert KL, Bhattacharjee S (1996) How to model an internetwork. In: Proceedings of the 15th IEEE conference on computer communications (INFOCOM), pp 594–602
3. Netrality.com: Internet Exchanges – The glue that holds the internet together. https://netrality.com/data-centers/internet-exchanges-the-glue-that-holds-the-internet-together/
4. Norton WB (2011) The internet peering playbook: connecting to the core of the Internet. DrPeering Press, California
5. Li Z, Huang Y, Liu G, Wang F, Zhang ZL, Dai Y (2012) Cloud transcoder: bridging the format and resolution gap between internet videos and mobile devices. In: Proceedings of the 22nd SIGMM workshop on network and operating systems support for digital audio and video (NOSSDAV), pp 33–38
6. Li Z, Wang W, Xu T, Zhong X, Li XY, Liu Y, Wilson C, Zhao BY (2016) Exploring cross-application cellular traffic optimization with Baidu TrafficGuard. In: Proceedings of the 13th USENIX symposium on networked systems design and implementation (NSDI), pp 61–76
7. Ha S, Rhee I, Xu L (2008) CUBIC: a new TCP-friendly high-speed TCP variant. ACM SIGOPS Oper Syst Rev 42(5):64–74
8. Cardwell N, Cheng Y, Gunn CS, Yeganeh SH, Jacobson V (2017) BBR: congestion-based congestion control. Commun ACM 60(2):58–66
9. Li Z, Wilson C, Xu T, Liu Y, Lu Z, Wang Y (2015) Offline downloading in China: a comparative study. In: Proceedings of the 15th ACM internet measurement conference (IMC), pp 473–486
10. Ly C, Hsu C, Hefeeda M (2010) Improving online gaming quality using detour paths. In: Proceedings of the 18th ACM international conference on multimedia (ACM-MM), pp 55–64
11. Langley A, Riddoch A, Wilk A, Vicente A, et al (2017) The QUIC transport protocol: design and Internet-scale deployment. In: Proceedings of the ACM international conference on the applications, technologies, architectures, and protocols for computer communication (SIGCOMM), pp 183–196
12. Chen G, Li Z (2007) Peer-to-peer network: structure, application and design. Tsinghua University Press, Beijing
13. Liu Z, Dhungel P, Wu D, Zhang C, Ross K (2010) Understanding and improving incentives in private P2P communities. In: Proceedings of the 30th IEEE international conference on distributed computing systems (ICDCS), pp 610–621
14. Menasche DS, Rocha DA, Antonio A, Li B, Towsley D, Venkataramani A (2013) Content availability and bundling in swarming systems. IEEE/ACM Trans Netw 21(2):580–593
15. Li Z, Huang Y, Liu G, Wang F, Liu Y, Zhang ZL, Dai Y (2013) Challenges, designs and performances of large-scale Open-P2SP content distribution. IEEE Trans Parall Distrib Syst 24(11):2181–2191

16. Blum N, Lachapelle S, Alvestrand H (2021) WebRTC: real-time communication for the open web platform. Commun ACM 64(8):50–54
17. Yang X, Wang X, Li Z, Liu Y, Qian F, Gong L, Miao R, Xu T (2021) Fast and light bandwidth testing for Internet users. In: Proceedings of the 18th USENIX symposium on networked systems design and implementation (NSDI), pp 1011–1026
18. Huang Y, Li Z, Liu G, Dai Y (2011) Cloud download: using cloud utilities to achieve high-quality content distribution for unpopular videos. In: Proceedings of the 19th ACM international conference on multimedia (ACM-MM), pp 213–222
19. Li Z, Liu G, Ji Z, Zimmermann R (2015) Towards cost-effective cloud downloading with Tencent big data. J Comput Sci Technol 30(6):1163–1174
20. Xiao A, Liu Y, Li Y, Qian F, Li Z, Bai S, Liu Y, Xu T, Xin X (2019) An in-depth study of commercial MVNO: measurement and optimization. In: Proceedings of the 17th annual international conference on mobile systems, applications, and services (MobiSys), pp 457–468
21. Li Y, Zheng J, Li Z, Liu Y, Qian F, Bai S, Liu Y, Xin X (2020) Understanding the ecosystem and addressing the fundamental concerns of commercial MVNO. IEEE/ACM Trans Netw 28(3):1364–1377
22. Li Y, Lin H, Li Z, Liu Y, Qian F, Gong L, Xin X, Xu T (2021) A nationwide study on cellular reliability: measurement, analysis, and enhancements. In: Proceedings of the ACM SIGCOMM conference, pp 597–609
23. Lu Z, Li Z, Yang J, Xu T, Zhai E, Liu Y, Wilson C (2017) Accessing Google scholar under extreme internet censorship: a legal avenue. In: Proceedings of the 18th ACM/IFIP/USENIX middleware conference: industrial track, pp 8–14
24. Gao D, Lin H, Li Z, Qian F, Chen QA, Qian Z, Liu W, Gong L, Liu Y (2021) A nationwide census on WiFi security threats: prevalence, riskiness, and the economics. In: Proceedings of the 27th ACM annual international conference on mobile computing and networking (MobiCom), pp 242–255
25. Dang F, Li Z, Liu Y, Zhai E, Chen QA, Xu T, Chen Y, Yang J (2019) Understanding fileless attacks on Linux-based IoT devices with HoneyCloud. In: Proceedings of the 17th annual international conference on mobile systems, applications, and services (MobiSys), pp 482–493

Part II
Metric 1 Speed: Bandwidth Is the First

Chapter 2
Fast and Light Bandwidth Testing for Mobile Internet

Abstract Bandwidth testing measures the access bandwidth of end hosts, which is crucial to emerging Internet applications for network-aware content delivery. However, today's bandwidth testing services (BTSes) are slow and costly for mobile Internet users, especially 5G users. The inefficiency and high cost of BTSes root in their methodologies that use excessive temporal and spatial redundancies for combating noises in Internet measurement. This chapter presents FastBTS to make BTS fast and cheap while maintaining high accuracy. Its key idea is to accommodate and exploit the noise rather than repetitively and exhaustively suppress the impact of noise. This is achieved by a novel statistical sampling framework (termed *fuzzy rejection sampling*), based on elastic bandwidth probing and denoised sampling from high-fidelity windows. Our evaluation shows that with only 30 test servers, FastBTS achieves the same level of accuracy compared to the state-of-the-art BTS (SpeedTest.net) that deploys $\sim$12,000 servers. Most importantly, FastBTS makes bandwidth tests 5.6$\times$ faster and 10.7$\times$ more data-efficient.

Keywords Bandwidth testing · Bandwidth measurement · Fuzzy rejection sampling

2.1 Introduction

Access link bandwidth of Internet users commonly constitutes the bottleneck of Internet content delivery, especially for emerging applications such as AR/VR. In traditional residential broadband networks, the access bandwidth is largely stable and matches ISPs' service plans. In recent years, however, it becomes less transparent and more dynamic, driven by virtual network operators (VNOs), user mobility, and infrastructure dynamics [1].

To effectively measure the access bandwidth, bandwidth testing services (BTSes) have been widely developed and deployed. BTSes serve as a core component of many applications that conduct network-aware content delivery [2, 3]. BTSes' data are cited in government reports, trade press [4], and ISPs' advertisements [5]; they play a key role in ISP customers' decision-making [6]. During COVID-19, BTSes

© The Author(s), under exclusive license to Springer Nature Singapore Pte Ltd. 2023   19
Z. Li et al., *Content Distribution for Mobile Internet: A Cloud-based Approach*,
https://doi.org/10.1007/978-981-19-6982-9_2

are top "home networking tips" to support telework [7, 8]. The following lists a few common use cases of BTSes:

- VNO has been a popular operation model that resells network services from base carrier(s). The shared nature of VNOs and their complex interactions with the base carriers make it challenging to ensure service qualities [9–11]. Many ISPs and VNOs today either build their own BTSes [12] or recommend end users to use public BTSes. For example, SpeedTest.net, a popular BTS, serves more than 500M unique visitors per year [13].
- Wireless access is becoming ubiquitous, exhibiting heterogeneous and dynamic performance. To assist users to locate good coverage areas, cellular carriers offer "performance maps" [14], and several commercial products (e.g., WiFiMaster used by 800M mobile devices [3]) employ crowd-sourced measurements to probe bandwidth.
- Emerging bandwidth-hungry apps (e.g., UHD videos and VR/AR), together with bandwidth-fluctuating access networks (e.g., 5G), make BTSes an integral component of modern mobile platforms. For example, the newly released Android 11 provides 5G apps with a bandwidth estimation API that offers "a rough guide of the expected peak bandwidth for the first hop of the given transport [15]."

Most of today's BTSes work in three steps: (1) setup, (2) bandwidth probing, and (3) bandwidth estimation. During the setup process, the user client measures its latency to a number of candidate test servers and selects one or more servers with low latency. Then, it probes the available bandwidth by uploading and downloading large files to and from the test server(s) and records the measured throughput as samples. Finally, it estimates the overall downlink/uplink bandwidth.

The key challenge of BTSes is to deal with *noises* of Internet measurements incurred by congestion control, link sharing, etc. Spatially, the noise inflates as the distance increases between the user client and the test server. Temporally, the throughput samples may be constantly fluctuating over time—the shorter the test duration is, the severer the impact on throughput samples the noise can induce. An effective BTS needs to accurately and efficiently measure the access bandwidth from noisy throughput samples.

Today's BTSes are slow and costly. For example, a 5G bandwidth test using SpeedTest.net for a 1.15 Gbps downlink takes 15 seconds of time and incurs 1.94 GB of data usage on end users to achieve satisfying test accuracy. To deploy an effective BTS, hundreds to thousands of test servers are typically needed. Such a level of cost (both at the client and server sides) and long test duration prevent BTSes from being a foundational, ubiquitous Internet service for high-speed, metered networks. Based on our measurements and reverse engineering of 20 commercial BTSes (Sect. 2.2), we find that the inefficiency and cost of these BTSes fundamentally root in their methodology of relying on temporal and/or spatial redundancy to deal with noises:

- Temporally, most BTSes rely on a *flooding-based* bandwidth probing approach, which simply injects an excessive number of packets to ensure that the bottleneck link is saturated by test data rather than noise data. Also, their test processes often intentionally last for a long time to ensure the convergence of the probing algorithm.

- Spatially, many BTSes deploy dense, redundant test servers close to the probing client, in order to avoid "long-distance" noises. For example, FAST.com and SpeedTest.net deploy $\sim$1000 and $\sim$12,000 geo-distributed servers, respectively, while WiFiMaster controversially exploits a large Internet content provider's CDN server pool.

In this chapter, we present FastBTS to make BTS fast and cheap while maintaining high accuracy. Our key idea is to accommodate and exploit the noise through a novel statistical sampling framework, which eliminates the need for long test duration and exhaustive resource usage for suppressing the impact of noise. Our insight is that the workflow of BTS can be modeled as a process of *acceptance–rejection sampling* [16] (or *rejection sampling* for short). During a test, a sequence of throughput samples are generated by bandwidth probing and exhibit a measured distribution $P(x)$, where x denotes the throughput value of a sample. They are filtered by the bandwidth estimation algorithm, in the form of an acceptance–rejection function (ARF), which retains the accepted samples and discards the rejected samples to model the target distribution $T(x)$ for calculating the final test result.

The key challenge of FastBTS is that $T(x)$ cannot be known beforehand. Hence, we cannot apply traditional rejection sampling algorithm that assumes a $T(x)$ and uses it as an input. In practice, our extensive measurement results show that, while the noise samples are scattered across a wide throughput interval, the true samples tend to concentrate within a narrow throughput interval (termed as a *crucial interval*). Therefore, one can reasonably model $T(x)$ using the crucial interval, as long as $T(x)$ is persistently covered by $P(x)$. We name the above-described technique *fuzzy rejection sampling*.

FastBTS implements fuzzy rejection sampling with the architecture shown in Fig. 2.1. First, it narrows down $P(x)$ as the boundary of $T(x)$ to bootstrap $T(x)$ modeling. This is done by an elastic bandwidth probing (EBP) mechanism to tune the transport-layer data probing rate based on its deviation from the currently estimated bandwidth. Second, we design a crucial interval sampling (CIS) algorithm, acting as the ARF, to efficiently calculate the optimal crucial interval with throughput samples (i.e., performing denoised sampling from high-fidelity throughput windows). Also, the data-driven server selection (DSS) and adaptive multi-homing (AMH) mechanisms are used to establish multiple parallel connections with different test servers when necessary. DSS and AMH together can help saturate the access link, so that $T(x)$ can be accurately modeled in a short time, even when the access bandwidth exceeds the capability of each test server.

We have built FastBTS as an end-to-end BTS, consisting of the FastBTS app for clients, and a Linux kernel module for test servers. We deploy the FastBTS backend

Fig. 2.1 An architectural overview of FastBTS. The arrows show the workflows of a bandwidth test in FastBTS (Reprinted with permission from [17])

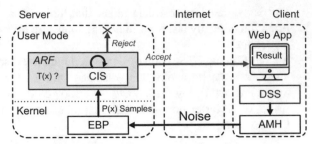

using 30 geo-distributed budget servers, and the FastBTS app on 100+ diverse client hosts. Our key evaluation results are:[1]

- On the same testbed, FastBTS yields 5–72% higher average accuracy than the other BTSes under diverse network scenarios (including 5G), while incurring 2.3–8.5× shorter test duration and 3.7–14.2× less data usage.
- Employing only 30 test servers, FastBTS achieves comparable accuracy to the production system of SpeedTest.net with ∼12,000 test servers, while incurring 5.6× shorter test duration and 10.7× less data usage.
- FastBTS flows incur little (<6%) interference to concurrent non-BTS flows—EBP only ramps up fast when the data rate is well below the available bandwidth; it slowly grows the data rate when it is about to hit the bottleneck bandwidth.

We have released all the source code at https://FastBTS.github.io and have built an online prototype system at http://FastBTS.thucloud.com.

2.2 Understanding State-of-the-Art BTSes

2.2.1 Methodology

We measure a BTS using the following metrics: (1) *Test accuracy* measures how well the result (r) reported by a BTS matches the ground-truth bandwidth R. We calculate the accuracy as $\frac{r}{R}$. In practice, we observe that all BTSes (including FastBTS) tend to underestimate the bottleneck bandwidth due to factors such as TCP slow start and congestion control, so the accuracy values are less than 1.0. (2) *Test duration* measures the time needed to perform a bandwidth test—from starting a bandwidth test to returning the test result. (3) *Data usage* measures the consumed network traffic for a test. This metric is of particular importance to metered LTE and 5G links.

---

[1] In this chapter, we focus on the downlink bandwidth test due to its importance to a typical Internet user compared to the uplink.

Obtaining Ground Truth Measuring test accuracy requires ground-truth data. However, it is challenging to know all the ground-truth bandwidths for large measurements. We use best possible estimations for different types of access links:

- *Wired LANs for in-lab experiments.* We regard the (known) physical link bandwidth, with the impact of (our injected) cross traffic properly considered, as the ground truth.
- *Commercial residential broadband and cloud networks.* We collect the bandwidth claimed by the ISPs or cloud service providers from the service contract, denoted as T_C. We then verify T_C by conducting long-lived bulk data transfers (average value denoted as T_B) before and after a bandwidth test. In more than 90% of our experiments, T_B and T_C match, with their difference being less than 5%; thus, we regard T_C as the ground truth. Otherwise, we choose to use T_B.
- *Cellular networks (LTE and 5G).* Due to a lack of T_C and the high dynamics of cellular links, we leverage the results provided by SpeedTest.net as a baseline reference. Being the state-of-the-art BTS that owns a massive number of ($\sim$12,000) test servers across the globe, SpeedTest.net's results are widely considered as a close approximation to the ground-truth bandwidth [18–23].

2.2.2 Analyzing Deployed BTSes

We study 20 deployed BTSes, including 18 widely used, web-based BTSes and 2 Android 11 BTS APIs.[2] We run the 20 BTSes on three different PCs and four different smartphones listed in Table 2.1 (WiFiMaster and Android APIs are only run on smartphones). To understand the implementation of these BTSes, we jointly analyze: (1) the network traffic (recorded during each test), (2) the client-side code, and (3) vendors' documentation. A typical analysis workflow is as follows. We first examine the network traffic to reveal which server(s) the client interacts with during the test, as well as their interaction durations. We then inspect the captured HTTP(S) transactions to interpret the client's interactions with the server(s) such as server selection and file transfer. We also inspect client-side code (typically in JavaScript). However, this attempt may not always succeed due to code obfuscation used by some BTSes such as SpeedTest. In this case, we use the Chrome developer tool to monitor the entire test process in the debug mode. With the above efforts, we are able to "reverse engineer" the implementations of all the 20 BTSes.

---

[2] The 18 web-based BTSes are ATTtest [12], BWP [24], CenturyLink [25], Cox [26], DSLReports [27], FAST [28], NYSbroadband [29], Optimum [30], SFtest [31], SpeakEasy [32], Spectrum [33], SpeedOf [34], SpeedTest [35], ThinkBroadband [36], Verizon [37], Xfinity [38], XYZtest [39], and WiFiMaster [3]. They are selected based on Alexa ranks and Google page ranks. In addition, we also study two BTS APIs in Android 11: `getLinkDownstreamBandwidthKbps` and `testMobileDownload`.

Table 2.1 Client devices used for testing the 20 BTSes. The test results are obtained from SpeedTest.net

Device	Location	Network	Ground truth
PC-1	U.S.A.	Residential broadband	100 Mbps
PC-2	Germany	Residential broadband	100 Mbps
PC-3	China	Residential broadband	100 Mbps
Samsung GS9	U.S.A.	LTE (60 Mhz/1.9 Ghz)	60–100 Mbps
Xiaomi XM8	China	LTE (40 Mhz/1.8 Ghz)	58–89 Mbps
Samsung GS10	U.S.A.	5G (400 Mhz/28 Ghz)	0.9–1.2 Gbps
Huawei HV30	China	5G (160 Mhz/2.6 Ghz)	0.4–0.7 Gbps

(Reprinted with permission from [17])

Our analysis shows that a bandwidth test in these BTSes is typically done in three phases: (1) setup, (2) bandwidth probing, and (3) bandwidth estimation. In the setup phase, the BTS sends a list of candidate servers (based on the client's IP address or geo-location) to the client who then PINGs each candidate server over HTTP(S). Next, based on the servers' PING latency, the client selects one or more candidate servers to perform file transfer(s) to collect throughput samples. The BTS processes the samples and returns the result to the user.

2.2.3 Measurement Results

We select 9 (out of 20) representative BTSes for more in-depth characterizations, as listed in Table 2.2. These 9 selected BTSes well cover different designs (in terms of the key bandwidth test logic) of the remaining 11 ones. We deploy a large-scale testbed to comprehensively profile 8 representative BTSes, except Android API-A (we will discuss it separately). Our testbed is deployed on 108 geo-distributed VMs from multiple public cloud services providers (CSPs, including Azure, AWS, Ali Cloud, Digital Ocean, Vultr, and Tencent Cloud) as the client hosts. Note that we mainly employ VMs as client hosts because they are globally distributed and easy to deploy. Per their service agreements, the CSPs offer three types of access link bandwidths: 1 Mbps, 10 Mbps, and 100 Mbps (36 VMs each). The ground truth in Fig. 2.4 is obtained according to the methodology in Sect. 2.2.1. We denote one *test group* as using one VM to run back-to-back bandwidth tests across all the 8 BTSes in a random order. We perform in one day 3240 groups of tests, i.e., 108 VMs × 3 different time-of-day (0:00, 8:00, and 16:00) × 10 repetitions.

We summarize our results in Table 2.2. We discover that all but one of the BTSes adopt *flooding-based* approaches to combat the test noises from a temporal perspective, leading to enormous data usage. Meanwhile, they differ in many aspects: (1) bandwidth probing mechanism, (2) bandwidth estimation algorithm, (3) connection management strategy, (4) server selection policy, and (5) server pool size.

Table 2.2 A brief summary of the 9 representative BTSes. "Testbed" and "5G" denote the large-scale cloud-based testbed and the 5G scenario, respectively. * means that WiFiMaster and Andriod API-B share the similar bandwidth test logic with ThinkBroadBand (TBB)

BTS	# servers	Bandwidth test logic	Duration	Accuracy (Testbed/5G)	Data usage (Testbed/5G)
TBB*	12	Average throughput in all connections	8 s	0.59/0.31	42 MB/481 MB
SpeedOf	116	Average throughput in the last connection	8–230 s	0.76/0.22	61 MB/256 MB
BWP	18	Average throughput in the fastest connection	13 s	0.81/0.35	74 MB/524 MB
SFtest	19	Average throughput in all connections	20 s	0.89/0.81	194 MB/2013 MB
ATTtest	75	Average throughput in all connections	15–30 s	0.86/0.53	122 MB/663 MB
Xfinity	28	Average all throughput samples	12 s	0.82/0.67	107 MB/835 MB
FAST	~1000	Average stable throughput samples	8–30 s	0.80/0.72	45 MB/903 MB
SpeedTest	~12,000	Average refined throughput samples	15 s	0.96/0.92	150 MB/1972 MB
Android API-A	0	Directly calculate using system configs	<10 ms	NA/0.09	0/0

(Reprinted with permission from [17])

2.2.4 Case Studies

We present our case studies of five major BTSes with the largest user bases selected from Table 2.2.

ThinkBroadBand [36] This BTS first selects a test server with the lowest latency to the client among its server pool. Then, it starts an 8-second bandwidth test by delivering a 20-MB file toward the client; if the file transfer takes less than 8 seconds, the test is repeated to collect more data points. After the 8 seconds, it calculates the average throughput (i.e., data transfer rate) during the whole test process as the estimated bandwidth.

WiFiMaster [3] WiFiMaster's BTS is largely the same as that of ThinkBroadBand. The main difference lies in the test server pool. Instead of deploying a dedicated test server pool, WiFiMaster exploits the CDN servers of a large Internet content provider (Tencent) for frequent bandwidth tests. It directly downloads fixed-size ($\sim$47 MB) software packages as the test files and measures the average download speed as the estimated bandwidth.

Our measurements show that the accuracy of ThinkBroadBand and WiFiMaster is low. The accuracy is merely 0.59, because the single HTTP connection during the test can easily be affected by network spikes and link congestion that lead to significant underestimation. In addition, using the average throughput for bandwidth estimation cannot rule out the impact of slow start and thus requires a long test duration.

Android APIs [2, 40] To cater to the needs of bandwidth estimation for bandwidth-hungry apps (e.g., UHD videos and VR/AR) over 5G, Android 11 offers two "Bandwidth Estimator" APIs to "make it easier to check bandwidth for uploading and downloading content [2]."

API-A, `getLinkDownstreamBandwidthKbps`, statically calculates the bandwidth by "taking into account link parameters (radio technology, allocated channels, etc.) [15]." It uses a pre-defined dictionary (`KEY_BANDWIDTH_STRING_ARRAY`) to map device hardware information to bandwidth values. For example, if the user device is connected to the new-radio non-standalone mmWave 5G, API-A searches the dictionary that records `NR_NSA_MMWAVE:145000,60000`, indicating that the downlink bandwidth is 145,000 Kbps and the uplink bandwidth is 60,000 Kbps. This API provides a static "start-up on idle" estimation [2]. We test the performance of API-A in a similar manner as introduced in Sect. 2.2.3 with the 5G phones in Table 2.1. The results show that API-A bears rather poor accuracy (0.09) in realistic scenarios.

API-B, `testMobileDownload`, works in a similar way as ThinkBroadBand. It requires the app developer to provide the test servers and the test files.

FAST [28] is an advanced BTS with a pool of about 1000 test servers. It employs a two-step server selection process: the client first picks five nearby servers based on its IP address and then PINGs these five candidates to select the latency-wise nearest server for the bandwidth probing phase.

FAST progressively increases the concurrency according to the client network condition during the test. The client starts with a 25-MB file over a single connection. When the throughput reaches 0.5 Mbps, a new connection is created to transfer another 25-MB file. Similarly, at 1 Mbps, a third connection is established. For each connection, when the file transfer completes, it repeatedly requests another 25-MB file (the concurrency never decreases).

FAST estimates the bandwidth as follows. As shown in Fig. 2.2, it collects a throughput sample every 200 ms and maintains a 2-second window consisting of 10 most recent samples. After 5 seconds, FAST checks whether the in-window throughput samples are stable: $S_{max} - S_{min} \leq 3\% \cdot S_{avg}$, where S_{max}, S_{min}, and S_{avg} correspond to the maximum, minimum, and average value across all samples

Fig. 2.2 Test logic of FAST
(Reprinted with permission
from [17])

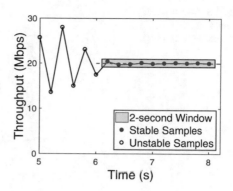

in the window, respectively. If the above inequality holds, FAST terminates the test
and returns S_{avg}. Otherwise, the test will continue until reaching a time limit of 30
seconds; at that time, the last 2-second window's S_{avg} will be returned to the user.

Unfortunately, our results show that the accuracy of FAST is still unsatisfactory.
The average accuracy is 0.80, as shown in Table 2.2 and Fig. 2.4. We ascribe this to
two reasons: (1) Though FAST owns ~1000 servers, they are mostly located in the
USA and Canada. Thus, FAST can hardly assign a nearby server to clients outside
North America. In fact, FAST achieves relatively high average accuracy (0.92) when
serving the clients in North America; however, it has quite low accuracy (0.74)
when measuring the access link bandwidth of the clients in other places around the
world. (2) We observe that FAST's window-based mechanism for early generation
of the test result is vulnerable to throughput fluctuations. Under unstable network
conditions, FAST can only use throughput samples in the last two seconds (rather
than the entire 30-second samples) to calculate the test result.

SpeedTest [35] is considered the most advanced industrial BTS [18–22]. It deploys
a pool of ~12,000 servers. Similar to FAST, it also employs the two-step server
selection process: it identifies 10 candidate servers based on the client's IP address
and then selects the latency-wise nearest from them. It also progressively increases
the concurrency level: it begins with 4 parallel connections for quickly saturating
the available bandwidth and establishes a new connection at 25 Mbps and 35 Mbps,
respectively. It uses a fixed file size of 25 MB and a fixed test duration of 15 seconds.

SpeedTest's bandwidth estimation algorithm is different from that of FAST.
During the bandwidth probing phase, it collects a throughput sample every 100 ms.
Since the test duration is fixed to 15 seconds, all the 150 samples are used to
construct 20 slices, each covering the same traffic volume, illustrated as the area
under the throughput curve in Fig. 2.3. Then, 5 slices with the lowest average
throughput and 2 slices with the highest average throughput are discarded. This
leaves 13 slices remaining, whose average throughput is returned as the final test
result. This method may help mitigate the impact of throughput fluctuations, but
the two fixed thresholds for noise filtering could be deficient under diverse network
conditions (Fig. 2.4).

Fig. 2.3 Test logic of
SpeedTest (Reprinted with
permission from [17])

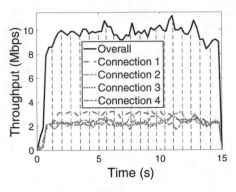

Fig. 2.4 Test accuracy of
nine BTSes (Reprinted with
permission from [17])

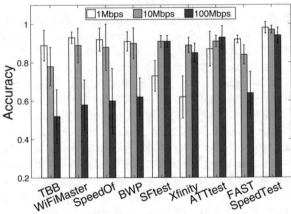

Overall, SpeedTest exhibits the highest accuracy (0.96) among the measured
BTSes. A key contributing factor is its large server pool (Sect. 2.5.2).

2.3 Design of FastBTS

FastBTS is a fast and lightweight BTS with a fundamentally new design. FastBTS
accommodates and exploits noises (instead of suppressing them) to significantly
reduce the resource footprint and accelerate the tests, while retaining high test
accuracy. The key technique of FastBTS is *fuzzy rejection sampling* that automatically identifies true samples that represent the target distribution and filters out
false samples due to measurement noises, without a priori knowledge of the target
distribution. Figure 2.1 shows the main components of FastBTS and the workflow
of a bandwidth test:

- *Crucial interval sampling (CIS)* implements the acceptance–rejection function
  of fuzzy rejection sampling. CIS is built upon a key observation based on our

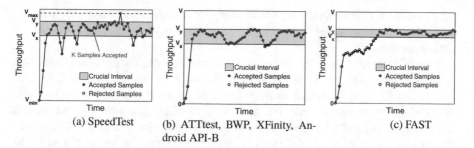

Fig. 2.5 Common scenarios where the true samples fall in a crucial interval. In our measurement, more than 96% cases fall into the three patterns (Reprinted with permission from [17])

measurement study (see Sects. 2.2.3 and 2.2.4): *while the noise samples may be widely scattered, the desired bandwidth samples tend to concentrate within a narrow throughput interval.* CIS searches for a *dense* and *narrow* interval that covers the majority of the desirable samples, and uses computational geometry to drastically reduce the searching complexity.

- *Elastic bandwidth probing (EBP)* generates throughput samples that persistently[3] obey the distribution of the target bandwidth. We design EBP by optimizing BBR's bandwidth estimation algorithm [42] —different from BBR's static bandwidth probing policy, EBP reaches the target bandwidth much faster, while being non-disruptive.
- *Data-driven server selection (DSS)* selects the server(s) with the highest bandwidth estimation(s) through a data-driven model. We show that a simple model can significantly improve server selection results compared to the de facto approach that ranks servers by round-trip time.
- *Adaptive multi-homing (AMH)* adaptively establishes multiple parallel connections with different test servers. It is important for saturating the access link when the last-mile access link is not the bottleneck, e.g., 5G [43].

2.3.1 Crucial Interval Sampling (CIS)

CIS is designed based on the key observation: while noise samples are scattered across a wide throughput interval, the desirable samples tend to concentrate within a narrow interval, referred to as the *crucial interval*. As shown in Fig. 2.5, in each subfigure, although the crucial interval is narrow, it can cover the vast majority of the desirable samples. Thus, while the target distribution $T(x)$ is unknown, we can approximate $T(x)$ with the crucial interval. Also, as more noise samples

---

[3] Here "persistently" means that a certain set (or range) of samples constantly recur to the measurement data during the test process [41].

accumulate, the test accuracy would typically increase as randomly scattered noise samples help better "contrast" the crucial interval, leading to its improved approximation.

Crucial Interval Algorithm. Based on the above insights, our designed bandwidth estimation approach for FastBTS aims at finding this crucial interval ($[V_x, V_y]$) that has both *a high sample density* and *a large sample size*. Assuming there are N throughput samples ranging from V_{min} to V_{max}, our aim is formulated as maximizing the *product of density and size*. We denote the size as $K(V_x, V_y)$, i.e., the number of samples that fall into $[V_x, V_y]$. The density can be calculated as the ratio between $K(V_x, V_y)$ and $N' = N(V_y - V_x)/(V_{max} - V_{min})$, where N' is the "baseline" corresponding to the number of samples falling into $[V_x, V_y]$ *if* all N samples are uniformly distributed in $[V_{min}, V_{max}]$. To prevent a pathological case where the density is too high, we enforce a lower bound of the interval: $V_y - V_x$ should be at least L_{min}, which is empirically set to $(V_{max} - V_{min})/(N - 1)$. Given the above, the objective function to be maximized is

$$F(V_x, V_y) = Density \times Size = C \cdot \frac{K^2(V_x, V_y)}{V_y - V_x}, \qquad (2.1)$$

where $C = (V_{max} - V_{min})/N$ is a constant. Once the optimal $[V_x, V_y]$ is calculated, we can derive the bandwidth estimation by averaging all the samples falling into this interval.

FastBTS computes the crucial interval as bandwidth probing (Sect. 2.3.2) is in progress, which serves as the acceptance–rejection function (ARF) of rejection sampling. When a new sample is available, the server computes a crucial interval by maximizing Eq. (2.1). It thus produces a series of intervals $[V_{x3}, V_{y3}]$, $[V_{x4}, V_{y4}]$, $\cdots$, where $[V_{xi}, V_{yi}]$ corresponds to the interval generated when the i-th sample is available.

Searching Crucial Interval with Convex Hull. We now consider how to actually solve the maximization problem in Eq. (2.1). To enhance the readability, we use L to denote $V_y - V_x$, use K to denote $K(V_x, V_y)$, and let the maximum value of $F(V_x, V_y)$ be F_{max}, which lies in $(0, \frac{C \cdot N^2}{L_{min}}]$.

Clearly, a naïve exhaustive search takes $O(N^2)$ time. Our key result is that this can be done much more efficiently in $O(N \log N)$ by strategically searching on a convex hull dynamically constructed from the samples. Our high-level approach is to perform a binary search for F_{max}. The initial midpoint is set to $\lfloor \frac{C \cdot N^2}{2 \cdot L_{min}} \rfloor$. In each binary search iteration, we examine whether the inequality $\frac{C \cdot K^2}{L} - m \geq 0$ holds for any interval(s), where $0 < m \leq F_{max}$ is the current midpoint. Based on the result, we adjust the midpoint and continue with the next iteration.

We next see how each iteration is performed exactly. Without loss of generality, we assume that the throughput samples are sorted in ascending order. Suppose we choose the i-th and j-th samples ($i < j$) from the N sorted samples as the endpoints of the interval $[V_i, V_j]$. Then the inequality $\frac{C \cdot K^2}{L} - m \geq 0$ can be transformed as

$$\frac{C \cdot (j - i + 1)^2}{V_j - V_i} - m \geq 0. \tag{2.2}$$

We further rearrange it as

$$i^2 - 2i + \frac{m}{C} V_i - 2ij \geq \frac{m}{C} V_j - 2j - j^2 - 1. \tag{2.3}$$

It is not difficult to discover that the right side of the inequality is only associated with the variable j, while the left side just relates to the variable i except the term $-2ij$. Therefore, we adopt the following coordinate conversion:

$$\begin{cases} k(j) = 2j \\ b(j) = \frac{m}{C} V_j - 2j - j^2 - 1 \\ x(i) = i \\ y(i) = i^2 - 2i + \frac{m}{C} V_i. \end{cases} \tag{2.4}$$

With the abovementioned coordinate conversion, the inequality (2.3) can be transformed as $y(i) - k(j) \cdot x(i) \geq b(j)$. Then, determining whether the inequality holds for at least one pair of (i, j) is equivalent to finding the maximum of $f(i) = y(i) - k(j) \cdot x(i)$ for each $1 < j \leq N$.

As depicted in Fig. 2.7a, we regard $\{x(i)\}$ and $\{y(i)\}$ as coordinates of N points on a two-dimensional plane (these points do not depend on j). It can be shown using the linear programming theory that for any given j, the largest value of $f(i)$ always occurs at a point that is on the convex hull formed by $(x(i), y(i))$. This dictates an algorithm where for each $1 < j \leq N$, we check the points on the convex hull to find the maximum of $f(i)$.

Since i must be less than j, each time we increment j (the outer loop), we progressively add one point $(x(j - 1), y(j - 1))$ to the (partial) convex hull, which is shown in Fig. 2.7b. Then among all the existing points on the convex hull, we search backward from the point with the largest $x(i)$ value to the smallest $x(i)$ to find the maximum of $f(i)$ and stop searching when $f(i)$ starts to decrease since the points are on the convex hull (the inner loop).

As demonstrated in Fig. 2.7c, an analytic geometry explanation of this procedure is to determine a line with a fixed slope $y = k(j)x + B$, s.t. the line intersects with a point on the convex and the intercept B is maximized, and the maximized intercept corresponds to the maximum of $f(i)$.

Also, once the maximum of $f(i)$ is found at $(x(i'), y(i'))$ for a given j, all points that are to the right of $(x(i'), y(i'))$ can be removed from the convex hull—they must not correspond to the maximum of $f(i)$ for all $j' > j$. This is because: (1) the slope of the convex hull's edge decreases as i increases and (2) $k(j)$ increases as j increases. Therefore, using amortized analysis, we can show that in each binary search iteration, the overall processing time for all points is $O(N)$ as j grows from 1 to N. This leads to an overall complexity of $O(N \log N)$ for the whole algorithm.

Fast Result Generation FastBTS selects a group of samples that well fit $T(x)$ as soon as possible while ensuring data reliability. Given two intervals $[V_{xi}, V_{yi}]$, and $[V_{xj}, V_{yj}]$, we regard their similarity as the Jaccard coefficient [44]. FastBTS then keeps track of the similarity values of consecutive interval pairs, i.e., $S_{3,4}, S_{4,5}, \cdots$ If the test result stabilizes, the consecutive interval pairs' similarity value will keep growing from a certain value β, satisfying $\beta \leq S_{i,i+1} \leq \cdots \leq S_{i+k,i+k+1} \leq 1$. If the above sequence is observed, FastBTS determines that the result has stabilized and reports the bottleneck bandwidth as the average value of the throughput samples belonging to the most recent interval. The parameters β and k pose a tradeoff between accuracy and cost in terms of test duration and data traffic.

Specifically, increasing β and k can yield a higher test accuracy while incurring a longer test duration and more data usage. Currently, we empirically set $\beta = 0.9$ and $k = 2$, which are found to well balance the tradeoff between the test duration and the accuracy. Nevertheless, when dealing with those relatively rare cases that are not covered by this work, BTS providers are recommended to do pre-tests in order to find the suitable parameter settings before putting CIS mechanism into actual use.

Solutions to Caveats There do exist some "irregular" bandwidth graphs in prior work [4, 45, 46] where CIS may lose efficacy. For instance, due to in-network mechanisms such as data aggregation and multipath scheduling, the millisecond-level throughput samples can vary dramatically (i.e., sometimes the throughput is about to reach the link capacity and sometimes the throughput approaches zero). To mitigate this issue, we learn from some BTSes (e.g., SpeedTest) and use a relatively large time interval (50 ms) to smooth the gathered throughput samples. However, even with smoothed samples, CIS is still likely to be inaccurate if the actual access bandwidth is outside the crucial interval, or the interval becomes too wide to give a meaningful bandwidth estimation. In our experiences, such cases are rare (less than 4% in our measurements in Sect. 2.2.3). However, to ensure that our tests are stable in all scenarios, we design solutions to those pathological cases.

Figure 2.6 shows all types of the pathological cases of CIS we observe, where $P(x)$ deviates from $T(x)$ over time. FastBTS leverages three mechanisms to resolve these cases: (1) elastic bandwidth probing (Sect. 2.3.2) reaches bottleneck bandwidth in a short time, effectively alleviating the impact of slow-start effect in Fig. 2.6a; (2) data-driven server selection (Sect. 2.3.3) picks the expected highest-throughput server(s) for bandwidth tests, minimizing the requirement of additional connection(s) in Fig. 2.6c; (3) adaptive multi-homing (Sect. 2.3.4) establishes concurrent connections with different servers, avoiding the underestimations in Fig. 2.6b and c (Fig. 2.7).

2.3.2 Elastic Bandwidth Probing (EBP)

In rejection sampling, $P(x)$ determines the boundary of $T(x)$. A bandwidth test measures $P(x)$ using bandwidth probing based on network conditions. It shares

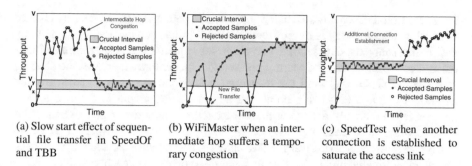

(a) Slow start effect of sequential file transfer in SpeedOf and TBB

(b) WiFiMaster when an intermediate hop suffers a temporary congestion

(c) SpeedTest when another connection is established to saturate the access link

Fig. 2.6 Pathological scenarios where the true samples are not persistently covered by the crucial interval (less than 4% in our measurements) (Reprinted with permission from [17])

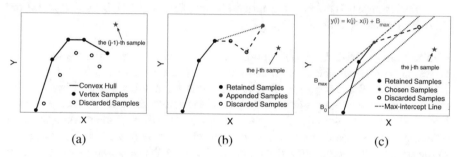

(a)   (b)   (c)

Fig. 2.7 (**a**) The current convex hull under transformed coordinates, where the axes X and Y correspond to $x(i)$ and $y(i)$ in Eq. (2.4), respectively. (**b**) Updating the convex hull with the $(j-1)$-th sample. (**c**) Searching for the max-intercept line (Reprinted with permission from [17])

a similar principle as congestion control at the test server's transport layer. The goal is to accommodate diverse noises over the live Internet, while saturating the bandwidth of the access link. FastBTS employs BBR [42], an advanced congestion control algorithm, as a starting point for probing design. FastBTS uses BBR's built-in bandwidth probing for bootstrapping.

On the other hand, bandwidth tests have different requirements compared with congestion control. For example, congestion control emphasizes stable data transfers over a long period, while a BTS focuses on obtaining accurate link capacity as early as possible with the lowest data usage. Therefore, we modify and optimize BBR to support bandwidth tests.

BBR Prime BBR is featured by two key metrics: bottleneck bandwidth $BtlBw$ and round-trip propagation time RT_{prop}. It works in four phases: Startup, Drain, ProbeBW (probing the bandwidth), and ProbeRTT. A key parameter $pacing\_gain$

(PG) controls TCP pacing so that the capacity of a network path can be fully utilized while the queuing delay is minimized. BBR multiplies its measured throughput by PG to determine the data sending rate in the subsequent RTT. After a connection is established, BBR enters the Startup phase and exponentially increases the sending rate (i.e., $PG = \frac{2}{ln2}$) until the measured throughput does not increase further, as shown in Fig. 2.8. At this point, the measured throughput is denoted as B_0, and a queue is already formed at the bottleneck of the network path. Then, BBR tries to drain it by reducing PG to $\frac{ln2}{2} < 1$ until there is expected to be no excess in-flight data. Afterward, BBR enters a (by default) 10-second ProbeBW phase to gradually probe $BtlBw$ in a number of cycles, each consisting of 8 $RTTs$ with $PGs = \{\frac{5}{4}, \frac{3}{4}, 1, 1, 1, 1, 1, 1\}$. We plot in Fig. 2.8 four such cycles tagged as ①②③④. Finally (10 seconds later), the *maximum* value of the measured throughput samples is taken as the network path's $BtlBw$, and BBR enters a 200-ms ProbeRTT phase to estimate RT_{prop}.

Limitations of BBR Directly applying BBR's $BtlBw$-based probing method to BTSes is inefficient. First, as illustrated in Fig. 2.8 (where the true $BtlBw$ is 100 Mbps), BBR's $BtlBw$ probing is conservative, making the probing process unnecessarily slow. A straightforward idea is to remove the 6 RTTs with $PG = 1$ in each cycle. Even with that, the probing process is still inefficient when the data (sending) rate is low. Second, when the current data rate (e.g., 95 Mbps) is close to the true $BtlBw$ (e.g., 100 Mbps), using the fixed PG of $\frac{5}{4}$ causes the data rate to far overshoot its limit (e.g., to 118.75 Mbps). This may not be a severe issue for data transfers but may significantly slow down the convergence of $BtlBw$ and thus lengthen the test duration. Third, BBR takes the maximum of all throughput samples in each cycle as the estimated $BtlBw$. The simple maximization operation is vulnerable to outliers and noises (this is addressed by CIS in Sect. 2.3.1).

Elastic Data Rate Pacing We design *elastic pacing* to make bandwidth probing faster, more accurate, and more adaptive. Intuitively, when the data rate is low, it ramps up quickly to reduce the probing time; when the data rate approaches the

Fig. 2.8 Elastic bandwidth probing vs. BBR's original scheme (Reprinted with permission from [17])

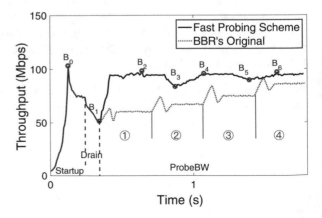

estimated bottleneck bandwidth, it performs fine-grained probing by reducing the step size, toward a smooth convergence. This is in contrast to BBR's static probing policy.

We now detail our method. As depicted in Fig. 2.8, once entering the ProbeBW phase, we have recorded B_0 and B where B_0 is the peak data rate measured during the Startup phase and B is the current data rate. Let the ground-truth bottleneck bandwidth be B_T. Typically, B_0 is slightly higher than B_T due to queuing at the bottleneck link in the end of the Startup phase (otherwise, it will not exit Startup); also, B is lower than B_T due to the Drain phase. We adjust the value of B by controlling the *pacing gain* (PG) of the data sending rate, but the pivotal question here is the adjustment policy, i.e., how to make B approach B_T quickly and precisely.

Our idea is inspired by the spring system [47] in physics where the restoring force of a helical spring is proportional to its elongation. We thus regard PG as the restoring force and B's deviation from B_0 as the elongation (we do not know B_T so we approximate it using B_0). Therefore, the initial PG is expected to grow to

$$PG_{grow-0} = (PG_m - PG_0) \times \left(1 - \frac{B}{B_0}\right) + PG_0, \qquad (2.5)$$

where $1 - \frac{B}{B_0}$ denotes the normalized distance between B_0 and B, and PG_0 represents the default value (1.0) of PG. We set the upper bound of PG (PG_m) as $\frac{2}{ln2}$ that matches BBR's PG in the (most aggressive) Startup phase. As Eq. (2.5) indicates, the spring system indeed realizes our idea: it increases the data rate rapidly when B is well below B_0, and cautiously reduces the probing step as B grows.

To accommodate a corner scenario where B_0 is lower than B_T ($< 1\%$ cases in our experiments), we slightly modify Eq. (2.5) to allow B to overshoot B_0 marginally:

$$PG_{grow-0} = max\left\{(PG_m - PG_0') \times \left(1 - \frac{B}{B_0}\right) + PG_0', PG_0'\right\}, \qquad (2.6)$$

where PG_0' equals $1 + \epsilon$, with ϵ being empirically set to 0.05.

When the data rate overshoots the bottleneck bandwidth (i.e., the number of in-flight bytes exceeds the bandwidth-delay product), we reduce the data rate to suppress the excessive in-flight bytes. This is realized by inverting PG to $PG_{drop-0} = \frac{1}{PG_{grow-0}}$. This process continues until no excessive in-flight data is present. At that moment, B will again drop below B_T, so we start a new cycle to repeat the aforementioned data rate growth process.

To put things together, in our design, the ProbeBW phase consists of a series of cycles each consisting of only two stages: *growth* and *drop*. Each stage has a variable number of RTTs, and the six RTTs with $PG = 1$ in the original BBR algorithm are removed. The transitions between the two stages are triggered by the formation and disappearance of excessive in-flight bytes (i.e., the queueing delay). In the i-th cycle, the PGs for the two stages are

$$
\begin{cases}
PG_{grow-i} = max \left\{ (PG_m - PG'_0) \times \left(1 - \frac{B}{B_i}\right) + PG'_0, \; PG'_0 \right\}, \\
PG_{drop-i} = \frac{1}{PG_{grow-i}},
\end{cases}
\tag{2.7}
$$

where B is the data rate at the beginning of a growth stage, and B_i is the peak rate in the previous cycle's growth stage. Interestingly, by setting $B_0 = +\infty$, we can make the growth and drop stages identical to BBR's Startup and Drain phases, respectively. Our final design thus only consists of a single phase (ProbeBW) with two stages. The ProbeRTT phase is removed because it does not help our bandwidth probing.

Compared with traditional bandwidth probing mechanisms, EBP can saturate available bandwidth more quickly as it ramps up the sending rate when the current rate is much lower than the estimated bandwidth. Meanwhile, when the sending rate is about to reach the estimated bandwidth, EBP carefully increases the rate in order to be less aggressive to other flows along the path than other bandwidth probing mechanisms.

2.3.3 Data-Driven Server Selection (DSS)

FastBTS includes a new server selection method. We find that selecting the test server(s) with the lowest PING latency, widely used in the existing BTSes, is ineffective. Our measurement shows that latency and the available bandwidth are not highly correlated—the servers yielding the highest throughput may not always be those with the lowest PING latency.

FastBTS takes a *data-driven approach* for server selection (DSS): each test server maintains a database (model) containing {latency, throughput} pairs obtained from the setup and bandwidth probing phases of past tests. Then in a new setup phase, the client still PINGs the test servers, while each server returns an expected throughput value based on the PING latency by looking up the database. The client will then rank the selected server(s) based on their expected throughput values.

As demonstrated in Fig. 2.9, the actual DSS algorithm is conceptually similar to CIS introduced in Sect. 2.3.1, whereas we empirically observe that only considering the density can yield decent results. Specifically, given a latency measurement l, the server searches for a width w that maximizes the density defined as $K(l, w)/2w$, where $K(l, w)$ denotes the number of latency samples falling in the latency interval $[l - w, l + w]$. The expected throughput is calculated as an average of all samples in $[l - w, l + w]$. In addition, the server also returns the maximum throughput (using the 99-percentile value) belonging to $[l - w, l + w]$ to the client. Both values will be used in the bandwidth probing phase (Sect. 2.3.4). During bootstrapping when servers have not yet accumulated enough samples, the client can fall back to

Fig. 2.9 Data-driven server selection that takes both historical latency and throughput information into account (Reprinted with permission from [17])

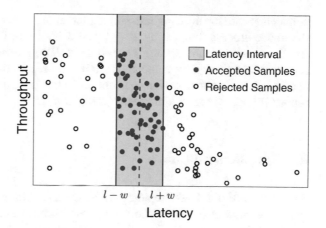

the traditional latency-based selection strategy. To keep their databases up-to-date, servers can maintain only most recent samples.

2.3.4   Adaptive Multi-Homing (AMH)

For high-speed access networks such as 5G, the last-mile access link may not always be the bottleneck. To saturate the access link, we design an adaptive multi-homing (AMH) mechanism to dynamically adjust the concurrency, i.e., the number of concurrent connections between the servers and the client.

AMH starts with a single connection to cope with possibly low-speed access links. For this single connection C_1, when CIS (Sect. 2.3.1) has accomplished using the server S_1 (the highest-ranking server, see Scct. 2.3.3), the reported bottleneck bandwidth is denoted as BW_1. At this time, the client establishes another connection C_2 with the second highest-ranking server S_2 while retaining C_1. C_2 also works as described in Sect. 2.3.2. Note we require S_1 and S_2 to be in different ASes to minimize the likelihood that S_1 and S_2 share the same Internet-side bottleneck. Moreover, we pick the server with the second highest bandwidth estimation as S_2 to saturate the client's access link bandwidth with the fewest test servers. After that, we view C_1 and C_2 together as an "aggregated" connection, with its throughput being $BW_2 = BW_{2,1} + BW_{2,2}$, where $BW_{2,1}$ and $BW_{2,2}$ are the real-time throughput of C_1 and C_2.

By monitoring $BW_{2,1}$, $BW_{2,2}$, and BW_2, FastBTS applies intelligent throughput sampling and fast result generation (Sect. 2.3.1) to judge whether BW_2 has become stable. Once BW_2 stabilizes, AMH determines whether the whole bandwidth test process should be terminated based on the relationship between BW_1 and $BW_{2,1}$. If for C_1 the bottleneck link is not the access link, $BW_{2,1}$ should have a value similar to or higher than BW_1 (assuming the unlikeliness of C_1 and C_2 sharing the same Internet-side bottleneck [48]). In this case, the client establishes another connection with the third highest-ranking server S_3 (with a different AS) and repeats the above process (comparing $BW_{3,1}$ and BW_1 to decide whether to launch the fourth connection, and so on). Otherwise, if $BW_{2,1}$ exhibits a noticeable decline (empirically set to $>5\%$) compared to BW_1, we regard that C_1 and C_2 saturate the access link and incur cross-flow contention. In this case, the client stops probing and reports the access bandwidth as $max(BW_1, BW_2)$.

2.4 Implementation

As shown in Fig. 2.1, we implement *elastic bandwidth probing* (EBP) and *crucial interval sampling* (CIS) on the server side because EBP works at the transport layer and thus requires OS kernel modifications, and CIS needs to get fine-grained throughput samples from EBP in real time. We implement EBP and CIS in C and Node.js, respectively.

We implement *data-driven server selection* (DSS) and *adaptive multi-homing* (AMH) on the client side. End users can access the FastBTS service through REST APIs. We implement DSS and AMH in JavaScript to make them easy to integrate with web pages or mobile apps.

The test server is built on CentOS 7.6 with the Linux kernel version of 5.0.1. As mentioned in Sect. 2.3.2, we develop EBP by using BBR as the starting point. Specifically, we implement the calculation of *pacing_gain* according to Eq. (2.7) by modifying the bbr_update_bw function; we also modify bbr_set_state and bbr_check_drain to alter BBR's original cycles in the ProbeBW phase, so as to realize EBP's two-stage cycles. EBP is implemented as a loadable kernel module. CIS is a user-space program. To efficiently send in situ performance statistics including throughput samples, *Btlbw*, and RT_{prop} from EBP to CIS (both EBP and CIS are implemented on the server side in C and Node.js), we use the Linux Netlink Interface in netlink.h to add a raw socket and a new packet structure bbr_info that carries the above performance information. The performance statistics are also sent to the client by piggybacking with probing traffic, allowing users to examine the real-time bandwidth test progress.

2.5 Evaluation

2.5.1 Experiment Setup

We compare FastBTS with the 9 state-of-the-art BTSes studied in Sect. 2.2. For fair comparisons, we re-implement all the BTSes based on our reverse engineering efforts and use the same setup for all these re-implemented BTSes. To do so, we built the following testbeds.

Large-scale Testbed. We deploy a total of 30 test servers on 30 VMs across the globe (North America, South America, Asia, Europe, Australia, and Africa) with the same configurations (dual-core Intel CPU@2.5 GHz, 8-GB DDR memory, and 1.5+ Gbps outgoing bandwidth). The size of the server pool (30) is on par with 5 out of the 9 BTSes but is smaller than those of FAST and SpeedTest (Table 2.2), which we assume is a representative server pool size adopted by today's commercial BTSes. We deploy 100+ clients including 3 PCs, 4 smartphones, and 108 VMs (the same as those adopted in Sect. 2.2). For a fair comparison with FastBTS, we replicate the 9 other popular BTSes: SpeedOf, BWP, SFtest, ATTtest, Xfinity, FAST, SpeedTest, TBB, and Android API-A (see Sect. 2.2.3) and deploy them on the 30 test servers and the 100+ clients. We deploy API-A (Android specific) on 4 phones.

Tested Networks. We conduct extensive evaluations under heterogeneous networks. We detail their setups below:

- *Residential Broadband.* We deploy three PCs located in China, the U.S.A., and Germany (Table 2.1). All the PCs' access links are 100 Mbps residential broadband. The three clients communicate with (a subset of) the aforementioned 30 test servers to perform bandwidth tests. We perform in one day 90 groups of tests, consisting of 3 clients × 3 different time-of-day (0:00, 8:00, and 16:00) × 10 repetitions.
- *Data Center Networks.* We deploy 108 VMs belonging to different commercial cloud providers as the clients (Sect. 2.2.3). We perform a total number of 108 VMs × 3 time-of-day × 10 repetitions = 3240 groups of tests.
- *mmWave 5G* experiments were conducted at a downtown street in a large U.S. city, with a distance from the phone (Samsung GS10, see Table 2.1) to the base station of 30 m. This is a typical 5G usage scenario due to the small coverage of 5G base stations. The phone typically has line-of-sight to the base station unless being blocked by passing vehicles. The typical downlink throughput is between 0.9 and 1.2 Gbps. We perform in one day 120 groups of tests, consisting of 4 clients × 3 time-of-day × 10 repetitions.
- *Sub-6Ghz 5G* experiments were conducted in a Chinese city using an HV30 phone over China Mobile. The setup is similar to that of mmWave. We run 120 groups of tests.
- *LTE* experiments were conducted in both China (a university campus) and the U.S.A. (a large city's downtown area) using XM8 and GS9, respectively, each with 120 groups of tests.
- *HSR Cellular Access.* We also perform tests on high-speed rail (HSR) trains. We take the Beijing–Shanghai HSR line (a peak speed of 350 km/h) with two HV30 phones. We measure the LTE bandwidth from the train. We run 2 clients × 50 repetitions = 100 groups of tests.
- *LAN.* Besides the deployment of 30 VMs, we also create an in-lab LAN testbed to perform controlled experiments, where we can craft background traffic. The testbed consists of two test servers (S_1, S_2) and two clients (C_1, C_2), each equipping a 10 Gbps NIC. They are connected by a commodity switch with a 5 Gbps forwarding capability, thus being the bottleneck. When running

bandwidth tests on this testbed, we maintain two parallel flows: one 1 Gbps background flow between S_1 and C_1 and a bandwidth test flow between S_2 and C_2.

We use the three metrics described in Sect. 2.2.1 to assess BTSes: test duration, data usage, and accuracy. Also, the methodology for obtaining the ground truth is described in Sect. 2.2.1.

2.5.2 End-to-End Performance

LAN and Residential Networks As in Fig. 2.10a and b, FastBTS yields the highest accuracy (0.94 for LAN and 0.96 for residential network) among the nine BTSes, whose accuracy lies within 0.44–0.89 for LAN and 0.51–0.9 for residential network. The average test durations of FastBTS for LAN and residential network are 3.4 and 3.0 seconds, respectively, 2.4–7.4× shorter than the other BTSes. The average data usage of FastBTS is 0.9 GB for LAN and 27 MB for residential network, 3.1–10.5× less than the other BTSes. The short test duration and small data usage are attributed to EBP (Sect. 2.3.2), which allows a rapid data rate increase when the current data rate is far lower than the bottleneck bandwidth, as well as fast result generation, which strategically trades off accuracy for a shorter test duration.

Data Center Networks Figure 2.10c and d show the performance of different BTSes in CSPs' data center networks with the bandwidth of {1, 100} Mbps (per the CSPs' service agreements). FastBTS outperforms the other BTSes by yielding the highest accuracy (0.94 on average), the shortest test duration (2.67 seconds on average), and the smallest data usage (21 MB on average for 100-Mbps network). In contrast, the other BTSes' accuracy ranges between 0.46 and 0.91; their test duration is also much longer, from 6.2 to 20.8 seconds, and they consume much more data (from 44 to 194 MB) compared to FastBTS. In particular, we find that on low-speed network (1 Mbps), some BTSes such as Xfinity and SFtest establish too many parallel connections. This leads to poor performance due to the excessive contention across the connections. FastBTS addresses this issue through AMH (Sect. 2.3.4) that adaptively adjusts the concurrency level according to the network condition. The results of networks with 10 Mbps bandwidth are similar to those of 100 Mbps networks.

LTE and 5G Networks We evaluate the BTSes' performance on commercial LTE and 5G networks (both mmWave and sub-6Ghz for 5G). Over LTE, as plotted in Fig. 2.10e, FastBTS owns the highest accuracy (0.95 on average), the smallest data usage (28.23 MB on average), and the shortest test duration (2.73 seconds on average). The other nine BTSes are far less efficient: 0.62–0.92 for average accuracy, 41.8–179.3 MB for data usage, and 7.1–20.8 seconds for test duration. For instance, we discover that FAST bears a quite low accuracy (0.67) because its window-based mechanism is very vulnerable to throughput fluctuations in LTE. SpeedTest, despite

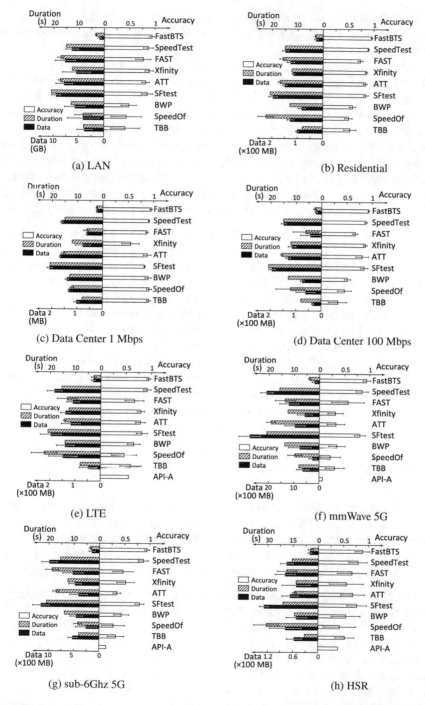

Fig. 2.10 Duration and test accuracy of FastBTS, compared with nine BTSes under various networks. "API-A" refers to Android API-A (Sect. 2.2.4) (Reprinted with permission from [17])

having a decent accuracy (0.92), incurs quite high data usage (166.3 MB) since it fixes the bandwidth test duration to 15 seconds regardless of the stability of the network.

Figure 2.10f shows the results for mmWave 5G. It is also encouraging to see that FastBTS outperforms the 9 other BTSes across all three metrics (0.94 vs. 0.07–0.87 for average accuracy, 194.7 vs. 101–2749 MB for data usage, and 4.0 vs. 8.9–26.2 seconds for test duration). Most of the BTSes have low accuracy (<0.6); Speedtest and SFtest bear relatively high accuracy (0.81 and 0.85). However, the high data usage issue due to their flooding nature is drastically amplified in mmWave 5G. For example, Speedtest incurs very high data usage—up to 2087 MB per test. The data usage for FAST is even as high as 2.75 GB. FastBTS addresses this issue through the synergy of its key features for fuzzy rejection sampling such as EBP and CIS. We observe similar results in the sub-6Ghz 5G experiments as shown in Fig. 2.10g.

HSR Cellular Access We also benchmark the BTSes on an HSR train running at a peak speed of 350 km/h from Beijing to Shanghai. As shown in Fig. 2.10h, the accuracy of all 10 BTSes decreases. This is attributed to two reasons. First, on HSR trains, the LTE bandwidth is highly fluctuating because of, e.g., frequent handovers caused by high mobility and the contention traffic from other passengers. Second, given such fluctuations, performing bulk transfer before and after a bandwidth test can hardly capture the ground-truth bandwidth, which varies significantly during the test. Nevertheless, compared to the other 9 BTSes, FastBTS still achieves the best performance (0.88 vs. 0.26–0.84 for average accuracy, 20.3 vs. 16–155 MB for data usage, and 4.6 vs. 10.6–32.4 seconds for test duration). The test duration is longer than the stationary scenarios because under high mobility, network condition fluctuation makes crucial intervals converge slower.

2.5.3 Individual Components

We evaluate the benefits of each component of FastBTS by incrementally enabling one at a time. When EBP is not enabled, we use BBR. When CIS is not enabled, we average the throughput samples to calculate the test result. When DSS is not enabled, test server(s) are selected based on PING latency. When AMH is not enabled, we apply SpeedTest's (single-homing) connection management logic.

Bandwidth Probing Schemes We compare BBR-based FastBTS and SpeedTest under mmWave 5G. The average data usage of BBR per test (735 MB) is 65% less than that of our replicated SpeedTest (2087 MB). Meanwhile, the accuracy of BBR slightly reduces from 0.85 to 0.81. The results indicate that BBR's $BtlBw$ estimation mechanism better balances the tradeoff between accuracy and data usage compared to flooding-based methods. We next compare BBR and EBP. We find that our EBP brings further improvements over BBR: under mmWave, EBP achieves an average data usage of 419 MB (compared 735 MB in BBR, a 42% reduction) and an average accuracy of 0.87 (compared to 0.81 in BBR, a 7% improvement). The

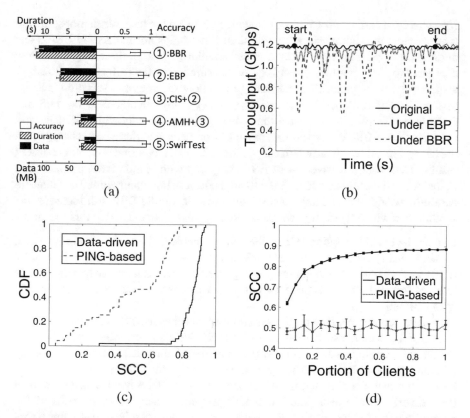

(a)   (b)

(c)   (d)

Fig. 2.11 (a) Impact of individual modules in 100-Mbps data center networks. (b) Intrusiveness between EBP and BBR. (c) Distributions of SCC_{gp} (PING-based) and SCC_{gd} (data-driven) when $P=20\%$; (d) P (portion of clients) vs. SCC_{gp} and SCC_{gd} (Reprinted with permission from [17])

advantages of EBP come from its elastic PG setting mechanism that is critical for adaptive bandwidth probing. Next, we compare BBR and EBP under data center networks. As shown in Fig. 2.11a, compared to BBR, EBP reduces the average test duration by 40% (from 11.3 to 6.6 seconds) and the data usage by 38% (from 107 to 66 MB), while improving the average accuracy by 6%.

Probing Intrusiveness We evaluate the probing intrusiveness of vanilla BBR and EBP using the LAN testbed (Sect. 2.5.1). Recall that we simultaneously run a 1 Gbps background flow and the bandwidth test flow that share a 5 Gbps bottleneck at the switch. Ideally, a BTS should measure the bottleneck bandwidth to be 4 Gbps without interfering with the background flow, whose average/standard deviation throughput is thus used as a metric to assess the intrusiveness of BBR and EBP. Our test procedure is as follows.

We first run the background flow alone for 1 minute and measure its throughput as $R_{Origin} = 1$ Gbps. We then run BBR and EBP with the background flow and measure the average (standard deviation) of the background flow throughput as

R_{BBR} (S_{BBR}) and R_{EBP} (S_{EBP}), respectively, during the test. We demonstrate the three groups' throughput samples with their timestamps normalized by BBR's test duration in Fig. 2.11b. EBP incurs a much smaller impact on the background flow compared to BBR, with R_{EBP} and R_{BBR} measured to be 0.97 Gbps and 0.90 Gbps, respectively. Also, under EBP, the background flow's throughput variation is lower than under BBR: S_{EBP}/R_{EBP} and S_{BBR}/R_{BBR} are calculated to be 0.03 and 0.15, respectively. This suggests that when probing the bandwidth, EBP is less intrusive than BBR. We repeat the above test procedure under other settings, with the background flow's bandwidth varying from 0.5 to 4 Gbps, and observe consistent results. The lower intrusiveness of EBP compared with vanilla BBR probably lies in that when the sending rate is about to hit the access link bandwidth, EBP tends to carefully reclaim the available bandwidth; however, vanilla BBR still increases the sending rate with a fixed step, which is more aggressive than EBP in this scenario.

Crucial Interval Sampling (CIS) We further enable CIS. As shown in Fig. 2.11a, by strategically removing outliers, CIS increases the average accuracy from 0.87 (EBP only) to 0.91. Due to the fast result generation mechanism, the test duration is reduced from 6.8 to 2.8 seconds, and the data usage is reduced by 2.8× (compared with EBP only).

We next compare CIS with the sampling approaches used by the other 9 BTSes (Sect. 2.5.1), which use a total of five bandwidth sampling algorithms because SFtest, ATTtest, and Xfinity employ the same trivial approach of simply averaging the throughput samples. To fairly compare them with CIS, we take a replay-based approach. Specifically, we select one "template" BTS from which we collect the network traces during the bandwidth probing phase; the time series of the aggregated throughput across all connections is then obtained from the traces and fed to all the sampling algorithms. We exclude SpeedOf and BWP from this experiment because they calculate the bandwidth based on the last or fastest connection that cannot be precisely reconstructed by our replay approach.

We next show the results by using SpeedTest as the template BTS. The simplest algorithm (averaging) bears the lowest accuracy (0.81) because it is poor at eliminating the noises caused by, for example, TCP congestion control; the accuracy values of FAST and SpeedTest are 0.82 and 0.84, respectively. In contrast, CIS owns the highest accuracy (0.91). This confirms the effectiveness of CIS's sampling approach. The efficiency and effectiveness of CIS lie in that, instead of incurring much redundancy in test duration and data usage to achieve a decent test accuracy, CIS keeps calculating the crucial interval of the gathered throughput samples. Once the crucial interval stabilizes, CIS immediately stops the test, thus significantly saving test duration and data usage.

Adaptive Multi-Homing (AMH) When AMH is further enabled, the test accuracy increases from 0.91 (EBP+CIS) to 0.93 (EBP+CIS+AMH), as shown in Fig. 2.11a. Meanwhile, since testing over more connections takes additional time, AMH slightly lengthens the average test duration from 2.8 to 3.1 seconds, with the average data usage increased from 23 to 28 MB. We repeat the above experiments over mmWave 5G networks where the bottleneck is more likely to shift to the Internet side. The results show that AMH improves the average accuracy from 0.84 to 0.91, while incurring moderate overhead by increasing the average data usage from 148 to 206 MB and the average test duration from 3.3 to 4.1 seconds. The results suggest that AMH is essential for high-speed networks such as mmWave 5G.

Data-driven Server Selection (DSS) We employ *cross-validation* for a fair comparison between the PING-based method and the DSS in three steps: (1) We do file transfers between every server and a randomly selected portion (P) of all clients to gather throughput samples. (2) Each client C runs a bandwidth test toward every server. In each test, the clients' historical test records (excluding the record of C) gathered in the previous step are utilized by each server to calculate the expected bandwidth, which are then returned to C. (3) Each client calculates three rankings of the servers based on the server-returned expected bandwidth: $Rank_g$, $Rank_p$, and $Rank_d$. $Rank_g$ refers to the server ranking based on the ground truth. $Rank_p$ is the ranking calculated based on PING latency; and $Rank_d$ is the ranking computed by DSS. We use the *Spearman Correlation Coefficient* (SCC [49]) to calculate the similarity SCC_{gp} between $Rank_g$ and $Rank_p$, as well as the similarity SCC_{gd} between $Rank_g$ and $Rank_d$.

The distributions of SCC_{gp} and SCC_{gd} when $P = 20\%$ are shown in Fig. 2.11c. We find that SCC_{gd} is much higher than SCC_{gp} in terms of the median (0.81 vs. 0.63), average (0.80 vs. 0.50), and maximum (0.93 vs. 0.88) values. Further, Fig. 2.11d shows that SCC_{gd} drops as P decreases; however, even when P decreases to 5%, SCC_{gd} (0.62) is still 24% larger than SCC_{gp} (0.5). These results show that even with limited historical data, DSS works reasonably well. We enable DSS in our experiments of Fig. 2.11a with $P = 20\%$. Compared to EBP+CIS+AMH, enabling DSS improves the average accuracy from 0.93 to 0.94; the test duration slightly reduces.

Overall Runtime Overhead The client-side overhead of FastBTS is negligible based on our measurement on Samsung Galaxy S9, S10, Xiaomi M8, and Huawei Honor V30. On the server side, the incurred overhead is also low. When $Btlbw$ is 100 Mbps, the CPU overhead is measured to be lower than 5% (single core, tested on Intel CPU@2.5 GHz, 8-GB memory). The CPU overhead is only 12% when $Btlbw$ is 5 Gbps.

2.6 Concluding Remarks

We present FastBTS, a novel bandwidth testing system, to make bandwidth testing fast and light as well as accurate. By accommodating and exploiting the test noises, FastBTS achieves the highest level of accuracy among commercial BTSes, while significantly reducing data usage and test duration. Further, FastBTS only employs 30 servers, 2–3 orders of magnitude fewer than the state of the arts.

Despite the above merits, FastBTS still bears several limitations at the moment. First, when testing a client's uplink bandwidth, FastBTS requires extra deployment efforts (in particular a kernel module of EBP, as demonstrated in Fig. 2.1) at the client side. Second, the performance of the data-driven server selection (DSS) mechanism can be affected by its cold start phase as well as the specific deployment of test servers. Third, when the selected test servers cannot saturate the client's downlink bandwidth, the adaptive multi-homing (AMH) mechanism may need several rounds to make the bandwidth probing process converge, thus leading to a relatively long test duration. We have been exploring practical ways to overcome these limitations.

References

1. SpaceX Starlink Speeds Revealed as Beta Users Get Downloads of 11 to 60Mbps. https://arstechnica.com/information-technology/2020/08/spacex-starlink-beta-tests-show-speeds-up-to-60mbps-latency-as-low-as-31ms/
2. Add 5G capabilities to your app. https://developer.android.com/about/versions/11/features/5g
3. WiFiMaster. https://en.wifi.com/wifimaster/
4. Bauer S, Clark D, Lehr W (2010) Understanding broadband speed measurements. MIT computer science & artificial intelligence lab, Technical Report
5. Understanding Internet Speeds. https://www.att.com/support/article/u-verse-high-speed-internet/KM1010095
6. Bischof ZS, Otto JS, Sánchez MA, et al (2011) Crowdsourcing ISP characterization to the network edge. In: Proceedings of SIGCOMM W-MUST workshop, pp 61–66
7. Home Network Tips for the Coronavirus Pandemic. https://www.fcc.gov/home-network-tips-coronavirus-pandemic
8. How Coronavirus Affects Internet Usage and What You Can Do to Make Your Wi-Fi Faster. https://www.nbcnewyork.com/news/local/how-coronavirus-affects-internet-usage-and-what-you-can-do-to-make-your-wi-fi-faster/2332117/
9. Zarinni F, Chakraborty A, Sekar V, et al (2014) A first look at performance in mobile virtual network operators. In: Proceedings of IMC, pp 165–172
10. Schmitt P, et al (2016) A study of MVNO data paths and performance. In: Proceedings of PAM, pp 83–94
11. Oshiba T (2018) Accurate available bandwidth estimation robust against traffic differentiation in operational MVNO networks. In: Proceedings of ISCC, pp 694–700
12. AT&T BTS. http://speedtest.att.com/speedtest/
13. BTS Insights. https://www.speedtest.net/insights
14. Nperf BTS. https://www.nperf.com/en/map/US/-/2420.ATT-Mobility/signal/?ll=37.59682400108367&lg=-109.44030761718751&zoom=8
15. Source of Android / NetworkCapabilities.java. https://cs.android.com/android/platform/superproject/+/master:frameworks/base/packages/Connectivity/framework/src/android/net/NetworkCapabilities.java
16. Casella G, Robert CP, Wells MT, et al (2004) Generalized accept-reject sampling schemes. In: A festschrift for Herman Rubin, pp 342–347
17. Yang X, Wang X, Li Z, Liu Y, Qian F, Gong L, Miao R, Xu T (2021) Fast and light bandwidth testing for internet users. In: Proceedings of the 18th USENIX symposium on networked systems design and implementation (NSDI), pp 1011–1026
18. Alimpertis E, Markopoulou A, Irvine U (2017) A system for crowdsourcing passive mobile network measurements. In: Proceedings of NSDI
19. Bajpai V, Schönwälder J (2015) A survey on internet performance measurement platforms and related standardization efforts. IEEE Commun Surv Tutorials 17(3):1313–1341

20. Canadi I, Barford P, Sommers J (2012) Revisiting broadband performance. In: Proceedings of IMC, pp 273–286
21. Sommers J, Barford P (2012) Cell vs. WiFi: on the performance of metro area mobile connections. In: Proceedings of IMC, pp 301–314
22. Goga O, et al (2012) Speed measurements of residential internet access. In: Proceedings of PAM, pp 168–178
23. Bauer S, et al (2016) Improving the measurement and analysis of gigabit broadband networks. SSRN 2757050
24. BWP BTS. https://www.bandwidthplace.com/
25. Centurylink BTS. https://www.centurylink.com/home/help/internet/internet-speed-test.html/
26. Cox BTS. https://www.cox.com/residential/support/internet/speedtest.html
27. DSLReports. http://www.dslreports.com/speedtest/
28. FAST BTS. https://fast.com/
29. NYSbroadband BTS. http://nysbroadband.spcedtestcustom.com/
30. Optimum BTS. https://www.optimum.net/pages/speedtest.html
31. HTML5 Speed Test by SourceForge. https://sourceforge.net/speedtest/
32. Speakeasy. https://www.speakeasy.net/speedtest/
33. Spectrum BTS. https://www.spectrum.com/internet/speedtest-only/
34. Speedof.me BTS. https://www.speedof.me/
35. SpeedTest BTS. https://www.speedtest.net
36. ThinkBroadband BTS. https://www.thinkbroadband.com/speedtest/
37. Verizon BTS. https://www.verizon.com/speedtest/
38. Xfinity BTS. http://speedtest.xfinity.com/
39. Speedtest.xyz BTS. https://speedtest.xyz/
40. BandwidthTest API in Android. https://cs.android.com/android/platform/superproject/+/master:frameworks/base/core/tests/bandwidthtests/src/com/android/bandwidthtest/BandwidthTest.java
41. Dai H, Shahzad M, Liu AX, et al (2016) Finding persistent items in data streams. In: Proceedings of VLDB, pp 289–300
42. Cardwell N, Cheng Y, Gunn CS, et al (2017) BBR: congestion-based congestion control. Commun ACM 60(2):58–66
43. Narayanan A, Carpenter J, Ramadan E, et al (2019) A first measurement study of commercial mmWave 5G performance on smartphones. Preprint arXiv:1909.07532
44. Levandowsky M, Winter D (1971) Distance between sets. Nature 234(5323):34–35
45. Dong M, Li Q, Zarchy D, et al (2015) PCC: re-architecting congestion control for consistent high performance. In: Proceedings of NSDI, pp 395–408
46. Huang J, et al (2013) An in-depth study of LTE: effect of network protocol and application behavior on performance. In: Proceedings of SIGCOMM, pp 363–374
47. Goldstein H, Poole C, Safko J (2002) Classical mechanics . American Association of Physics Teachers, Maryland
48. Hu N, Li L, Mao ZM, et al (2005) A measurement study of internet bottlenecks. In: Proceedings of INFOCOM, pp 1689–1700
49. Lehman A (2005) JMP for basic univariate and multivariate statistics: a step-by-step guide. SAS Institute, Cary

Chapter 3
Offline Downloading via Cloud and/or Smart APs

Abstract Although Internet access has become more ubiquitous in recent years, most users in China still suffer from low-quality connections, especially when downloading large files. To address this issue, hundreds of millions of China's users have resorted to technologies that allow for "*offline downloading*," where a proxy is employed to pre-download the user's requested file and then deliver the file at her convenience. In this chapter, we examine two typical implementations of offline downloading: the *cloud-based approach* and the *smart AP* (access point)-*based approach*. Using a large-scale dataset collected from a major cloud-based system and comprehensive benchmarks of popular smart APs, we find that the two approaches are complementary while also being subject to distinct performance bottlenecks. Driven by these results, we design and implement a proof-of-concept middleware called ODR (Offline Downloading Redirector) to help users get rid of performance bottlenecks. We feel that offline downloading has broad applicability to other areas of the world that lack broadband penetration. By deploying offline downloading technologies, coupled with our proposed ODR middleware, the Internet experiences for users in many parts of the world can be improved.

Keywords Offline downloading · Cloud downloading · Smart WiFi router

3.1 Introduction

Although Internet access has become more ubiquitous in recent years, many users still suffer from low-quality (i.e., low bandwidth, intermittent, or restricted) network connections [1, 2]. In particular, there is a huge gap of high-speed, fixed broadband penetration between developed and developing countries. By the end of 2014, the penetration rate of fixed broadband access in the developed world has reached 27.5% with as high as 25 Mbps of download bandwidth [3]. On the other hand, the rate is merely 6.1% in the developing world with relatively limited, unstable download bandwidth [4].

This digital divide prevents many Internet users in developing countries from accessing the full wealth of data and services available online, especially those *large files* (e.g., HD videos and large software) that require high-quality connections to download [5]. Researchers have studied various approaches to making the Internet more accessible, performant, and affordable, such as delay-tolerant networking (DTN) [6, 7]. Nevertheless, to date, these technologies have not been widely deployed or evaluated in practice.

Modern China exemplifies both the promise and challenges of increasing Internet penetration [8]. In the last ten years, 46% of China's population has come online [9], and China is now home to world-class Internet companies such as Tencent, Baidu, Alibaba, and Sina Weibo. However, a majority (over 72%) of China's Internet users have low-quality connections [10], due to low access bandwidth, unreliable/unstable data connection, and poor interconnectivity between ISPs (termed *ISP barrier*). The disparity between those who have access to high-speed broadband and those who do not is likely to increase over the next few years as more of China's rural population comes online.

To deal with the problems caused by low-quality Internet connections, hundreds of millions of China's users have resorted to technologies that allow for " *offline downloading*" of large files [11–13]. Offline downloading implements ideas from DTNs by outsourcing long downloads to a proxy, as demonstrated in Fig. 3.1. Specifically, when a user wants to acquire a file, the user first *requests* a proxy to *pre-download* the file on her behalf (typically using an HTTP/FTP/P2P link via a low-quality network connection). The proxy may have access to faster, cheaper, or more reliable connectivity than the user, so it is better suited to downloading the file from the Internet. The user can then *fetch* the file from the proxy at a later point in time, when local network conditions are conducive to the task.

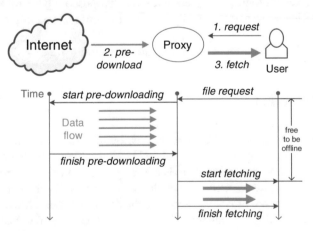

Fig. 3.1 Basic working principle of offline downloading, as well as the corresponding timing diagram (Reprinted with permission from [14])

In this chapter, we examine two implementations of offline downloading that are extremely popular in China [15, 16] (Sect. 3.3):

- *The cloud-based approach* leverages a geo-distributed, massive cloud storage pool as the proxy, which usually caches petabytes of files in a data center that is within or directly peered with the requesting user's ISP. This approach is adopted by Tencent Xuanfeng, Baidu CloudDisk, and Xunlei. As it requires expensive cloud infrastructure for data storage and delivery, it is mostly operated by big Internet companies such as Tencent and Baidu.

- *The smart AP-based approach* relies on a local smart WiFi AP as the proxy. It is adopted by HiWiFi, MiWiFi, Newifi, etc. A traditional AP only forwards data for its connected end devices such as laptops and smartphones. In contrast, a smart AP, if requested, also pre-downloads and caches data on an embedded/connected storage device (e.g., an SD card, a USB flash drive, or a hard disk drive). The user can then fetch the requested file at her convenience once it is successfully pre-downloaded. This approach incurs almost zero infrastructure cost but requires smart AP devices with redesigned hardware, OS, and application software.

Currently, there is a dispute over which approach better suits the Internet [17, 18]. This *selection dilemma* confuses the users, especially those who have little expertise in Internet content delivery. The key argument lies in the performance of the two approaches, in terms of (pre-)downloading *speed, delay*, and *failure ratio*. Both approaches have advocates that express complaints in news media and marketing reports. However, all these disputes either are limited to one particular offline downloading service/product [13, 19–22] or rely on oversimplified workloads and network environments [23–26]. The former make it hard to form a general and unified view of the factors that may affect offline downloading performance, while the latter do not present comprehensive or objective results.

In this chapter, we address the issue in a *quantitative* and *comparative* manner. First, we measure the workload characteristics of offline downloading (Sect. 3.4), based on a large-scale dataset collected from a major cloud-based system called Xuanfeng. Our analysis of this dataset provides useful insights on the optimization of offline downloading services. Second, we identify the key performance bottlenecks of both approaches, based on the complete running logs of Xuanfeng (Sect. 3.5) and comprehensive benchmarks of three popular smart APs (Sect. 3.6). Some of our key results include:

1. *The users' fetching processes are often impeded.* The cloud-based approach can usually accelerate downloading by 7–11 times but performs *poorly* (i.e., the user's fetching speed falls below 1 Mbps, or 125 KBps, and is thus unfit for HD video streaming) once there is a bandwidth bottleneck in the network path between the cloud and the user. Specifically, a high portion (28%) of Xuanfeng users suffer from this bottleneck, which is mainly caused by cross-ISP data delivery, low user-side access bandwidth, or a lack of cloud-side upload bandwidth. These users should utilize an additional smart AP to mitigate these impediments.

2. *The cloud's upload bandwidth is being overused.* The cloud-based approach is
   threatened by running out of its upload bandwidth due to *unnecessarily* sending
   highly popular files. A small percentage (0.84%) of highly popular files account
   for a large part (39%) of all downloads. As the user base grows, the cloud of
   Xuanfeng will have to reject more (>1.5%) users' fetching requests. Because a
   majority (87%) of requested files are hosted in peer-to-peer data swarms [27],
   many highly popular files can be directly downloaded by users with as good or
   greater performance than what is provided by cloud-based offline downloading
   services.
3. *Smart APs frequently fail during pre-downloading.* Although smart APs are
   immune to the above performance bottlenecks of the cloud-based approach,
   they frequently (42%) fail while pre-downloading *unpopular* files. This is
   mainly caused by insufficient seeds in a P2P data swarm and poor HTTP/FTP
   connections. Note that 36% of the offline downloading requests are issued for
   unpopular files. Thus, users who need to download unpopular files should choose
   the cloud-based approach, which is better at downloading unpopular files—
   the failure ratio (13%) is much lower owing to *collaborative caching* (refer to
   Sect. 3.3.1) in the massive cloud storage pool.
4. *Smart APs can be slower due to hardware/filesystem restrictions.* Surprisingly,
   a smart AP's pre-downloading speed can be restricted by its hardware and
   filesystem. This is because some types of storage devices (e.g., USB flash
   drive) and filesystems (e.g., NTFS) do not fit the pattern of frequent, small data
   writes during the pre-downloading process. These smart APs would benefit from
   upgraded storage devices and/or alternate filesystems, so as to release the full
   potential of offline downloading.

Driven by these results, we design and implement a proof-of-concept middleware called Offline Downloading Redirector (ODR) to help users to get rid
of performance bottlenecks (Sect. 3.7). As illustrated in Fig. 3.2, the basic idea
is to adaptively redirect the user's file request to where the best performance is
expected to be achieved, including the cloud (we use the Xuanfeng cloud in our
implementation), the smart AP, the user's local device, or a combination. ODR's

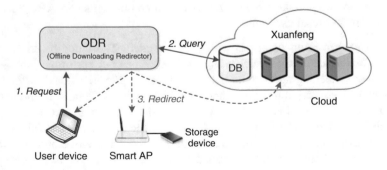

Fig. 3.2 Basic working principle of ODR (Reprinted with permission from [14])

primary goal is to minimize the downloading time and failure ratio; its secondary goal is to minimize the upload bandwidth burden on the cloud.

ODR makes redirection decisions based on two types of information. First, after receiving an offline downloading request, ODR queries the content database of Xuanfeng to obtain the popularity information of the requested file. Then, ODR examines whether there is a potential bandwidth bottleneck by analyzing the user's IP address, access bandwidth, storage device, and so forth. Note that ODR requires no modification to the existing cloud-based systems or smart AP devices. As a result, it is easy to deploy in practice.

To validate the efficacy of ODR, we replay an unbiased sample of Xuanfeng users' offline downloading requests using a prototype ODR system. The evaluation results indicate that ODR is able to effectively overcome the performance bottlenecks. First, the percentage of impeded fetching processes is reduced from 28 to 9%. Second, the cloud's upload bandwidth burden is reduced by 35% and thus no fetching request will need to be rejected. Third, the percentage of smart APs' failures in pre-downloading unpopular files is reduced from 42 to 13%. Last, the hardware/filesystem restrictions on smart APs' pre-downloading speeds are almost completely avoided.

Finally, we feel that offline downloading has broad applicability to other areas of the world that lack broadband penetration. By deploying offline downloading, coupled with our proposed ODR middleware, the Internet experiences for users in many parts of the world can be significantly improved.

3.2 Related Work

This section reviews previous studies of offline downloading, including both the cloud and smart AP-based approaches. We also discuss the hybrid approach that directly connects the smart AP to the cloud and compare it with our ODR. In addition, we describe a few offline downloading (based) services outside China. Finally, we briefly survey the state-of-the-art downloading techniques and compare them with offline downloading.

Cloud-Based Approach With the proliferation of cloud-based services, a number of studies have investigated the design and implementation of cloud-based offline downloading systems and their performance measurements.

Huang et al. [19] presented the early-stage system design of Xuanfeng in 2011, which focuses on guaranteeing data health and accelerating the downloading speed of unpopular videos. However, perhaps due to the startup stage of the system at that time (with a relatively small user base), their study did not notice the two critical performance bottlenecks, i.e., Bottleneck 1 and Bottleneck 2 uncovered in this chapter.

Ao et al. [13] conducted a long-term measurement study of Xuanfeng in 2012 and predicted that the system would be short of cloud-side upload bandwidth in the near future. Complementary to their study, our work provides in-depth insights into the cloud-side upload bandwidth burden and recognizes Bottleneck 2—the root cause of cloud bandwidth shortage. Furthermore, our proposed ODR middleware can significantly reduce cloud-side bandwidth consumption by asking users to download highly popular P2P files directly from their data swarms.

Zhou et al. [23] made a theoretical analysis of offline downloading service models, including the cloud-based model and the peer-assisted model. They argue that the former can help scale with file population, and the latter should be used to deal with popular files. An adaptive algorithm called AMS (Automatic Mode Selection) is proposed for selecting an appropriate model. Compared with AMS, ODR is more general and applicable: it requires no modification on the cloud side. Additionally, ODR is a deployed system rather than a theoretical algorithm.

Smart AP-Based Approach   Since the history of smart APs is extremely short (just two years), we are not aware of any systematic study on their downloading performances. Most of the existing evaluations [20–22, 24–26] are based on simplified network environments and unrealistic workloads (e.g., a few popular files). This is probably the reason why Bottleneck 3 in our study had not been discovered yet. Furthermore, Bottleneck 4 had never been identified in the existing evaluations of smart Aps.

Hybrid Approach   HiWiFi, MiWiFi, and Newifi all provide hybrid solutions for offline downloading. In these hybrid solutions, user-requested files are first downloaded by the cloud, and then the smart AP fetches the files from the cloud. That is to say, the downloading process always goes through the longest data flow: first from the Internet to the cloud and then to the smart AP of the user. In contrast, our ODR middleware adaptively selects the most efficient data flow for users to avoid performance bottlenecks. Therefore, ODR significantly outperforms the current hybrid approach by addressing the bottlenecks of both (cloud and smart AP-based) approaches while also inheriting their advantages.

Offline Downloading Outside China   Besides those developing countries (as mentioned in Sect. 3.1), developed countries can also benefit from offline downloading (based) services. For example, URL Droplet and the Amazon Silk web browser take advantage of the cloud to speed up file transfers. The former employs the Dropbox cloud storage service to download and host files for its users; the latter utilizes Amazon's cloud servers to improve web page loading performance for Kindle Fire tablets and smartphones. On the other side, the smart AP-based approach is adopted by the Linksys Smart WiFi Router sold in the USA.

3.3 System Overview

This section provides an overview of the systems studied in this chapter, including the cloud-based offline downloading system (Xuanfeng) and three popular smart AP systems.

3.3.1 Overview of Xuanfeng

Xuanfeng is a major provider of cloud-based offline downloading service in China, possessing over 30 million users at the moment (including a small portion of overseas users). Its service can be accessed via either a PC client or a web-based portal. The former access method is dominant due to its full-fledged functionality (supporting almost all the common file transfer protocols such as HTTP/FTP and BitTorrent/eMule). In terms of business model, Xuanfeng exists as a value-added service of the Tencent company, i.e., any registered Tencent user can access it freely. Baidu CloudDisk and Xunlei are the main competitors of Xuanfeng. The former is also a free service, while the latter charges its users around $1.50 per month.

As depicted in Fig. 3.3, the system architecture of the Xuanfeng cloud mainly consists of three clusters of servers: (1) *pre-downloading servers*, (2) *storage servers*, and (3) *uploading servers*, as well as a database (DB) for maintaining the metadata information of users and cached files. The total cloud storage space (spread across nearly 500 commodity servers) is nearly 2 PB at the moment, caching around 5 million files. The cached files are replaced in an LRU (least recently used) manner.

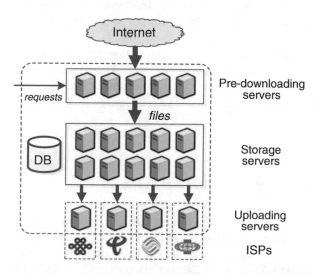

Fig. 3.3 System architecture of Xuanfeng cloud (Reprinted with permission from [14])

Collaborative Caching In the Xuanfeng cloud, all users' requested files are cached in a *collaborative* way. Specifically, every file is identified using the MD5 hash code of its content, which facilitates file-level deduplication across different users. Consequently, the vast majority (89%) of offline downloading requests can be instantly satisfied with cached files, and then no pre-downloading bandwidth cost is incurred. Xuanfeng does not utilize chunk-level deduplication to avoid trading high chunking complexity for low (<1%) storage space savings. The low storage savings come from the fact that there do exist a few videos sharing a portion of frames/chunks.

When a user-requested file cannot be found in the cloud cache, Xuanfeng assigns a *pre-downloader* to pre-download the file from the Internet. The Internet access bandwidth of a pre-downloader is around 20 Mbps (= 2.5 MBps), equivalent to the high-end, fixed broadband bandwidth in China.

Privileged Network Path China has a different Internet topology from Europe and the USA. It has a simple AS topology with a small number of major ISPs; each ISP has a giant AS built on top of a nationwide backbone network [28]. As a consequence, the performance of cross-ISP data delivery is significantly degraded, a problem that is known as the *ISP barrier* [29, 30]. To accelerate users' fetching processes, Xuanfeng tries to construct *privileged network paths* between the cloud and users by deploying uploading servers within the four major ISPs: Unicom, Telecom, Mobile, and CERNET.

To construct a privileged network path, Xuanfeng always attempts to select an uploading server that resides in the same ISP as the fetching user, so that the ISP barrier is avoided. However, privileged path construction may fail in two cases: (1) The fetching user is not within any of the four major ISPs; (2) The fetching user is within one of the four major ISPs (say CERNET), but the uploading servers in CERNET have exhausted their upload bandwidth at that time. In either case, Xuanfeng would select an alternative uploading server that has the shortest network latency from the user.

Once a privileged network path is set up, Xuanfeng sets no limitation on the fetching speed, with maximum speeds reaching 50 Mbps (= 6.25 MBps). However, at some "peak" point, all the uploading servers may have exhausted their upload bandwidth. In this case, Xuanfeng temporarily rejects new fetching requests rather than degrading the speeds of active downloads.

3.3.2   Overview of the Smart AP Systems

Though smart APs have only been on the market for around 2 years, they have quickly gained enormous popularity in China. HiWiFi, the first widely available smart AP device released in Mar. 2013 [31], is now striving toward 5 million sales [12]. Despite the late entry into the market (in May 2014), 100,000 MiWiFi devices were sold out in just 59 seconds [11].

As depicted in Fig. 3.4, the system architecture of popular smart APs is essentially made up of three parts: (1) Basic hardware, including CPU, RAM, NIC (network interface card) for xDSL, NIC for WiFi, and the storage device interface(s); (2) The operating system (typically OpenWrt); (3) Shell and the other applications. Table 3.1 lists the hardware configurations of the three popular smart APs we examine in this study. Among them, MiWiFi has the best configuration in terms of CPU, RAM, storage device, and WiFi data transfer. Accordingly, MiWiFi costs more than $100, while HiWiFi and Newifi each cost around $20.

All the three smart APs use OpenWrt, a Linux-based embedded OS. OpenWrt provides a fully writable filesystem and supports the lightweight Opkg package management system, which allows users to install any Opkg application. For instance, the three APs make use of wget and aria2 [32] to support HTTP/FTP and BitTorrent/eMule protocols. Also, a web interface is provided for users to specify offline downloading requests. In our benchmark experiments, we measure

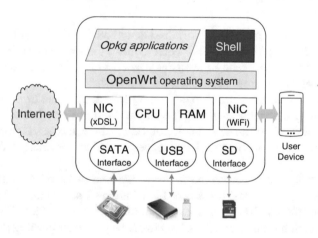

Fig. 3.4 System architecture of a commercial smart AP. A given smart AP device may not contain all potential storage device interfaces (Reprinted with permission from [14])

Table 3.1 Hardware configurations of the three popular smart APs studied in this chapter

Smart AP	CPU	RAM	Storage interface (and device)	WiFi protocol
HiWiFi (1S)	MT7620A @580 MHz	128 MB	An SD card interface	IEEE 802.11 b/g/n @2.4 GHz
MiWiFi	Broadcom4709 @1 GHz	256 MB	A USB 2.0 interface and an internal 1-TB SATA hard disk drive	IEEE 802.11 b/g/n/ac @2.4/5.0 GHz
Newifi	MT7620A @580 MHz	128 MB	A USB 2.0 interface	IEEE 802.11 b/g/n/ac @2.4/5.0 GHz

(Reprinted with permission from [14])

and record detailed performance of smart APs with Opkg tools/apps such as BASH, tcpdump, top, iostats, and scp.

3.4 Workload Characteristics

To understand the workload characteristics of offline downloading, we study a large-scale dataset collected from Xuanfeng. We assume that the smart AP-based offline downloading systems have similar workload characteristics to Xuanfeng, since most end users are not familiar with the technical details and cannot differentiate these services. The large-scale dataset contains the complete running logs of Xuanfeng during a whole week (Feb. 22–28, 2015), involving 4,084,417 offline downloading tasks, 783,944 users, and 563,517 unique files. Corresponding to the three stages of offline downloading (refer to Fig. 3.1), the dataset is composed of the following three parts:

1. The **trace of user requests (workload trace)** records all the offline download-ing requests issued by users. For each request, the logs record the user ID, IP address, access bandwidth (if available), request time, file type, file size, link to the original data source, and file transfer protocol.
2. The **pre-downloading trace** records the performance data of the proxy's pre-downloading user-requested files. It includes the start time, finish time, acquired file size, network traffic consumed, cloud cache hit status, average downloading speed, peak downloading speed, and success or failure for each pre-downloading process.
3. The **fetching trace** records the performance data of users' fetching processes from the proxy. It contains the user ID, IP address, access bandwidth (if avail-able), start time, finish/pause time, acquired file size, network traffic consumed, average fetching speed, and peak fetching speed for each fetching process.

This section studies the first part of the dataset. The second and third parts of the dataset will be examined in Sects. 3.5 and 3.6.

File Type In the workload trace, the majority (75%) of offline downloading requests is issued for videos; the other 15% are for software packages. The reason is intuitive: among all the requested files, videos are the largest in size, i.e., the most time and traffic consuming to download, so users are more inclined to issue offline downloading requests for videos. This suggests that offline downloading systems should be mainly optimized for videos.

File Size As shown in Fig. 3.5, the average size of requested files is 390 MB and the maximum size is 4 GB, which is consistent with our observation that most requested files are large videos. Nevertheless, we also find that up to 25% of the requested files are smaller than 8 MB in size, most of which are demo videos, pictures, documents, and small software packages.

Fig. 3.5 CDF of requested
file size. Min size: 4 B,
Median size: 115 MB,
Average size: 390 MB, and
Max size: 4 GB (Reprinted
with permission from [14])

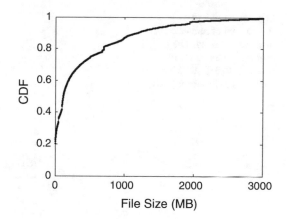

File Transfer Protocol The majority (87%) of requested files is hosted in P2P
data swarms, including BitTorrent (68%) and eMule (19%) swarms. The remaining
13% are hosted on HTTP or FTP servers. Thus, designers of offline downloading
systems should pay special attention to P2P-based file transfer protocols. Since P2P
suffers from several technical shortcomings (e.g., high dynamics and heterogeneities
among end-user devices and network connections), it is often difficult for users to
find peers (including both seeds and leechers) sharing the target files. As a result, the
downloading efficacy of P2P can be poor and unpredictable. For this reason, users
resort to offline downloading to obtain P2P files over the long run. On the contrary,
HTTP and FTP servers are usually stable with more predictable performance, so
online downloading is preferred. This explains the dominance of P2P in terms of
file transfer protocol.

File Popularity As mentioned in Sect. 3.3.1, Xuanfeng actively maintains a content database where every file is associated with a unique identifier (ID). The ID is
the MD5 hash code of the complete file content. Hence, files are considered *identical*
as long as they have the same ID. Fig. 3.6 (in $log(x)$ vs. $log(y)$ style) and Fig. 3.7
(in $log(x)$ vs. y^c style) indicate that the popularity distribution of requested files is
highly skewed, approximately following the well-known Zipf model [33] or the SE
(stretched exponential) model [34].

Let x denote the popularity ranking of a file, and y denote its popularity
(according to the **workload trace**). We have the following fitting equations:

$$\text{Zipf}: \quad log(y) = -a_1 \times log(x) + b_1,$$

$$\text{SE}: \quad y^c = -a_2 \times log(x) + b_2,$$

where $a_1 = 1.034$, $b_1 = 14.444$, $a_2 = 0.010$, $b_2 = 1.134$, and $c = 0.01$.

With regard to the average relative error of fitness, SE (13.7%) seems to be a
better fit than Zipf (15.3%), especially for those small-ranking (i.e., most popular)
files. The reason why SE fits the measurement data better than Zipf can be mainly

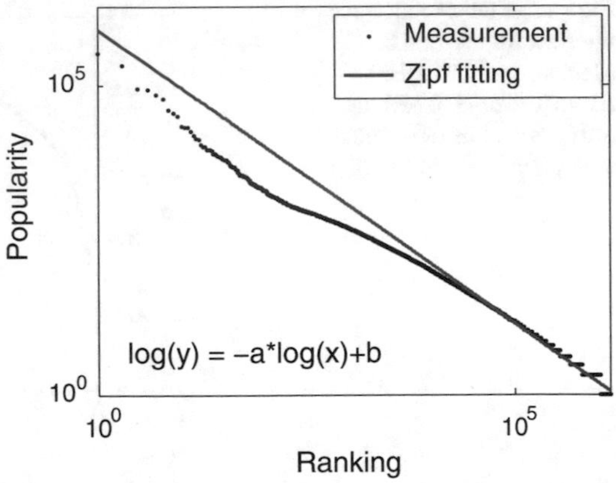

Fig. 3.6 Popularity
distribution of requested
files—Zipf fitting. The
average relative error of
fitness is 15.3% (Reprinted
with permission from [14])

Fig. 3.7 Popularity
distribution of requested
files—SE fitting. The average
relative error of fitness is
13.7% (Reprinted with
permission from [14])

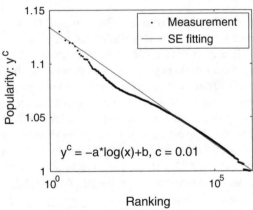

attributed to the *fetch-at-most-once* effect of P2P video files [35]. It is known
that 75% of the offline downloading requests are issued for videos and 87% of
the requested files are hosted in P2P data swarms. That is to say, P2P video
files dominate the workload of Xuanfeng. Specifically, a given Xuanfeng user
generally fetches a P2P video file for at most once, whereas web pages and other
small documents are often fetched repeatedly [33]. Therefore, the access pattern
of offline downloaded files deviates from the Zipf access pattern of web objects.
The above finding complements the analysis of file popularity in previous studies of
offline downloading [19, 23], which simply used the Zipf model to characterize the
workload.

3.5 Performance of the Cloud-Based System

This section presents the performance of Xuanfeng, including both the pre-downloading and fetching phases. In addition, we analyze the end-to-end performance by combining the two phases.

3.5.1 Pre-downloading Performance

Pre-downloading Speed Figure 3.8 (the upper curve) plots the distribution of pre-downloading speeds in Xuanfeng. The median speed is merely 25 KBps, which indicates that half of the pre-downloading processes are quite slow. The average speed (69 KBps) is higher than the median speed but is still far from satisfactory—keep in mind that, as mentioned in Sect. 3.3.1, the access bandwidth of a pre-downloader is around 20 Mbps (= 2.5 MBps). 21% of the pre-downloading processes even have a speed close to 0 KBps, which is mostly caused by pre-downloading failures.

Pre-downloading Delay Figure 3.9 (the lower curve) plots the distribution of the pre-downloading delay in Xuanfeng (excluding the cache hit cases where the pre-downloading delay is zero). The average delay is as high as 370 min, which is much longer than the length of a common movie (100–120 min). Obviously, such long delay is unfit for continuous video streaming [36, 37]. Also, the average delay is

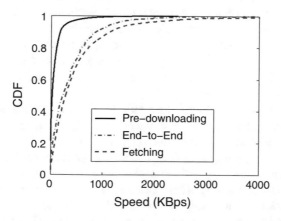

Fig. 3.8 CDF of pre-downloading and fetching speeds in Xuanfeng. As for the pre-downloading speed (excluding the cache hit cases), Min: 0 KBps, Median: 25 KBps, Average: 69 KBps, and Max: 2.37 MBps (≈20 Mbps). As for the fetching speed, Min: 0 KBps, Median: 287 KBps, Average: 504 KBps, and Max: 6.1 MBps (≈50 Mbps). As for the end-to-end speed, Min: 0 KBps, Median: 233 KBps, Average: 380 KBps, and Max: 6.1 MBps (≈50 Mbps) (Reprinted with permission from [14])

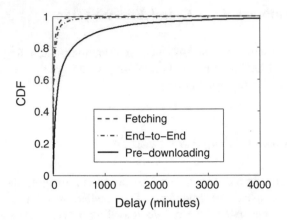

Fig. 3.9 CDF of pre-downloading, fetching, and end-to-end delay in Xuanfeng. As for the pre-downloading delay (excluding the cache hit cases), Min: 0 min, Median: 82 min, Average: 370 min, and Max: 10071 min. As for the fetching delay, Min: 0 min, Median: 7 min, Average: 27 min, and Max: 9724 min. As for the end-to-end delay, Min: 0 min, Median: 10 min, Average: 68 min, and Max: 19553 min (Reprinted with permission from [14])

much longer than the median delay (82 min), indicating that the pre-downloading delay of many requested files is extremely long.

Failure Ratio A *pre-downloading failure* occurs when the service gives up the pre-downloading attempt and notifies the requesting user of the failure. It is hard to theoretically define a failure if we allow the pre-downloading process to take infinite time. However, practical systems have to terminate the process if the expected completion time is not reasonable. In practice, Xuanfeng raises a pre-downloading failure for a requested file when *the corresponding pre-downloading progress stagnates for an hour*. This timeout rule is supported by our following observation in Xuanfeng: if the pre-downloading progress of a requested file stagnates for an hour, then this file can hardly be successfully pre-downloaded even if the timeout threshold is set to be one week.

The overall pre-downloading failure ratio of Xuanfeng is 8.7%. Note that if a user-requested file is already cached in the cloud storage pool, the pre-downloading is immediately successful. On the other hand, if we do not take the cache hit cases into account (i.e., we assume that the cloud storage pool does not exist), the overall pre-downloading failure ratio will increase to 16.4%. This confirms the importance of the massive cloud storage pool as well as the collaborative caching mechanism (refer to Sect. 3.3.1) in mitigating pre-downloading failures.

More importantly, we discover that the pre-downloading failure ratio correlates with the popularity of requested files, as shown in the scatter plot of Fig. 3.10. For the purposes of this discussion, we define a file to be *unpopular* if it was downloaded less than 7 times per week. *Popular* files are downloaded 7–84 times per week, while *highly popular* files are downloaded greater than 84 times per week. Given these definitions, we find that 93.2% of the files are unpopular, while only 0.84% of the

Fig. 3.10 Request popularity
versus pre-downloading
failure ratio. Request
popularity: [0, 7) →
unpopular files, [7, 84] →
popular files, and (84, MAX]
→ highly popular files
(Reprinted with permission
from [14])

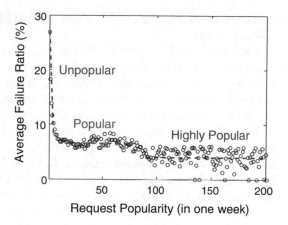

files are highly popular. However, only 36% of the offline downloading requests are
issued for the 93.2% unpopular files, while 39% of the requests are issued for the
0.84% highly popular files.

Network Traffic Cost As discussed in Sect. 3.4, only 13% of the requested files
are hosted in HTTP or FTP servers, while 87% are hosted in P2P data swarms.
For HTTP and FTP, the pre-downloading traffic is slightly (typically 7–10%) larger
than the file size; the overhead mainly comes from HTTP, FTP, TCP, and IP packet
headers. For P2P, its "tit-for-tat" policy [38] (i.e., a peer that downloads data from
others must upload data to others at the same time) causes the pre-downloading
traffic to be considerably (50–150%) larger than the file size. In the Xuanfeng
system, we observe that the overall pre-downloading traffic is 196% of the total
file size. That is to say, the overhead traffic is comparable to the file size.

3.5.2 Fetching Performance

Fetching Speed Figure 3.8 (the lower curve) shows the distribution of users' fetching speeds from the cloud. Owing to the privileged network paths constructed by
Xuanfeng (refer to Sect. 3.3.1), the median and average fetching speeds are as high
as 287 and 504 KBps. Given that the median and average pre-downloading speeds
are merely 25 and 69 KBps, Xuanfeng greatly improves *perceived* downloading
speeds (by 7–11 times in terms of median and average speeds) for China's Internet
users.

When videos are fetched from the proxy, Xuanfeng supports two different modes:
(a) *view as download* and (b) *view after download*. According to Xuanfeng users'
behaviors, most users tend to choose the former mode over the latter. Therefore,
to facilitate users' real-time video playback in a continuous manner, a *bandwidth
bottleneck* is recognized when the fetching speed falls below 125 KBps. The

125 KBps threshold corresponds with the typical 1 Mbps playback rate of large (HD) videos [39, 40].

Specifically, a high portion (28%) of fetching speeds are below 125 KBps. To explore why Xuanfeng exhibits poor performance during these fetching processes, we carefully examine the corresponding logs in the fetching trace and find that the bandwidth bottleneck is mainly caused by three issues: (1) cross-ISP data delivery, (2) low user-side access bandwidth, and (3) a lack of cloud-side upload bandwidth.

In detail, 9.6% of the fetching processes are limited by the ISP barrier. For these fetching processes, the users' IP addresses do not belong to any of the four ISPs supported by Xuanfeng. Besides, around 10.8% of the fetching processes are limited by low user-side access bandwidth[1] (<125 KBps). Additionally, there are 1.5% of the fetching requests rejected by the cloud due to the lack of upload bandwidth (refer to Sect. 3.3.1). These rejected requests explain why the minimum observed fetching speed is 0 KBps. Finally, the remaining unmentioned portion (= 28% − 9.6% − 10.8% − 1.5% = 6.1%) are owing to unknown reasons we have not figured out yet, possibly because of the network dynamics or system bugs.

Fetching Delay Figure 3.9 (the upper curve) shows the distribution of users' fetching delay. As a consequence of most users' high fetching speeds, the median fetching delay is as low as 7 min, and the average fetching delay is merely 27 min. Given that the median and average pre-downloading delays are as high as 82 and 370 min, Xuanfeng has significantly shortened *perceived* downloading delay (by 12–14 times in terms of median and average fetching delay) for China's Internet users. In summary, we find the first key performance bottleneck of offline downloading:

- *The cloud-based approach performs poorly once there is a bandwidth bottleneck in the privileged network path between the cloud and the user. This bottleneck is mainly caused by cross-ISP data delivery, low user-side access bandwidth, or a lack of cloud-side upload bandwidth.*

Shortage of Cloud Bandwidth In order to support high-speed fetching from the cloud to users' devices, Xuanfeng has purchased a total of 30 Gbps of upload bandwidth from the four major ISPs in China. In the 7th day of the measurement week, the peak cloud-side upload bandwidth burden exceeded 30 Gbps, as demonstrated in Fig. 3.11. Consequently, a small portion (1.5%) of fetching requests were rejected by Xuanfeng. As the user base continues to grow, Xuanfeng will have to reject more fetching requests, which unfortunately harms the user experience.

On the other hand, if we look deeply into the usage of cloud bandwidth, we find that *the current cloud-side upload bandwidth burden is not all necessary.* We calculate the cloud-side bandwidth used for delivering (uploading) highly popular files based on the fetching trace, plotted as the lower, blue curve in Fig. 3.11. We can see that, on average, nearly 40% of the cloud bandwidth is spent delivering

---

[1] Some users of Xuanfeng did not report their access bandwidth. For these users, we use the peak fetching speed recorded in the fetching trace to approximate their access bandwidth.

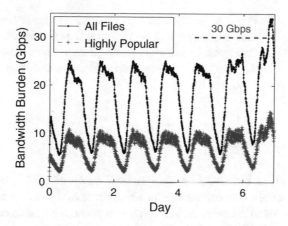

Fig. 3.11 Cloud-side upload bandwidth burden of Xuanfeng in the measurement week (including those rejected fetching requests). The time interval is 5 min. Note that for 1.5% of the fetching requests rejected by Xuanfeng in the 7th day, their incurred cloud-side upload bandwidth burden (which did not really happen) is estimated by approximately taking their average fetching speed as 504 KBps (i.e., the average speed of all the real fetching processes in Xuanfeng, refer to Fig. 3.8) (Reprinted with permission from [14])

highly popular files. The reason is that a small percentage (0.84%) of highly popular files account for a large part (39%) of all downloads, as discussed in Sect. 3.5.1.

In fact, because a majority (87%) of the requested files are hosted in P2P data swarms, many highly popular files can be directly downloaded by users with as good or greater performance than what the cloud provides [41, 42]. This is because P2P data sharing among end users can achieve the so-called *bandwidth multiplier effect* [41]. Specifically, by appropriately allocating a certain portion of cloud bandwidth (S_i) to a P2P data swarm i to seed the content, the Xuanfeng system can attain a higher aggregate content distribution bandwidth (D_i) by letting P2P users exchange data and distribute content among themselves. The ratio $\frac{D_i}{S_i}$ is referred to as the bandwidth multiplier for P2P data swarm i. The above observation and analysis lead to the second key performance bottleneck of offline downloading:

- *The cloud-based approach is threatened by running out of upload bandwidth due to unnecessarily sending highly popular files. As the user base continues to grow, the cloud will have to reject more (>1.5%) fetching requests.*

User-Side Network Overhead Xuanfeng minimizes the user-side network overhead, as its users only download requested files from the cloud and do not upload data to others. On average, a user's downloading traffic usage is slightly (7–10%) larger than the file size. This is especially useful for mobile P2P users with limited data plans or traffic caps. As mentioned in Sect. 3.5.1, for an average P2P user to download a file from the corresponding data swarm, the total traffic usage is 196% of the total file size. Therefore, by resorting to Xuanfeng rather than the original data swarm, an average P2P user could achieve considerable traffic usage saving that is comparable to 86–89% of the total file size.

3.5.3   End-to-End Performance

Finally, we analyze the *end-to-end speed and delay* of offline downloading in Xuanfeng. For a complete offline downloading process, the end-to-end delay is the sum of pre-downloading delay and fetching delay, and the end-to-end speed is the size of the requested file divided by the end-to-end delay.

As illustrated in Fig. 3.9, the CDF curve of end-to-end delay falls between the CDF curves of pre-downloading delay and fetching delay, which is within our expectation. More importantly, the distribution of end-to-end delay looks much closer to the distribution of fetching delay. This is because the vast majority (89%) of offline downloading requests can be instantly satisfied by the cloud cache, and thus the corresponding pre-downloading delay is almost zero (refer to Sect. 3.3.1). Similarly, Fig. 3.8 indicates that the CDF curve of end-to-end speed falls between the CDF curves of pre-downloading speed and fetching speed, and the distribution of end-to-end speed is much closer to the distribution of fetching speed.

From the above observations, we conclude that even from an end-to-end perspective, the offline downloading service provided by Xuanfeng can effectively improve the *perceived experiences* for its users.

3.6   Performance of the Smart APs

Now that we understand the dynamics and performance characteristics of Xuanfeng, we move on to examining smart AP-based offline downloading. In this section, we report our benchmark methodology and the performance of the three most popular smart APs in China: HiWiFi, MiWiFi, and Newifi.

3.6.1   Methodology

To comprehensively measure the performance of the three popular smart APs (during Mar. 1–22, 2015), we randomly sample 1000 real offline downloading

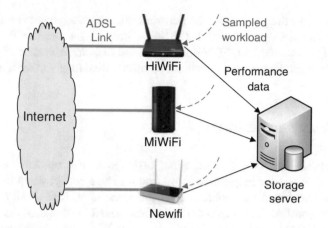

Fig. 3.12 Our benchmark environment. For each smart AP, its embedded/connected storage device is not plotted to make the figure tidy (Reprinted with permission from [14])

requests[2] issued by Unicom users in the **workload trace** of Xuanfeng (Sect. 3.4). These sampled requests (referred to as the **sampled workload**) are restricted to Unicom users because our benchmark experiments are conducted by replaying the **sampled workload** with smart APs on Unicom network connections. On the other hand, the data sources of these sampled requests are located across various ISPs in China. For every request record, we ignore its user ID, IP address, and request time (since these factors cannot be reproduced in our benchmarks) but reuse the user's access bandwidth, as well as the file type, file size, link to the original data source, and file transfer protocol.

To replay the **sampled workload** using the three smart APs, we utilize three independent residential ADSL links provided by the Unicom ISP, each of which was used exclusively by one smart AP, as depicted in Fig. 3.12. Each link has 20 Mbps (= 2.5 MBps) of Internet access bandwidth. When replaying an individual offline downloading request, we restrict the smart AP's pre-downloading speed within the recorded user access bandwidth, so as to approximate the real network connection status. We sequentially replay around 333 requests (request $i + 1$ is replayed after request i completes or fails) on each smart AP and record the performance data.

HiWiFi uses an embedded 8-GB SD card (Max Write/Read Speed: 15 MBps/30 MBps) as the storage device. The SD card can only be formatted as FAT (otherwise, HiWiFi does not work). Newifi uses an external 8-GB USB flash drive (Max Write/Read Speed: 10 MBps/20 MBps) via a USB 2.0 interface. The USB flash drive is formatted as NTFS. Since both HiWiFi and Newifi have a small storage capacity, we remove requested files from the storage device after they are completely downloaded or the corresponding pre-downloading task failures (refer

---

[2] Each selected request record should contain the user's access bandwidth information, so we can approximate the user's network connection characteristics during our benchmarks.

to Sect. 3.5.1). At the same time, the performance data is aggregated into a storage server. MiWiFi uses its internal 1-TB SATA hard disk drive (5400 RPM, Max Write/Read Speed: 30 MBps/70 MBps). This hard disk drive has been formatted as EXT4 by the manufacturer, and it cannot be reformatted to any other filesystem.

3.6.2   Benchmark Results

Since smart APs are located in the same LAN (local area network) as users, the performance of the fetching phase is seldom an issue except when multiple user devices are fetching from a smart AP at the same time. Specifically, a user can fetch from a smart AP by directly dumping from the AP's storage device or through a wired/WiFi LAN connection. Even the lowest WiFi fetching speed lies in 8–12 MBps, which is higher than the maximum fetching speed (i.e., 6.1 MBps) of Xuanfeng users. As a consequence, below we focus on the performance of the pre-downloading phase.

Pre-Downloading Failure Ratio The overall pre-downloading failure ratio of smart APs is 16.8%, which is higher than that of Xuanfeng (8.7%). More importantly, for unpopular files, the pre-downloading failure ratio of smart APs is as high as 42%, significantly higher than that of Xuanfeng (13%). Note that according to the **workload trace** of Xuanfeng, 36% of the offline downloading requests are issued for unpopular files. With these results, we discover the third key performance bottleneck of offline downloading:

- *Although smart APs are immune to the two bottlenecks of the cloud-based approach described in Sect. 3.5, they frequently fail in pre-downloading unpopular files. In contrast, the cloud-based approach performs much better at downloading unpopular files since it benefits from the massive geo-distributed cloud storage pool.*

Further, we delve into the details of the pre-downloading failures of smart APs. Among the 168 (= 1000×16.8%) failures, the vast majority (145, 86%) were caused by insufficient seeds in a P2P data swarm. This explains why the pre-downloading failure ratio of unpopular files is especially high. Besides, a non-negligible part (17, 10%) was ascribed to poor HTTP/FTP connections, i.e., the server at the other end failed to maintain a persistent/resumable download. The remainder (6, 4%) might be the result of system bugs in HiWiFi, MiWiFi, and Newifi.

Pre-downloading Speed and Delay As shown in Figs. 3.13 and 3.14, the pre-downloading speeds of smart APs are just a bit lower than those of Xuanfeng's pre-downloaders, and thus the pre-downloading delay of smart APs seems a bit longer than that of Xuanfeng. This is because smart APs work in a similar way as the pre-downloaders (i.e., they also download files using HTTP, FTP, and P2P

Fig. 3.13 CDF of smart
APs' pre-downloading
speeds. Min: 0 KBps;
Median: 27 KBps; Average:
64 KBps; Max: 2.37 MBps
($\approx$20 Mbps) for HiWiFi and
MiWiFi, and 0.93 MBps for
Newifi. As a comparison, the
CDF of cloud-based
pre-downloading speeds is
also plotted (Reprinted with
permission from [14])

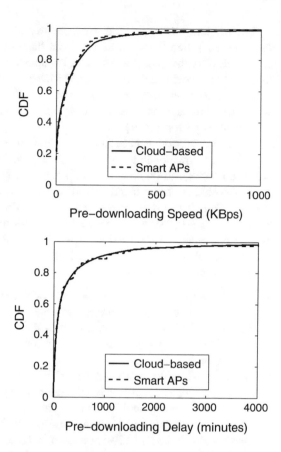

Fig. 3.14 CDF of smart
APs' pre-downloading delay.
Min: 0 min; Median: 77 min;
Average: 402 min; Max:
8297 min. As a comparison,
the CDF of cloud-based
pre-downloading delay is also
plotted (Reprinted with
permission from [14])

protocols; refer to Sect. 3.3.1), although their access bandwidths are generally lower
than 20 Mbps (or 2.5 MBps, i.e., a pre-downloader's access bandwidth).

However, one detail in Figs. 3.13 and 3.14 is worth discussing: the median
pre-downloading speed of smart APs (27 KBps) is *higher* than that of Xuanfeng
(25 KBps), but the average pre-downloading speed of smart APs (64 KBps) is *lower*
than that of Xuanfeng (69 KBps). Accordingly, the median pre-downloading delay
of smart APs (77 min) is *shorter* than that of Xuanfeng (82 min), but the average
pre-downloading delay of smart APs (402 min) is *longer* than that of Xuanfeng
(370 min). To demystify this counterintuitive phenomenon, we examine the pre-
downloading performance data of every task in the **sampled workload** and its
original performance data in the **pre-downloading trace**. Surprisingly, we uncover
the fourth key performance bottleneck of offline downloading:

- *A smart AP's pre-downloading speed can be restricted by its hardware and/or
  filesystem, since some types of storage devices and filesystems do not fit the
  pattern of frequent, small data writes during pre-downloading.*

In particular, among all the experimented storage devices, USB flash drive is the slowest. When Newifi uses the USB flash drive (in the NTFS format) as its storage device, the max pre-downloading speed is merely 0.93 MBps, much lower than that of HiWiFi and MiWiFi (2.37 MBps). This finding is basically consistent with Sundaresan et al. 's study results on broadband Internet performance in 2011, which also indicate that a user's home network equipment can significantly affect downloading performance [43].

To comprehensively understand the influence of hardware and filesystem on Newifi's pre-downloading speed, we replay the top 10 popular requests in the **sampled workload** on Newifi while setting no restriction on its pre-downloading speed (so the maximum speed should be nearly 2.37 MBps). We conducted replays with the USB flash drive formatted as FAT, NTFS, and EXT4, respectively, as well as with the USB flash drive replaced by a USB hard disk drive (5400 RPM, Max Write/Read Speed: 10 MBps/25 MBps). The resulting maximum pre-downloading speeds, as well as the corresponding **iowait** ratios, are listed in Table 3.2. We make three observations as follows:

- The NTFS filesystem severely harms Newifi's maximum pre-downloading speed, no matter whether the storage device is a USB flash drive or a USB hard disk drive. This is mainly attributed to the incompatibility between NTFS and Newifi's **OpenWrt** operating system (refer to Sect. 3.3.2) that utilizes the EXT4 filesystem.
- When Newifi uses a USB flash drive as its storage device, FAT and EXT4 filesystems also appear to have degraded its maximum pre-downloading speed. The major reason should be the unsuitability of the USB flash drive on handling frequent, small data writes during pre-downloading. This is reflected by the high **iowait** ratios (66.3 and 55%) as shown in Table 3.2. Besides, we observe that the receiver-side TCP sliding window (the typical size is 14608 bytes) is almost full in most of the time during the pre-downloading process.
- When Newifi uses a USB hard disk drive, its maximum pre-downloading speed is considerably enhanced (compared with using a USB flash drive) even when the hard disk drive is formatted as NTFS. No matter which filesystem is used, the **iowait** ratio is relatively low.

Based on the above observations, we suggest that Newifi-like smart APs upgrade their storage devices and/or change their default filesystems to more performant variants, so as to release the full potential of offline downloading. Currently, because Newifi only has a USB 2.0 interface (refer to Table 3.1), using a USB hard disk drive coupled with the EXT4 filesystem seems to be the best fit. On the other hand, if Newifi upgrades its storage interface to USB 3.0 in the future, using a USB 3.0 flash drive formatted as EXT4 might be a more cost-effective choice, given that a USB flash drive is usually much smaller and cheaper than a USB hard disk drive.

Table 3.2 Max pre-downloading speeds and the corresponding iowait ratios for HiWiFi, MiWiFi, and Newifi, with different storage devices and filesystems

Max pre-downloading speed (MBps)	FAT	NTFS	EXT4
HiWiFi + SD card	2.37	–	–
MiWiFi + SATA hard disk drive	–	–	2.37
Newifi + USB flash drive	**2.12**	**0.93**	**2.13**
Newifi + USB hard disk drive	2.37	**1.13**	2.37
iowait ratio	FAT (%)	NTFS (%)	EXT4 (%)
HiWiFi + SD card	42.1	–	–
MiWiFi + SATA hard disk drive	–	–	29.7
Newifi + USB flash drive	**66.3**	15.1	**55**
Newifi + USB hard disk drive	42	9.8	17.4

Bold values indicate that the pre-downloading speed is lower than what is supposed to be (Reprinted with permission from [14])

3.7 The ODR Middleware

Motivated by the study in Sects. 3.5 and 3.6, we design and implement a proof-of-concept middleware called ODR (Offline Downloading Redirector) to help users get rid of performance bottlenecks. We evaluate the performance of ODR using real-world workloads.

3.7.1 Design and Implementation

ODR is implemented as a middleware independent of any specific cloud-based offline downloading system or smart AP and thus can be deployed on any dedicated servers or virtual machines. ODR takes users' offline downloading requests and adaptively decides in which way the requested files should be downloaded to achieve the best expected downloading experience.

Specifically, when a user wants to download a file from the Internet, she first accesses the web service of ODR (by opening the front web page) and inputs the HTTP/FTP/P2P link to the original data source. In addition, ODR asks for other auxiliary information including the user's IP address, access bandwidth, smart AP type, storage device, and filesystem type.[3] All the aforementioned information is straightforward for common users, except the access bandwidth. Fortunately, as the majority of China's Internet users has installed PC-assistant software such as Tencent PC Manager, Baidu PhoneGuard, and 360 Security Guard. With simple instructions, ODR is able to guide users how to obtain the approximate value of access bandwidth with the PC-assistant software.

---

[3] ODR maintains a web cookie at the user side (if her web browser permits), so that the user does not need to repeatedly input the auxiliary information every time.

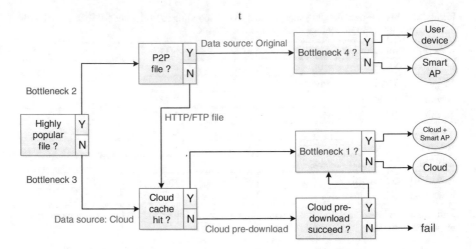

Fig. 3.15 Workflow of ODR. "Y": Yes; "N": No. Bottleneck 1, Bottleneck 2, Bottleneck 3, and Bottleneck 4 denote the four performance bottlenecks of offline downloading mentioned in our key results (refer to Sect. 3.1) (Reprinted with permission from [14])

On receiving an offline downloading request, ODR first queries the content database to obtain the latest popularity statistics of the requested file. We use the Xuanfeng database in our implementation, while keep in mind that the performance of ODR would be further enhanced if it is able to use multiple cloud services (e.g., Xuanfeng + Xunlei + Baidu CloudDisk) at once. ODR calculates the decisions based on the popularity of the file and the auxiliary information provided by the user. The decision is then returned to users via the front web page of the ODR service.

Figure 3.15 plots the state transition diagram of ODR's decision-making process, which involves a series of conditions and branches as follows.

Handling Highly Popular Files First and foremost, users are concerned with the downloading success of a requested file. As downloading failure ratio is tightly related with popularity (Sects. 3.5.1 and 3.6.2), ODR needs to examine whether the requested file is highly popular. If yes, ODR is likely to be successful at downloading the file, and therefore we can make efforts to mitigate the cloud-side upload bandwidth burden (addressing Bottleneck 2).

To deal with Bottleneck 2, if the highly popular file is hosted in a P2P data swarm, ODR suggests the user to directly download the file from the abundant peers sharing the file. On the contrary, if the highly popular file is hosted in an HTTP/FTP server, ODR would suggest the user to fall back on the cloud, so as to avoid making the HTTP/FTP server a bottleneck.

Further, to minimize the expected (pre-)downloading time, ODR considers the user-side access bandwidth, as well as the smart AP's storage device and filesystem type (addressing Bottleneck 4 in Fig. 3.15). For example, when the user-side access bandwidth reaches 20 Mbps (= 2.5 MBps), if the smart AP uses a USB flash drive as its storage device or its storage device is formatted as NTFS, ODR would suggest the user to directly download the file using her local device (given that it is usually inconvenient for the user to change the storage device and filesystem of a smart AP during pre-downloading). On the other hand, when the user-side access bandwidth is below 0.93 MBps (refer to Table 3.2), ODR would suggest the user to utilize their smart AP.

Handling Less Popular Files When a requested file is not highly popular, the success of downloading is our primary concern (addressing Bottleneck 3). To this end, ODR leverages the cloud storage pool to minimize the failure ratio of (pre-)downloading:

- *Case 1*: If the requested file is already cached in the cloud, ODR should further detect whether there is a bandwidth bottleneck between the cloud and the user by analyzing the user-side access bandwidth and ISP information (addressing Bottleneck 1). If the user-side access bandwidth is low (<1 Mbps $= 125$ KBps) or the user is located in a different ISP other than the four ISPs supported by the cloud, ODR would suggest the user to leverage both the cloud and their smart AP to mitigate the impediments of Bottleneck 1 ("Cloud + Smart AP" in Fig. 3.15, i.e., the file should be first pre-downloaded by the smart AP from the cloud and then fetched by the user from the smart AP). Otherwise, ODR suggests the user to fetch from the cloud.
- *Case 2*: If the requested file is not cached in the cloud, ODR suggests the user to first use the cloud for pre-downloading. After the file is successfully pre-downloaded by the cloud, the user will be notified, and then she can ask ODR again for further suggestions (either directly fetching from the cloud, or from the cloud to a smart AP and then to her local device). If the cloud fails to download the file, the user will be notified of a pre-downloading failure.

Note that ODR never delivers file contents by itself, which makes its operation lightweight in terms of bandwidth and traffic consumption. For our implementation, we rent a low-end virtual machine from Aliyun.com (a major cloud service provider in China) to host the entire ODR service. This virtual machine has a public IP address and 1 Mbps ($= 125$ KBps) of Internet access bandwidth. The monthly operation cost of ODR is merely $20.

Limitation By proposing the ODR middleware, our major goal is to demonstrate the potential benefits for a hybrid approach that can effectively address the limitations of the two existing conventional approaches while inheriting their respective advantages. Therefore, the above design and implementation of ODR are basically a *coarse-grained* solution to optimize the offline downloading performance and overhead, where the optimization granularity is a whole offline downloading request/task.

ODR can further benefit from more fine-grained alternative optimization solutions at the chunk, TCP data flow, or sub-stream levels. For instance, a more dynamic solution proposed by Huang et al. [44] (i.e., a buffer-based adaptive bit rate selection algorithm for video streaming) can be used instead of the current hard coded decision procedure of ODR. Moreover, a simple solution (called "mobile phone content pre-staging" [45]) that has been proposed in the past is to simply defer downloads to later times when the download bandwidth is better if the users are not particularly time sensitive. In addition, there are even standards efforts such as Low Extra Delay Background Transport (LEDBAT, IETF RFC 6817 [46]) that seeks to utilize the available bandwidth on an end-to-end path while limiting the resulting penalty of delay increase on that path. ODR can learn from LEDBAT to further mitigate the cloud-side upload bandwidth burden.

3.7.2   Performance Evaluation

To evaluate the performance of ODR, we replay the sampled workload (refer to Sect. 3.6.1) using the deployed ODR middleware during Mar. 23–Apr. 13, 2015. The environment is similar to that in Fig. 3.12. For each smart AP, we use a common laptop (with Quad-core Intel i5 CPU @1.70 GHz, 4-GB RAM, and 7200-RPM 500-GB hard disk drive) as the user device. Figure 3.16 shows the overall performance results of ODR, compared with the performances of Xuanfeng and the three popular smart APs.

First, the percentage of impeded fetching processes (Bottleneck 1) is reduced from 28 to 9%. The remainder (9%) is mostly due to the intrinsic dynamics of the Internet. In detail, Fig. 3.17 shows the fetching speed distribution using ODR. Compared with the fetching speed distribution of Xuanfeng, the median fetching speed is enhanced from 287 to 368 KBps. Limited by our benchmark environment, the max fetching speed using ODR is 20 Mbps (= 2.5 MBps), which is lower than that in Xuanfeng (i.e., 50 Mbps = 6.25 MBps). This is why the average fetching speed using ODR (509 KBps) is comparable to that of Xuanfeng (504 KBps).

With regard to Bottleneck 2, the cloud-side upload bandwidth burden under the sampled workload is reduced by 35%, which is attributable to the fact that the cloud no longer needs to deliver highly popular P2P files. If Xuanfeng had

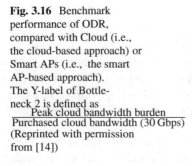

Fig. 3.16 Benchmark performance of ODR, compared with Cloud (i.e., the cloud-based approach) or Smart APs (i.e., the smart AP-based approach). The Y-label of Bottleneck 2 is defined as
$$\frac{\text{Peak cloud bandwidth burden}}{\text{Purchased cloud bandwidth (30 Gbps)}}$$
(Reprinted with permission from [14])

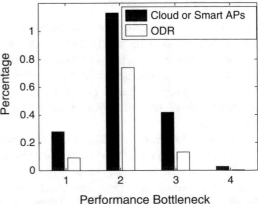

Fig. 3.17 CDF of fetching
speeds using ODR. Min:
0 KBps; Median: 368 KBps;
Average: 509 KBps; Max:
2.37 MBps (≈20 Mbps). As a
comparison, the CDF of
cloud-based fetching speeds
is also plotted (Reprinted
with permission from [14])

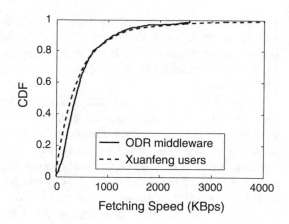

integrated ODR, its peak upload bandwidth burden could decrease from 34 Gbps
(refer to Fig. 3.11) to around 22 Gbps, and thus Xuanfeng would not need to reject
any fetching request, given their current workload.

Further, the percentage of smart APs' failures in pre-downloading unpopular files
(Bottleneck 3) is reduced from 42 to 13%. In addition, Bottleneck 4 (caused by
unsuitable storage devices or filesystems) is almost completely avoided with the use
of ODR.

In a nutshell, the integration of ODR into offline downloading services results in a
marked reduction of performance bottlenecks, as well as considerable improvement
on the quality of service.

Limitation We acknowledge that ODR occasionally makes incorrect redirection
decisions due to the inherent dynamics of Internet that may degrade performance.
Fortunately, the percentage of such decisions is negligible (<1%) in our evaluation.
Thus, we believe that the performance of ODR is acceptable in practice, especially
given the significant advantages of the system.

3.8 Conclusion

In recent years, the Internet has gained enormous penetration all over the world.
However, basic Internet services, such as downloading (large) files, remain an issue
in most developing countries as a consequence of low-quality network connections.
To improve users' downloading experiences, offline downloading services have
been proposed and widely deployed in China.

The idea of offline downloading is mainly embodied in two different types of
approaches: (1) the cloud-based approach and (2) the smart AP-based approach.
Unfortunately, the two approaches are confusing to end users since they offer
different strengths and weaknesses (the so-called selection dilemma). Our study
addresses this dilemma with in-depth analysis of a large-scale cloud-based offline

downloading system, as well as comprehensive benchmark experiments of three popular smart APs. Our study shows that the two approaches are subject to distinct performance bottlenecks, while also being complementary to each other. Driven by the study, we build an ODR middleware to help users achieve the best expected performance.

In the future, we envision that offline downloading will become a widely used technology for enhancing the Internet experiences of users across both the developing world and the developed world. For example, people start to build a variety of useful Internet services on top of cloud-based offline downloading systems, such as cloud-based media converters (e.g., Cloud Transcoder [47]) and cloud-accelerated web browsers (e.g., QQ mobile web browser, UCWeb browser, and Amazon Silk web browser). Our study of offline downloading provides solid experiences and valuable heuristics for the developers of similar and relevant services.

References

1. Grover S, Park MS, Sundaresan S, Burnett S, Kim H, Ravi B, Feamster N (2013) Peeking behind the NAT: an empirical study of home networks. In: Proceedings of the 13th ACM internet measurement conference (IMC), pp 377–390
2. Zaki Y, Chen J, Pötsch T, Ahmad T, Subramanian L (2014) Dissecting web latency in Ghana. In: Proceedings of the 14th ACM internet measurement conference (IMC), pp 241–248
3. FCC raises broadband definition to 25Mbps, Chairman mocks ISPs. http://www.extremetech.com/mobile/198583-fcc-raises-broadband-definition-to-25mbps-chairman-mocks-isps
4. Key ICT indicators for developed and developing countries and the world (totals and penetration rates). http://www.itu.int/en/ITU-D/Statistics/Documents/statistics/2014/ITU_Key_2005-2014_ICT_data.xls
5. Bischof ZS, Bustamante FE, Stanojevic R (2014) Need, want, can afford C broadband markets and the behavior of users. In: Proceedings of the 14th ACM internet measurement conference (IMC), pp 73–86
6. Delay-tolerant networking (DTN) Wiki Page. http://en.wikipedia.org/wiki/Delay-tolerant_networking
7. Isaacman S, Martonosi M (2011) Low-infrastructure methods to improve internet access for mobile users in emerging regions. In: Proceedings of the 20th international world wide web conference (WWW), pp 473–482
8. China's Broadband Penetration Is Increasingly Lagging Behind Developed Nations, Says MIIT's Research Head. http://techcrunch.com/2013/03/21/china-broadband-laggin
9. Statistics of China Internet Users. http://www.internetlivestats.com/internet-users/china
10. The State of Broadband 2014—A Report by the Broadband Commission. http://www.broadbandcommission.org/documents/reports/bb-annualreport2014.pdf
11. 100,000 MiWiFi smart AP devices are sold out in just 59 seconds. http://bbs.xiaomi.cn/thread-9658495-1-1.html
12. HiWiFi smart AP is striving towards 5,000,000 sales. http://www.pcpop.com/doc/1/1002/1002782.shtml

13. Ao N, Xu Y, Chen C, Guo Y (2012) Offline downloading: a non-traditional cloud-accelerated and peer-assisted content distribution service. In: Proceedings of the IEEE international conference on cyber-enabled distributed computing and knowledge discovery (CyberC), pp 81–88
14. Li Z, Wilson C, Xu T, Liu Y, Lu Z, Wang Y (2015) Offline downloading in China: a comparative study. In: Proceedings of the 15th ACM internet measurement conference (IMC), pp 473–486
15. Offline Downloading: the Baidu Wikipedia page. http://baike.baidu.com/view/2718066.htm
16. Offline (movie) Downloading for MiWiFi. http://www.mi.com/miwifi/movie-download
17. A Collection of the Best Offline Downloading Tools. http://jingyan.baidu.com/article/636f38bb295e9bd6b84610e9.html
18. How to Offline Download? Which is the Best Offline Downloading Tool? http://jingyan.baidu.com/article/a65957f4fe63c424e67f9b92.html
19. Huang Y, Li Z, Liu G, Dai Y (2011) Cloud download: using cloud utilities to achieve high-quality content distribution for unpopular videos. In: Proceedings of the 19th ACM international conference on multimedia (ACM-MM), pp 213–222
20. An Evaluation Report of HiWiFi. http://news.mydrivers.com/1/279/279305_all.htm
21. An Evaluation Report of MiWiFi. http://www.geekpark.net/read/view/195133
22. An Evaluation Report of NewiFi. http://www.itbear.com.cn/n112446c93.aspx
23. Zhou Y, Fu Z, Chiu DM, Huang Y (2013) An adaptive cloud downloading service. IEEE Trans Multimed 15(4):802–810
24. Three Faults of HiWiFi. http://digi.tech.qq.com/a/20131112/002037.htm
25. HiWiFi vs. Newifi: A Benchmark Test. http://test.smzdm.com/pingce/p/20574
26. A Comparison of Nine Smart APs. http://net.zol.com.cn/478/4788494.html
27. Chen G, Li Z (2007) Peer-to-peer network: structure, application and design. Tsinghua University Press, Beijing
28. Tian Y, Dey R, Liu Y, Ross K (2013) Topology mapping and geolocating for China's internet. IEEE Trans Parallel Distrib Syst 24(9):1908–1917
29. Xie H, Yang R, Krishnamurthy A, Liu YG, Silberschatz A (2008) P4P: provider portal for applications. ACM SIGCOMM Comput Commun Rev 38(4):351–362
30. Choffnes D, Bustamante FE (2008) Taming the torrent: a practical approach to reducing cross-ISP traffic in peer-to-peer systems. ACM SIGCOMM Comput Commun Rev 38(4):363–374
31. HiWiFi Introduction and History. http://www.hiwifi.com/about
32. aria2: The next generation download utility. http://aria2.sourceforge.net
33. Breslau L, Cao P, Fan L, Phillips G, Shenker S (1999) Web caching and Zipf-like distributions: evidence and implications. In: Proceedings of the 18th IEEE international conference on computer communications (INFOCOM), pp 126–134
34. Guo L, Tan E, Chen S, Xiao Z, Zhang X (2008) The stretched exponential distribution of internet media access patterns. In: Proceedings of the 27th ACM symposium on principles of distributed computing (PODC), pp 283–294
35. Gummadi KP, Dunn RJ, Saroiu S, Gribble SD, Levy HM, Zahorjan J (2003) Measurement, modeling, and analysis of a peer-to-peer file-sharing workload. ACM SIGOPS Oper Syst Rev 37(5):314–329
36. Li Z, Cao J, Chen G (2008) ContinuStreaming: achieving high playback continuity of gossip-based peer-to-peer streaming. In: Proceedings of the 22nd IEEE international parallel and distributed processing symposium (IPDPS), pp 1–12
37. Ganjam A, Jiang J, Liu X, Sekar V, Siddiqi F, Stoica I, Zhan J, Zhang H (2015) C3: Internet-scale control plane for video quality optimization. In: Proceedings of the 12th USENIX symposium on networked systems design and implementation (NSDI), pp 131–144
38. Cohen B (2003) Incentives build robustness in BitTorrent. In: Proceedings of the 1st workshop on economics of peer-to-peer systems, pp 68–72
39. Huang TY, Handigol N, Heller B, McKeown N, Johari R (2012) Confused, timid, and unstable: picking a video streaming rate is hard. In: Proceedings of the 12th ACM internet measurement conference (IMC), pp 225–238

40. Krishnan S, Sitaraman R (2013) Video stream quality impacts viewer behavior: inferring causality using quasi-experimental designs. IEEE/ACM Trans Netw 21(6):2001–2014
41. Li Z, Zhang T, Huang Y, Zhang ZL, Dai Y (2012) Maximizing the bandwidth multiplier effect for hybrid cloud-P2P content distribution. In: Proceedings of the 20th IEEE/ACM international workshop on quality of service (IWQoS), pp 1–9
42. Li Z, Huang Y, Liu G, Wang F, Liu Y, Zhang ZL, Dai Y (2013) Challenges, designs, and performances of large-scale open-P2SP content distribution. IEEE Trans. Parallel Distrib Syst 24(11):2181–2191
43. Sundaresan S, De Donato W, Feamster N, Teixeira R, Crawford S, Pescapè A (2011) Broadband internet performance: a view from the gateway. ACM SIGCOMM Comput Commun Rev 41(4):134–145
44. Huang TY, Johari R, McKeown N, Trunnell M, Watson M (2014) A buffer-based approach to rate adaptation: evidence from a large video streaming service. In: Proceedings of ACM SIGCOMM, pp 187–198
45. Finamore A, Mellia M, Gilani Z, Papagiannaki K, Erramilli V, Grunenberger Y (2013) Is there a case for mobile phone content pre-staging? In: Proceedings of the 9th ACM conference on emerging networking experiments and technologies (CoNEXT), pp 321–326
46. Low Extra Delay Background Transport (LEDBAT), IETF RFC 6817. http://datatracker.ietf.org/doc/rfc6817
47. Li Z, Huang Y, Liu G, Wang F, Zhang ZL, Dai Y (2012) Cloud transcoder: bridging the format and resolution gap between internet videos and mobile devices. In: Proceedings of the 22nd SIGMM workshop on network and operating system support for digital audio and video (NOSSDAV), pp 33–38

Part III
Metric 2 Cost: Never Waste on Traffic Usage

Chapter 4
Cross-Application Cellular Traffic Optimization

Abstract As mobile cellular devices and traffic continue growing rapidly, providers are putting more efforts to optimize traffic, with the hopes of improving user experiences while reducing congestion and bandwidth costs. This chapter presents the design, deployment, and experiences with Baidu TrafficGuard, a cloud-based mobile proxy that reduces cellular traffic using a network-layer VPN. The VPN connects a client-side proxy to a centralized traffic processing cloud. TrafficGuard works transparently across heterogeneous applications and effectively reduces cellular traffic by 36% and overage instances by 10.7 times for roughly 10 million Android users in China. We discuss a large-scale cellular traffic analysis effort, how the resulting insights guided the design of TrafficGuard, and our experiences with a variety of traffic optimization techniques over one year of deployment.

Keywords Cellular traffic optimization · Web optimization proxy

4.1 Introduction

Mobile cellular devices are changing today's Internet landscape. Growth in cellular devices today greatly outpaces that of traditional PCs, and global cellular traffic is growing by double digits annually, to an estimated 15.9 Exabytes in 2018 [1]. This growing traffic demand has led to significant congestion on today's cellular networks, resulting in bandwidth caps, and throttling at major wireless providers. The challenges are more dramatic in developing countries, where low-capacity cellular networks often fail to deliver basic quality of service needed for simple applications [2–4].

While this is a well-known problem, only recently have we seen efforts to address it at scale. Google took the unprecedented step of prioritizing mobile-friendly sites in its search algorithm [5]. This will likely spur further efforts to update popular websites for mobile devices. Recent reports estimate that most enterprise web pages are designed for PCs, and only 38% of the web pages are mobile-friendly [6]. More recently, Google released details on their Flywheel proxy service for compressing content for the Chrome mobile browser [7].

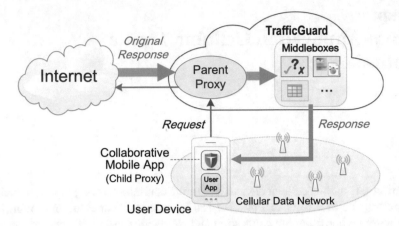

Fig. 4.1 Architectural overview of TrafficGuard (Reprinted with permission from [14])

Competition in today's mobile platforms has led to numerous "walled-gardens," where developers build their own suites of applications that keep users within their ecosystem. The ongoing trend limits the benefits of app-specific proxies, even ones with user bases as large as Google Chrome [7–9]. In contrast, an alternative approach is to transparently intercept and optimize network traffic across all apps at the OS/network layer. Although some examples of this approach exist (e.g., Opera Max, Windows Data Sense, and Onavo), little is known about their design or impact on network performance.

This chapter describes the design, deployment, and experiences with Baidu TrafficGuard, a third-party cellular traffic proxy widely deployed for Android devices in China.[1] As shown in Fig. 4.1, TrafficGuard is a cloud-based proxy that redirects traffic through a VPN to a client-side mobile app (http://shoujiweishi. baidu.com). It currently supports all Android 4.0+ devices and does not require root privileges. Inside the cloud, a series of software middleboxes are utilized to monitor, filter, and reshape cellular traffic. TrafficGuard was first deployed in early 2014, and its Android app has been installed by roughly 10M users.

In designing a transparent mobile proxy for cellular traffic optimization, Traffic-Guard targets four key goals:

- First, traffic optimization should not harm user experiences. For example, image compression through pixel scaling often distorts web page and UI (user interface) rendering in user apps. Similarly, traffic processing should not introduce unacceptable delays.

---

[1] Cellular data usage in Asia differs from that of US/European networks, in that HTTP traffic dominates 80.4% of the cellular traffic in China and 74.6% in South Korea [10]. In comparison, HTTPS accounts for more than 50% of the cellular traffic in the USA [11–13].

- Second, our techniques must generalize to different apps, so proprietary APIs or data formats should be avoided. For example, Flywheel achieves significant traffic savings by transcoding images to the WebP format. Though WebP offers high compression, not all apps support this format.
- Third, we wish to limit client-side resource consumption, in terms of memory, CPU, and battery. Note that the client needs to collaborate well with the cloud using a certain amount of resources.
- Finally, we wish to reduce system complexity, resource consumption, and monetary costs on the cloud side. In particular, the state information maintained for each client should be carefully determined.

In this chapter, we document considerations in the design, implementation, and deployment of TrafficGuard. *First*, we analyze aggregate cellular traffic measurements over 110 K users to understand the characteristics of cellular traffic in China. This gave us insights on the efficacy and impact of traditional data compression, as well as the role of useless content such as broken images in cellular traffic. *Second*, we adopt a lightweight, adaptive approach to image compression, where more considerate compression schemes are constructed to achieve a sweet spot on the image-quality versus file-size tradeoff. This helps us achieve traffic savings comparable to Flywheel (27%) at roughly 10–12% of the computation overhead. *Third*, we develop a customized VPN tunnel to efficiently filter users' unwanted traffic, including overnight, background, malicious, and advertisement traffic. *Finally*, we implement a cloud–client paired proxy system and integrate best-of-breed caching techniques for duplicate content detection. The cloud–client paired design allows us to finely tune the tradeoff between traffic optimization and state maintenance.

TrafficGuard is the culmination of these efforts. For installed users, it reduces the overall cellular traffic by an average of 36% and instances of traffic overage (i.e., going beyond the users' allotted data caps) by 10.7 times. Roughly, 55% of the users saw more than a quarter reduction in traffic, and 20% of the users saw their traffic reduced by half. TrafficGuard introduces relatively small latency penalties (a median of 53 ms and a mean of 282 ms) and has little to no impact on the battery life of user devices.

While already successful in its current deployment, TrafficGuard can achieve even higher efficiency if cellular carriers (are willing to) integrate it into their infrastructure. As demonstrated in Fig. 4.2, carriers could deploy TrafficGuard between the GGSN (Gateway GPRS Support Node) and the SGSN (Serving GPRS Support Node). Then the optimized traffic is further transferred to the RNC (Radio Network Controller) and BTS (Base Transceiver Station). This would greatly simplify both the cloud-side and client-side components of TrafficGuard and further reduce latency penalties for users.

Finally, we note that while Baidu does not have an internal IRB (Institutional Review Board) review process, all reasonable steps were taken at Baidu to protect user privacy during this study. All users who participated in the study opted in as volunteers with informed consent, and full traffic traces were limited to one week of

Fig. 4.2 Potential integration of TrafficGuard into a 3G cellular carrier. Integration for 4G would be similar (Reprinted with permission from [14])

measurements (all other datasets are anonymized logs). Wherever possible, analysis was limited to anonymized metadata only. When necessary, content analysis was done on aggregate data, and fully decoupled from any user identifiers or personally identifiable information.

4.2   State-of-the-Art Systems

This section surveys state-of-the-art mobile traffic proxy systems. As listed in Table 4.1, we compare seven systems with TrafficGuard. We focus on five of the most important and ubiquitous features supported by these systems: (1) image compression, (2) text compression, (3) content optimization, (4) traffic filtering, and (5) caching. In each case, we highlight the strengths and shortcomings of different approaches.

Since most mobile traffic proxy systems are closed-source, we rely on a variety of methods to determine their features. The implementation of Google Flywheel is described in [7]. For Opera Turbo, UCBrowser, and QQBrowser, we are able to uncover most of their features through carefully controlled experiments. Specifically, we set up our own web server, used these proxies to browse our own content hosted by the server, and carefully compared the data sent by the server with what was received by our client device. Unfortunately, Opera Max, Microsoft Data Sense, and Onavo Extend use encrypted proxies, and thus we can only discover a subset of their implementation details.

First, we examine the techniques of image compression. Three systems transcode images to WebP, which effectively reduces network traffic [7]. However, this only works for user apps that support WebP (e.g., Google Chrome). Similarly, Opera Max and Onavo Extend transcode PNGs to JPEGs, and Onavo Extend also transcodes large GIFs to JPEGs. Taking a different approach, UCBrowser rescales large images ($>700 \times 700$ pixels) to small images ($<150 \times 150$ pixels). Although rescaling reduces traffic, it could harm user experiences by significantly degrading image qualities. In contrast to these systems, TrafficGuard uses an adaptive quality reduction approach that is not CPU intensive, reduces traffic across apps, and generally does not harm user experiences (see Sect. 4.5.1).

Second, we find that all the seven systems compress textual content, typically with gzip. However, our large-scale measurement findings (in Sect. 4.3.2.2) reveal that the vast majority of textual content downloaded by smartphone users is very

Table 4.1 Comparison of state-of-the-art mobile traffic proxy systems

System	Image compression	Text compression	Content optimization	Traffic filtering	Caching
Google Flywheel	Transcoding to WebP	Yes	Lightweight error page	Safe browsing	Server side
Opera Turbo	Transcoding to WebP	Yes	Pre-executing JavaScript	Ad blocking	Non-existing or unknown
UCBrowser	Pixel scaling	Yes	No	Ad blocking	Non-existing or unknown
QQBrowser	Transcoding to WebP	Yes	No	Ad blocking	Non-existing or unknown
Opera Max [?] (China's version)	Transcoding PNG to JPEG	Yes	No	Restricting overnight traffic	Non-existing or unknown
Microsoft data sense	Non-existing or unknown	Yes	No	Restricting background traffic and ad blocking	Non-existing or unknown
Onavo Extend	Transcoding PNG and large GIF to JPEG	Yes	No	No	Client side
TrafficGuard	Adaptive quality reduction	No	Attempting to discard useless content	Restricting overnight and background traffic, ad blocking, safe browsing	Server side, and VBWC on both sides

(Reprinted with permission from [14])

short, meaning that compression would be ineffective. Thus, TrafficGuard does not compress texts, since the CPU overhead of decompression is not worth the low (1.36%) HTTP traffic savings.

Third, we explore the *content optimization* strategies employed by mobile traffic proxies. We define *content optimization* as attempts to reduce network traffic by altering the semantics or functionality of content. For example, Flywheel replaces HTTP 404 error pages with a lightweight version. More aggressively, Opera Turbo executes JavaScript objects at the proxy, so that clients do not need to download and execute them. Although this can reduce traffic, it often breaks the original functionality of websites and user apps, e.g., in the controlled experiments we often noticed that JavaScript functions such as onscroll() and oninput() were not properly executed by Opera Turbo. Rather than adopting these approaches, TrafficGuard validates HTTP content and attempts to discard useless content such as broken images (see Sect. 4.5.2).

Fourth, we observe that many of the target systems implement traffic filtering. Four systems block advertisements, plus Flywheel using Google Safe Browsing to block malicious content. Opera Max attempts to restrict apps' traffic usage during the night, when users are likely to be asleep. Microsoft Data Sense takes things a step further by also restricting traffic from background apps, under the assumption that apps that are not currently interactive should not be downloading lots of data. We discover that all these filtering techniques are beneficial to users (see Sect. 4.3.2.4), and thus we incorporate all of them into TrafficGuard (see Sect. 4.5.3).

Finally, we study the caching strategies of the existing systems. Flywheel maintains a server-side cache of recently accessed objects, while Onavo Extend maintains a local cache (of 100 MB by default). In contrast, TrafficGuard adopts server-side strategies by maintaining a cache at the proxy (see Sect. 4.4), as well as implementing value-based web caching (VBWC) between the client and the server (see Sect. 4.5.4). Although we evaluated other sophisticated caching strategies, we ultimately chose VBWC because it offers excellent performance and is straightforward to implement.

4.3 Measuring Cellular Traffic

This section presents a large-scale measurement study of cellular traffic usage by Android smartphone users. Unlike prior studies [10, 15–19], our analysis focuses on content and metadata. We identify several key performance issues and tradeoffs that guide the design of TrafficGuard.

4.3.1 Dataset Collection

The ultimate goal of TrafficGuard is to improve smartphone users' experiences by decreasing network usage and filtering unwanted content. To achieve this goal, we decided to take a measurement-driven methodology, i.e., we first observed the actual cellular traffic usage patterns of smartphone users, and then used the data to drive our design and implementation decisions.

When we first deployed TrafficGuard between Jan. 5 and Mar. 31, 2014, the system only monitored users' cellular traffic; it did not filter or reshape traffic at all. We randomly invited users to test TrafficGuard from ~100M existing mobile users of Baidu. We obtained informed consent from volunteers by prominently informing them that full traces of their cellular traffic would be collected and analyzed. We assigned a unique ClientToken to each user device that installed the mobile app of TrafficGuard.

We used two methods to collect packet traces from volunteers. For an HTTP request, the TrafficGuard app would insert the ClientToken into the HTTP header. The TrafficGuard cloud would then record the request, remove the injected header, complete the HTTP request, and store the server's response. However, for non-HTTP requests (most of which are HTTPS), it was not possible for the TrafficGuard cloud to read the injected ClientToken. Thus, the TrafficGuard app locally recorded the non-HTTP traffic and uploaded it to the cloud in a batch along with the ClientToken once per week. These uploads were restricted to WiFi to avoid wasting volunteers' cellular data. In both cases, we also recorded additional metadata such as the specific app that initiated each request, and whether that app was working in the foreground or background.

We collected packet traces from volunteers for one week: Mar. 21–27, 2014. In total, this dataset contains 320M requests from 0.65M unique ClientTokens. However, we observe that many user devices in the dataset only used their cellular connections for short periods of time. To avoid bias, we focus on the traces belonging to 111,910 *long-term* users who used their cellular connections in at least four days during the collection period. This final dataset is referred to as TGdataset, whose general statistics are listed in Table 4.2.

Table 4.2 General statistics of our collected TGdataset

Collection period	03/21–03/27, 2014
Unique users	111,910
Total requests	162M
Dataset size	1324 GB (100%)
Non-HTTP traffic (plus TCP/IP)	259 GB (19.6%)
HTTP traffic (plus TCP/IP)	1065 GB (80.4%)
HTTP header traffic	107 GB (8.1%)
HTTP body traffic	875 GB (66.1%)

(Reprinted with permission from [14])

4.3.2 Content Analysis

Below, we analyze the content and metadata in TGdataset. We observe that today's cellular traffic can be effectively optimized in multiple ways.

4.3.2.1 General Characteristics

We begin by presenting some general characteristics of TGdataset. As listed in Table 4.2, 80.4% of the TGdataset is HTTP traffic, most of which corresponds to the bodies of HTTP messages. This finding is positive for two reasons. First, it means content metadata (e.g., Content-Length and Content-Type) is readily available for us to analyze. Second, it is clear that the TrafficGuard system will be able to analyze and modify the vast majority of cellular traffic, since it is in plaintext.

Table 4.3 presents information about the types of HTTP content in TGdataset. We observe that images are the second most frequent type of content, but consume 71% of the entire HTTP traffic. Textual content is the most frequent, while nonimage binary content accounts for the remainder of HTTP traffic. We manually analyzed many of the octet-streams in our dataset and found that they mainly consist of software and video streams.

4.3.2.2 Size and Quality of Content

Next, we examine the size and quality of content in TGdataset and relate these characteristics to the compressibility of content.

Images Four image types dominate in our dataset: JPEG, WebP, PNG, and GIF. Certainly, all four types of images are already compressed. However, we observe that 40% of the images are *large*, which we define as images of $w \times h$ pixels such that $w \times h \geq 250,000 \wedge w \geq 150 \wedge h \geq 150$ (refer to Sect. 4.5.1 for more details of

Table 4.3 Statistics of HTTP content in TGdataset

Type	Percentage of requests (%)	Percentage of HTTP traffic (%)	Size (KB) Median	Size (KB) Mean
Image	**32**	**71**	**5.7**	**15.5**
Text	**49**	**15.7**	**0.2**	**2.2**
Octet-stream	10	5.5	0.4	3.8
Zip	8.1	5.1	0.5	4.3
Audio and video	0.03	2.6	407	614
Other	0.87	0.1	0.3	0.7

Bold values denote the dominant scenarios of network traffic usage (Reprinted with permission from [14])

image categorization). Some images even have over 4000×4000 pixels (exceeding 10 MB in size) in extreme cases.

More importantly, we observe that many JPEGs have high *quality factors* (QFs). QF determines the strength of JPEG's lossy-compression algorithm, with QF $= 100$ causing minimal loss but a larger file size. The median QF of JPEGs in TGdataset is 80, while the average is 74. Such high-quality images are unnecessary for most cellular users, considering their limited data plans and screen sizes. This presents us with an optimization opportunity that TrafficGuard takes advantage of (see Sect. 4.5.1).

Textual Content The six most common types of textual content in TGdataset are: JSON, HTML, PLAIN, JavaScript, XML, and CSS. Compared with images, textual content is much smaller: the median size is merely 0.2 KB. Compressing the short texts with the size less than 0.2 KB (e.g., with gzip, bzip2, or 7-zip) cannot decrease their size; in fact, the additional compression metadata may even *increase* the size of such textual data.

Surprisingly, we find that compressing the other, larger half (>0.2 KB) of textual content with gzip brings limited benefits—it only reduced the HTTP traffic of texts by 8.7%, equal to 1.36% ($= 8.7\% \times 15.7\%$) of total HTTP traffic. Similarly, using bzip2 and 7-zip could not significantly increase the compression rate. However, decompressing texts on user devices does necessitate additional computation and thus causes battery overhead. Given the limited network efficiency gains and the toll on battery life, we opt to not compress texts in TrafficGuard, unlike all other systems as listed in Table 4.1.

Other Content For the remaining octet-stream, zip, audio and video content, we find that compression provides negligible benefits, since almost all of them are already compressed. Although it is possible to reduce network traffic by transcoding, scaling, or reducing the quality of multimedia content [8], we do not explore these potential optimizations in this work.

4.3.2.3 Content Validation

Delving deeper into the content downloaded by our volunteers, we discover a surprisingly high portion of useless content, particularly *broken* images. We define an image to be broken if it cannot be decoded by any of the three widely used image decoders: imghdr, Bitmap, and dwebp. As shown in Table 4.4, 10.6% of the images are broken, wasting 3.2% of all image traffic in our dataset (their average size is much smaller than that of correct images). Note that we also observe a small fraction of *blank* and *incomplete* images that we can decode, as well as a few *inconsistent* images that are actually not images, but we do not consider to obey our strict definition of correctness.

Table 4.4 Validity and usefulness of images

Type	Percentage of requests (%)	Percentage of image traffic (%)	Image size (KB): Median	Mean
Correct	87	95.9	5.4	14.8
Broken	**10.6**	**3.2**	**0.13**	**3.2**
Blank	2.3	0.57	0	0
Incomplete	0.1	0.21	0.01	5.0
Inconsistent	0.04	0.16	4.8	33

Bold values indicate the undesirable scenario leading to network traffic waste (Reprinted with permission from [14])

4.3.2.4   Traffic Filtering

As we note in Sect. 4.2, the existing mobile traffic proxies have adopted multiple strategies for traffic filtering. In this section, we investigate the potential of four particular filtering strategies by analyzing TGdataset.

Overnight Traffic Prior studies have observed that many smartphones generate data traffic late at night, even when users are not using the devices [15, 17, 19]. If we conservatively assume that our volunteers are asleep between 0 and 6 AM, then 11.4% of traffic in our dataset can potentially be filtered without noticeable impact on users. Based on this finding, we implemented a feature in TrafficGuard that allows users to specify a night time period during which cellular traffic is restricted (see Sect. 4.5.3).

Background Traffic Users expect foreground apps to consume data since they are interactive, but background apps may also consume network resources. Although this is expected in some cases (e.g., a user may stream music while also browsing the web), undesirable data consumption by background apps has become such a common complaint that numerous articles exist to help mitigate this problem [20–23]. In TGdataset, we observe that 26.7% of the cellular traffic is caused by background apps. To this end, we implemented dual filters in TrafficGuard specifically designed to reduce the network traffic of background apps (see Sect. 4.5.3).

Malicious Traffic A recent study of Google Play reveals that more than 25% of the Android apps are malicious, including spammy, re-branded, and cloned apps [24]. We compare all the HTTP requests in TGdataset against a proprietary blacklist containing 29M links maintained by major Internet companies (including Baidu, Google, Microsoft, Symantec, Tencent, etc.) and find that 0.85% of the requests were issued for malicious content. We addressed this issue in TrafficGuard by filtering out HTTP requests for blacklisted URLs.

Advertisement Traffic In addition to malicious content, we also find that 4.15% of the HTTP requests in TGdataset were for ads. We determined this by comparing all the requested HTTP URLs in our dataset against a proprietary list of 102M known advertising URLs (similar to the well-known EasyList [25]). Ad blocking is a morally complicated practice, and thus we give TrafficGuard users the choice of whether to opt in to ad filtering. Users' configuration data reveal that the majority (67%) of users has chosen to block ads. On the other hand, we did get pushback from a small number of advertisers; when this happened, usually, we would remove the advertisers from our ad block list after verification.

4.3.2.5   Caching Strategies

Finally, we explore the feasibility of two common caching strategies. Unfortunately, we find neither technique offers satisfactory performance, which motives us to implement a more sophisticated caching strategy.

Name-Based Traditional web proxies such as Squid implement *name-based* caching of objects (i.e., objects are indexed by their URLs). However, this approach is known to miss many opportunities for caching [26, 27]. To make matters worse, we observe that over half of the content in TGdataset is not cacheable by Squid due to HTTP protocol issues. This situation is further exacerbated by the fact that many start-of-the-art HTTP libraries do not support caching at all [28]. Thus, although TrafficGuard uses Squid in the back-end cloud, we decided to augment it with an additional, object-level caching strategy (known as VBWC, see Sect. 4.5.4).

HTTP ETag ETag was introduced in HTTP/1.1 to mitigate the shortcomings of named-based caching. Unfortunately, the effectiveness of ETag is still limited by two constraints. First, as ETags are assigned arbitrarily by web servers, they do not allow clients to detect identical content served by multiple providers. This phenomenon is called content *aliasing* [29]. We observe that 14.16% of the HTTP requests in TGdataset are for aliased content, corresponding to 7.28% of the HTTP traffic. Second, we find that ETags are sparsely supported: only 5.76% of the HTTP responses include ETags.

4.4   System Overview

Our measurement findings in Sect. 4.3.2 provide useful guidelines for optimizing cellular traffic across apps. Additionally, we observe that some techniques used by prior systems (e.g., text compression) are not useful in practice. These findings guide the design of TrafficGuard for optimizing users' cellular traffic.

This section presents an overview of TrafficGuard, which consists of a front-end mobile app on users' devices and a set of back-end services. Below, we present the basic components of each end, with an emphasis on how these components

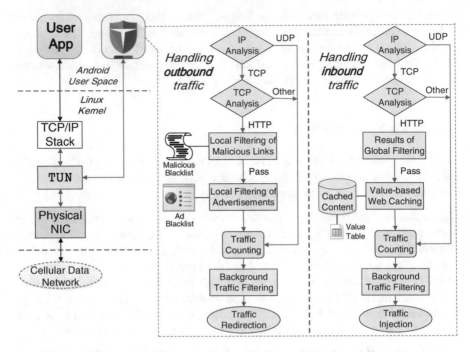

Fig. 4.3 Basic design of the child proxy (Reprinted with permission from [14])

support various traffic optimization mechanisms. Additional details about specific traffic optimization mechanisms are explained in Sect. 4.5.

Mobile App: The Client-Side Support The TrafficGuard mobile app is comprised of a user interface and a *child proxy*. The user interface is responsible for displaying cellular usage statistics and allows users to configure TrafficGuard settings. The settings include enabling/disabling specific traffic optimization mechanisms, as well as options for specific mechanisms (the details are discussed in Sect. 4.5). We also leverage the user interface to collect feedback from users, which help us continually improve the design.

The child proxy does the real work of traffic optimization on the client side. It intercepts incoming and outgoing HTTP requests at the cellular interface, performs computations on them, and forwards (some) requests to the back-end cloud via a customized VPN tunnel. As shown in Fig. 4.3, the client-side VPN tunnel is implemented using the TUN virtual network-level device that intercepts traffic from or injects traffic to the TCP/IP stack. HTTP GET requests[2] are captured by the child

---

[2] Non-GET HTTP requests (e.g., POST, HEAD, and PUT) and non-HTTP requests do not benefit from TrafficGuard's filtering and caching mechanisms, so the child proxy forwards them to the TCP/IP stack for regular processing. Furthermore, TrafficGuard makes no attempt to analyze SSL/TLS traffic for privacy reasons.

proxy, encapsulated, and then sent to the back-end cloud for further processing. Accordingly, the child proxy is responsible for receiving responses from the back-end.

The mobile app provides client-side support for traffic optimization. First, it allows users to monitor and restrict cellular traffic at night and from background apps in a real-time manner. Users are given options to control how aggressively TrafficGuard filters these types of traffic. Second, it provides local filtering of malicious links and unwanted ads using two small blacklists of the most frequently visited malicious and advertising URLs. Requests for malicious URLs are dropped; users are given a choice of whether to enable ad blocking, in which case requests for ads-related URLs are also dropped

Third, the child proxy acts as the client side of a value-based web cache [29] (VBWC, see Sect. 4.5.4 for details). At a high level, the child proxy maintains a key-value store that maps MD5 hashes to pieces of content. The back-end cloud may return "VBWC Hit" responses to the client that contain the MD5 hash of some content, rather than the content itself. In this case, the child proxy retrieves the content from the key-value store using the MD5 hash and then locally constructs an HTTP response containing the cached content. The reconstructed HTTP response is then returned to the corresponding user app. This process is fully transparent to user apps.

Web Proxy: The Back-End Support As shown in Fig. 4.4, the cloud side of TrafficGuard consists of two components: a cluster of parent proxy servers that decapsulate users' HTTP GET requests and fetch content from the Internet and a series of software middleboxes that process HTTP responses.

Once an HTTP GET request sent by the child proxy is received, the parent proxy decapsulates it and extracts the *original* HTTP GET request. Next, middleboxes compare the original HTTP GET request against large blacklists of known malicious and ads-related URLs. Note that this HTTP GET request has passed the client-side filtering with small blacklists. Together, this two-level filtering scheme prevents TrafficGuard users from wasting memory loading large blacklists on their own devices. If a URL hits either blacklist, it is reported back to the mobile app so the user can be notified.

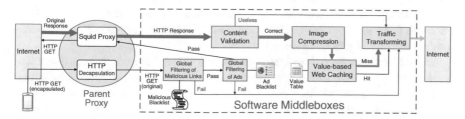

Fig. 4.4 Cloud-side overview of TrafficGuard. HTTP requests are generally processed from *left* to *right* by a cluster of parent proxy servers and a series of software middleboxes implemented on *top* of Nginx (Reprinted with permission from [14])

An HTTP request that passes the blacklist filters is forwarded to a Squid proxy, which fetches the requested content from the original source. The Squid proxy implements name-based caching of objects using an LRU (Least Recently Used) scheme, which helps reduce latency for popular objects. Once the content has been retrieved by Squid, it is further processed by middleboxes that validate content (Sect. 4.5.2) and compress images (Sect. 4.5.1).

Lastly, before the content is returned to users, it is indexed by VBWC (Sect. 4.5.4). VBWC maintains a separate index of content for every active user, which contains the MD5 hash of each piece of content recently downloaded by that user. For a given user, if VBWC discovers that some content is already indexed, it returns that MD5 in a "VBWC Hit" response to the mobile app, instead of the actual content. The child proxy then constructs a valid HTTP response message containing the cached content. Otherwise, the MD5 is inserted into the table, and the actual content is sent to the user.

4.5   Mechanisms

This section presents the details of specific traffic optimization mechanisms in TrafficGuard. Since many of the mechanisms include user-configurable parameters, we gathered users' configuration data between Jul. 4 and Dec. 27, 2014. This dataset is referred to as TGconfig.

4.5.1   Image Compression

Overview Image compression is the most important traffic reduction mechanism implemented by TrafficGuard, since our TGdataset shows that cellular traffic is dominated by images. Based on our observation that the majority of JPEGs have quality factors (QFs) that are excessively high for display on smartphone screens, TrafficGuard adaptively compresses JPEGs by reducing their QFs to an acceptable level. Additionally, TrafficGuard transcodes PNGs and GIFs to JPEGs with an acceptable QF. TrafficGuard does *not* transcode PNGs with transparency data or animated GIFs to avoid image distortion. TrafficGuard ignores WebP images since they are already highly compressed.

TrafficGuard's approach to image compression has three advantages over alternative strategies. First, as JPEG is the dominant image format supported by almost all (>99% to our knowledge) user apps, TrafficGuard does not need to transcode images back to their original formats on the client side. Second, our approach costs only 10–12% as much CPU as Flywheel's WebP-based transcoding method (see Sect. 4.6.3). Finally, our approach does not alter the pixel dimensions of images. This is important because many UI layout algorithms (e.g., CSS) are sensitive to the pixel dimensions of images, so rescaling images may break web page and app UIs.

Categorizing Images The challenge of implementing our adaptive QF reduction strategy is deciding how much to reduce the QFs of images. Intuitively, the QFs of large images can be reduced more than small images, since the resulting visual artifacts will be less apparent in larger images. Thus, following the approach of Ziproxy (an open-source HTTP proxy widely used to compress images), we classify images into four categories according to their width (w) and height (h) in pixels:

- *Tiny* images contain <5000 pixels, i.e., $w \times h < 5000$.
- *Small* images include images with less than 50,000 pixels (i.e., $5000 \le w \times h < 50,000$), as well as "slim" images with less than 150 width or height pixels (i.e., $w \times h \ge 5000 \wedge (w < 150 \vee h < 150)$).
- *Mid-size* images contain less than 250,000 pixels, that is $50,000 \le w \times h < 250,000 \wedge w \ge 150 \wedge h \ge 150$.
- *Large* images contain no less than 250,000 pixels, that is $w \times h \ge 250,000 \wedge w \ge 150 \wedge h \ge 150$.

QF Reduction Scheme After images are divided into the above four categories, we need to determine a proper *QF (reduction) scheme* for transcoding images in each category. Our goal is to maximize compression by reducing QF, while also minimizing the reductions of user-perceived image quality. To measure quality, we use structural similarity (SSIM) [30], which assesses the visual similarity between a compressed image and the original (1 means the two images are identical). We calculate SSIM and *compression ratio* ($= \frac{\text{Size of images after compression}}{\text{Size of images before compression}}$) corresponding to consecutive QFs, based on all the correct images in TGdataset. The results are in Figs. 4.5 and 4.6.

We define a QF scheme *ImgQFScheme* = $\{T, S, M, L\}$ to mean that tiny, small, mid-size, and large images are compressed to QF = T, S, M, and L, respectively. In practice, we constructed three QF schemes that vary from high compression, less quality to low compression, high quality: *ImgQFLow* = $\{30, 25, 25, 20\}$, *ImgQFMiddle* = $\{60, 55, 50, 45\}$, and *ImgQFHigh* = $\{90, 90, 85, 80\}$. We then

Fig. 4.5 Average SSIM corresponding to consecutive QFs (Reprinted with permission from [14])

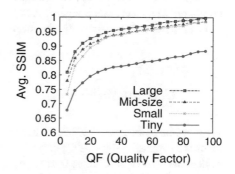

Fig. 4.6 Average
compression ratio
corresponding to consecutive
QFs (Reprinted with
permission from [14])

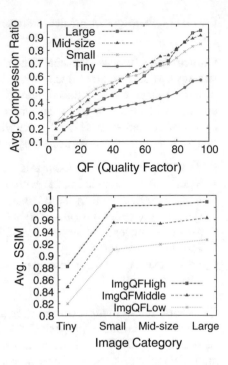

Fig. 4.7 Average SSIM
corresponding to the three QF
schemes (Reprinted with
permission from [14])

compressed all the correct images in TGdataset using each scheme to evaluate their
impact on image quality and size.

Figure 4.7 examines the impact of each QF scheme on image quality. Prior
work has shown that image compression with SSIM ≥ 0.85 is generally considered
acceptable by users [7]. As shown in Fig. 4.7, all three QF schemes manage to stay
above the 0.85 quality threshold for small, mid-size, and large images. The two
cases where image quality becomes questionable concern tiny images, which are
the hardest case for any compression strategy. Overall, these results suggest that in
most cases, even the aggressive *ImgQFLow* scheme will produce images with an
acceptable level of fidelity.

Figure 4.8 examines the image size reduction enabled by each QF scheme, as
compared to the original images. As expected, more aggressive QF schemes provide
more size reduction, especially for large images.

4.5.2   Content Validation

As mentioned in Sect. 4.3.2.3, TrafficGuard users encounter a non-trivial amount
of broken images when using apps. The back-end cloud of TrafficGuard naturally
notices most broken images during the image analysis, transcoding, and compression process. In these cases, the cloud simply discards the broken image and sends

Fig. 4.8 Average
compressed size
corresponding to the three QF
schemes (Reprinted with
permission from [14])

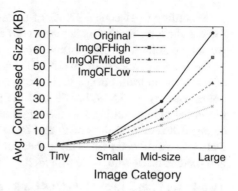

a "Broken Warning" response to the client. From the requesting app's perspective, broken images appear to be missing due to a network error and are handled as such.

4.5.3 Traffic Filtering

In this section, we present the implementation details of the four types of filters employed by TrafficGuard. Most traffic filtering in our system occurs on the client side (in the child proxy), including first-level filtering of malicious URLs and ads, and throttling of overnight and background traffic. Only second-level filtering of malicious URLs and ads occurs on the cloud side.

Restricting Overnight Traffic The mobile app of TrafficGuard automatically turns the user's cellular data connection off between the hours of t_1 and t_2, which are configurable by the user. This feature is designed to halt device traffic during the night, when the user is likely to be asleep. TrafficGuard pops up a notification just before t_1, alerting the user that her cellular connection will be turned off in ten seconds. Unless the user explicitly cancels the action, her cellular data connection will not be resumed until t_2. According to TGconfig, nearly 20% of the users have enabled the overnight traffic filter, and 84% of them adopt the default night duration of 0–6 AM.

Throttling Background Traffic To prevent malicious or buggy apps from draining users' limited data plans, TrafficGuard throttles traffic from background apps. Specifically, the TrafficGuard app has a configurable *warning bound* (B_1) and a *disconnection bound* (B_2), with $B_2 \gg B_1$. TrafficGuard also maintains a count c of the total bytes transferred by background apps. If c increases to B_1, TrafficGuard notifies the user that background apps are consuming a significant volume of traffic. If c reaches B_2, another notification is created to alert the user that her cellular data connection will be closed in ten seconds. Unless the user explicitly cancels this action or manually reopens the cellular data connection, her cellular data connection will not be resumed. After the user responds to the B_2 notification, c is reset to zero.

According to TGconfig, 97.6% of the users have enabled the background traffic filter, indicating that users actually care about background traffic usage. Initially, we set the default warning bound $B_1 = 1.0$ MB. However, we observed over 57% of the users decreased B_1 to 0.5 MB, indicating that they wanted to be reminded of background traffic usage more frequently. Conversely, the initial disconnection bound was $B_2 = 5$ MB, but 69% of the users raised B_2 to 20 MB, implying that the initial default setting was too aggressive. Based on this implicit feedback, we changed the default values of B_1 and B_2 to 0.5 and 20 MB. In comparison, Microsoft Data Sense only maintains a disconnection bound (B_2) to restrict background traffic, and there is no default value provided.

Two-Level Filtering of Malicious Links and Ads   To avoid wasting cellular traffic on unwanted content, TrafficGuard always prevents users from accessing malicious links, while giving users the choice of whether to opt in to ad blocking. In Sect. 4.4, we have presented high-level design of the two-level filtering. Here we talk about two more nuanced implementation issues.

The first issue is about the sizes of the local, small blacklists. Both lists have to be loaded in memory by the child proxy for quick searching, so they must be much shorter than the cloud-side large blacklists (which contain 29M malicious URLs and 102M ads-related URLs). To balance memory overhead with effective local traffic filtering, we limit the maximum size of the local blacklists to 40 MB. Consequently, the local blacklists usually contain around 1M links, which we observe can identify 72–78% of the malicious and ads links.

The second issue concerns updates to blacklists. As mentioned in Sect. 4.3.2.4, the large blacklists are maintained by an industrial union that typically updates them once per month. Accordingly, the TrafficGuard cloud automatically creates updated small blacklists and pushes them to mobile users.

4.5.4   Value-Based Web Caching (VBWC)

Early in 2003, Rhea et al. proposed VBWC to overcome the shortcomings of traditional HTTP caching [29]. The key idea of VBWC is to index objects by their *hash values* rather than their URLs, since an object may have many *aliases*. VBWC has a much better hit rate than HTTP caching because it handles aliased content. However, prior to TrafficGuard, VBWC has not been widely deployed in practice due to two problems: (1) the *complexity* of segmenting an object into KB-sized blocks and choosing proper block boundaries; (2) its *incompatibility* with the HTTP protocol, since VBWC requires that the proxy and the client maintain significant state information, i.e., a mapping from hash values to cached content.

Reducing Complexity   To determine whether TrafficGuard's VBWC implementation should segment content into blocks (and if so, at what granularity), we conduct trace-driven simulations using the content in TGdataset. Specifically, we played back each user's log of requests and inserted the content into VBWC using 8, 32,

128 KB, and full content segmentation strategies. To determine segment boundaries, we ran experiments with simple fixed-size segments [29] and variable-sized, Rabin-fingerprinting-based segments [31]. We also examined the handprinting-based approach that combines Rabin-fingerprinting and deterministic sampling [32].

Through these simulations, we discovered that 13% of the HTTP requests would hit the VBWC cache if we stored content whole, i.e., with no segmentation. Surprisingly, even if we segmented content into 8 KB blocks using the Rabin-fingerprinting (the most aggressive caching strategy we evaluated), the hit rate only increased to 15%. The handprinting-based approach exhibited similar performance to Rabin-fingerprinting when a typical number ($k = 4$) of handprint samples are selected, while incurring a bit lower computation overhead. By carefully analyzing the cache hit results, we find that the whole-content hashing is good enough for two reasons: (1) images dominate the size of cache hit objects in TGdataset; (2) there are almost no partial matches among images. Thus, we conclude that a simple implementation of content-level VBWC is sufficient to achieve high hit rates.

Addressing Incompatibility As discussed above, VBWC is incompatible with standard HTTP clients and proxies. Fortunately, we have complete control over the TrafficGuard system, particularly the cloud–client paired proxies, which enabled us to implement VBWC. The front-end child proxy takes care of encapsulating HTTP requests from user apps and decapsulating responses from the back-end cloud, meaning that VBWC is transparent to user apps. In practice, the mobile app of TrafficGuard maintains a 50-MB content cache on the client's file system, along with an in-memory table mapping content hashes to filenames that is a few KB large.

Ideally, every change to the cloud-side mapping table triggers a change to the client-side mapping table accordingly. But in practice, for various reasons (e.g., network packet loss), this pair of tables may be different at some time, so we need to synchronize them with proper overhead. In TrafficGuard, the client-side mapping table is loosely synchronized with the cloud-side mapping table on an hourly basis, making the synchronization traffic negligible and VBWC mostly effective.

4.6 Evaluation

In this section, we evaluate the traffic reduction, system overhead, and latency penalty brought by TrafficGuard.

4.6.1 Data Collection and Methodology

We evaluate the performance of TrafficGuard using both real-system logs and trace-driven simulations. We collect working logs from TrafficGuard's back-end cloud servers between Dec. 21 and 27, 2014, which include traces of 350M HTTP requests issued from 0.6M users, as well as records of CPU and memory utilization over time on the cloud servers. We refer to this dataset as TGworklog. On the other hand, as the client-side traffic optimization mechanisms mainly help users reduce traffic by suppressing unwanted requests, it is not possible to accurately record the corresponding saved traffic (which never occurred in reality). Instead, we rely on trace-driven simulations using TGdataset to estimate the client-side and overall traffic savings.

4.6.2   Traffic Reduction

Client Side   First, we examine the effectiveness of TrafficGuard's client-side mechanisms at reducing traffic. In TGdataset, 11.4% of the cellular traffic is transferred at night, and according to TGconfig, 20% of the users have enabled overnight traffic filtering. Thus, we estimate that users eliminate 2.3% ($= 11.4\% \times 20\%$) of the cellular traffic using the overnight traffic filter.

Moreover, we observe that 1% of the users in TGdataset regularly exceed the disconnection bound $B_2 = 20\,\text{MB}$ per day of background traffic. The resulting overage traffic amounts to 5.33% of the cellular traffic. In TGconfig, 97.6% of the users have enabled background traffic filtering. Therefore, we estimate that the background traffic filter reduces cellular traffic by 5.2% ($= 5.33\% \times 97.6\%$). Note that this background traffic saving is an *underestimation*, since we do not take the potential effect of B_1 ($= 0.5\,\text{MB}$, the warning bound) into account.

Additionally, in TGdataset, malicious content accounts for 0.8% of the HTTP traffic, while ads account for 4%. According to TGconfig, 67% of the users have chosen to drop ads. Consequently, after all malicious content and unwanted ads are filtered, 3.48% ($= 0.8\% + 4\% \times 67\%$) of the HTTP traffic can be saved. This is equal to 2.8% ($= 3.48\% \times 80.4\%$) of the total cellular traffic.

Overall   Next, we evaluate how much traffic TrafficGuard is able to reduce overall through trace-driven simulations. We play back all the requests in TGdataset and record how many bytes are saved by each mechanism: traffic filtering, content validation, image compression, and VBWC. As shown in Fig. 4.9, TrafficGuard is able to reduce HTTP traffic by 43% and non-HTTP traffic by 7.4% when all four mechanisms are combined. In summary, the overall cellular traffic usage is reduced by 36%, from 1324 to 845 GB.

As expected, image compression is the most important mechanism when used in isolation. 38% of the image traffic is reduced by our adaptive quality reduction approach. In other words, our approach saves a comparable portion ($27\% = 38\% \times 71\%$) of HTTP traffic as compared to Flywheel's WebP-based transcoding method, at a small fraction of the CPU cost (see Sect. 4.6.3).

To understand how traffic savings are spread across users, we plot the distribution of cellular traffic reduction ratios for our users in Fig. 4.10. 55% of the users saved

Fig. 4.9 Total cellular traffic usage optimized by each mechanism (Reprinted with permission from [14])

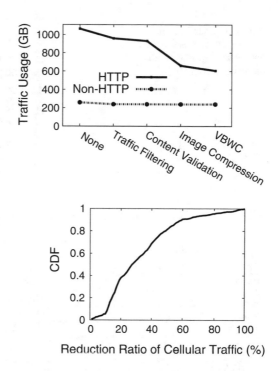

Fig. 4.10 Distribution of users' cellular traffic reduction ratios (Reprinted with permission from [14])

over a quarter of cellular traffic, and 20% of the users saved over a half (most of whom benefit a lot from traffic filtering and VBWC).

Using TrafficGuard's built-in user-feedback facility, we asked users to report their cellular data caps. 95% of the long-term volunteers in TGdataset reported their caps to us. Using this information, we plot Fig. 4.11, which shows the percentage of each user's data cap that would be used with and without TrafficGuard (again, based on trace-driven simulations). We observe that 58.2% of the users exceed their usage caps under normal circumstances and that TrafficGuard grants significant practical benefits for these users, e.g., users who would normally be using 200–300% of their allocation (and thus pay overage fees) are able to stay below 100% usage with TrafficGuard. Overall, TrafficGuard reduces the number of users who exceed their data caps by 10.7×.

At last, we wonder how TrafficGuard's traffic reduction gains are spread across user apps. Table 4.5 lists the top 10 apps ordered by popularity (the fraction of users with the app) as well as by the fraction of traffic eliminated. We observe that TrafficGuard is able to eliminate 12–42% of traffic for popular apps, but that the apps with the greatest traffic savings (52–84%) tend to be unpopular. This indicates that the developers of popular apps may already be taking steps to optimize their network traffic, while most unpopular apps can hardly become mobile-friendly in the near future.

Fig. 4.11 Users' cellular
traffic usage relative to their
data caps (Reprinted with
permission from [14])

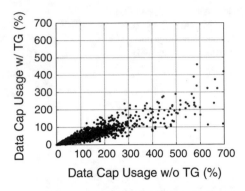

Table 4.5 Top 10 applications served by TrafficGuard, ordered by popularity and by greatest
traffic reduction

By user ratio (UR)			By traffic saving ratio (TSR)		
App name	UR (%)	TSR (%)	App name	UR (%)	TSR (%)
WeChat	74	22	Android Browser	0.11	84
QQ	66	22	Zhihu Q&A	0.15	81
Baidu search	29	21	iAround	0.03	63
Taobao	23	42	No. 1 Store	0.26	61
QQBrowser	22	27	Baidu news	0.45	57
Sogou Pinyin	20	12	Tiexue military	0.01	56
Baidu browser	16	30	WoChaCha	0.34	54
Toutiao news	14	22	Mogujie store	0.91	53
Sohu news	10	30	Koudai store	0.26	53
QQ zone	10	33	Papa photo	0.02	52

(Reprinted with permission from [14])

4.6.3   System Overhead

Cloud-Side Overhead The major cost of operating TrafficGuard lies in provision-
ing back-end cloud servers and supplying them with bandwidth. TrafficGuard has
been able to support ~0.2M users who send ~90M requests per day using only 23
commodity servers (HP ProLiant DL380). The configuration of each server is: 2*4-
core Xeon CPU E5-2609 @2.50 GHz, 4*8-GB memory, and 6*300-GB 10K-RPM
SAS disk (RAID-6).

Figure 4.12 illustrates the CPU/memory utilization of cloud servers on a typical
day. Mainly thanks to our lightweight image compression strategy, the CPU
utilization stays below 40%. Further, to compare the computation overhead of our
image compression strategy with Flywheel's WebP-based transcoding (based on the
cwebp encoder), we conduct offline experiments on two identical server machines
using 1M correct images randomly picked from TGdataset as the workload. Images
are compressed one by one without intermission. The results in Fig. 4.13 confirm
that the computation overhead (= average CPU utilization × total running time) of

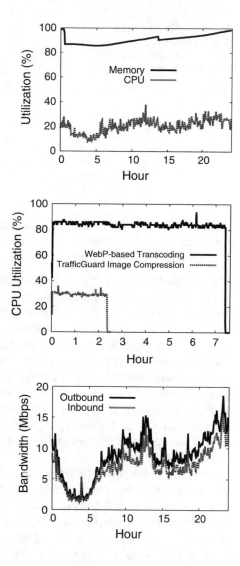

Fig. 4.12 CPU and memory overhead of the back-end servers (Reprinted with permission from [14])

Fig. 4.13 CPU overhead of different image compression strategies (Reprinted with permission from [14])

Fig. 4.14 Inbound and outbound bandwidth for back-end servers (Reprinted with permission from [14])

TrafficGuard image compression is only a small portion (10–12%) of that of WebP-based transcoding.

Memory utilization is typically >90% since content is in-memory cached whenever possible. Using a higher memory capacity, say 1 TB per server, can accelerate the back-end processing and thus decrease the corresponding latency penalty. Nonetheless, as shown in Fig. 4.25, the back-end processing latency constitutes only a minor portion of the total latency penalty, so we do not consider extending the memory capacity in the short term.

Figure 4.14 reveals the inbound/outbound bandwidth for back-end servers. Interestingly, we observe that a back-end server uses more outbound bandwidth

Fig. 4.15 Distribution of
client-side battery power
consumption (Reprinted with
permission from [14])

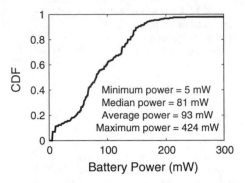

than inbound, though inbound traffic has been optimized. This happens because the
back-end has a 38% cache hit rate (with 4 TB of disk cache), so many objects are
downloaded from the Internet once but then downloaded by many clients.

Client-Side Overhead   The client-side overhead of TrafficGuard comes from three
sources: memory, computation, and battery usage. The memory usage is modest,
requiring 40 MB for local blacklists, and 10–20 MB for the VBWC mapping table.
Similarly, while running on a typical (8-core ARM CPU @1.7 GHz) Android
smartphone, TrafficGuard's single-core CPU usage is generally below 20% when
the cellular modem is active and almost zero when the network is inactive.

To understand the impact of TrafficGuard on battery life, we record the battery
power consumption of its mobile app when the child proxy is processing data
packets. As shown in Fig. 4.15, its working-state battery power is 93 mW on
average, given that the battery capacity of today's smartphones lies between 5
and 20 Wh and their working-state battery power lies between 500 mW and a few
watts [33, 34].

To understand specific facets of TrafficGuard's battery consumption, we conduct
micro-benchmarks on the client side with three popular, diverse apps: stock Android
Browser, WeChat, and Youku. In each case, we drove the app for five minutes
with and without TrafficGuard enabled while connected to a 4G network. Figures
4.16, 4.17, and 4.18 show the battery usage in each experiment. Meanwhile,
Figs. 4.19, 4.20, and 4.21 depict the corresponding CPU usage; Figs. 4.22, 4.23, and
4.24 plot the corresponding memory usage. All these results reveal that in cases
where TrafficGuard can effectively reduce network traffic (e.g., while browsing
the web), it also saves battery life or has little impact on battery life, because the
user app needs to process less traffic; accordingly, TrafficGuard does not increase
CPU/memory usage on the whole. However, in cases where TrafficGuard can hardly
reduce any traffic (e.g., Youku video streaming), it reduces battery life and increases
CPU/memory usage. Thus, we are planning to improve the design of TrafficGuard,
so that it can recognize and bypass the traffic from audio/video streams.

Fig. 4.16 Battery usage of
Android Browser with and
w/o TrafficGuard (Reprinted
with permission from [14])

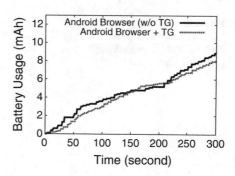

Fig. 4.17 Battery usage of
WeChat with and without
TrafficGuard (Reprinted with
permission from [14])

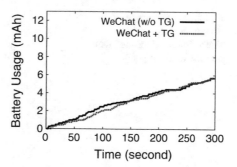

Fig. 4.18 Battery usage of
Youku with and without
TrafficGuard (Reprinted with
permission from [14])

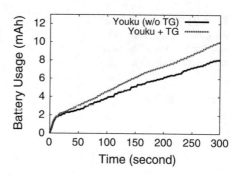

Fig. 4.19 CPU usage of
Android Browser with and
w/o TrafficGuard (Reprinted
with permission from [14])

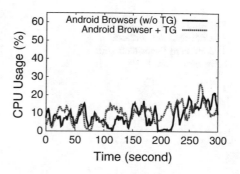

Fig. 4.20 CPU usage of
WeChat with and without
TrafficGuard (Reprinted with
permission from [14])

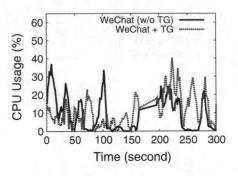

Fig. 4.21 CPU usage of
Youku with and without
TrafficGuard (Reprinted with
permission from [14])

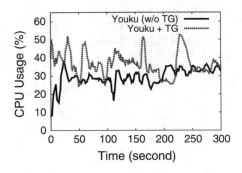

Fig. 4.22 Memory usage of
Android Browser with and
w/o TrafficGuard (Reprinted
with permission from [14])

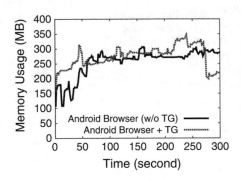

Fig. 4.23 Memory usage of
WeChat with and without
TrafficGuard (Reprinted with
permission from [14])

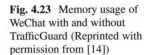
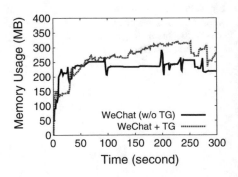

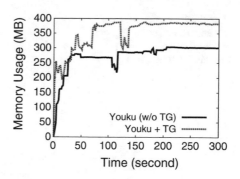

Fig. 4.24 Memory usage of Youku with and without TrafficGuard (Reprinted with permission from [14])

4.6.4 Latency Penalty

As TrafficGuard forwards HTTP GET requests to a back-end proxy rather than directly to the source, it may add response latency to clients' requests. In addition, client-side packet processing by the child proxy also brings extra latency. To put the latency penalty into perspective, first, we note three mitigating factors that effectively reduce latency: (1) TrafficGuard filters out ∼10.3% of the requests locally, which eliminates all latency except for client-side processing; (2) the ∼21.2% of the traffic that is not owing to HTTP GET requests is delivered over the Internet normally, thus only incurring the latency penalty for client-side processing; and (3) 38% of the HTTP GET requests hit the back-end Squid cache, thus eliminating the time needed to fetch the content from the Internet.

Next, to understand TrafficGuard's latency penalty in the worst-case scenario (unfiltered HTTP GETs that do not hit the Squid cache), we examine latency data from TGworklog. Figure 4.25 plots the total latency of requests that go through the TrafficGuard back-end and miss the cache, as well as the individual latency costs of four aspects of the system: (1) processing time on the client side, (2) processing time in the back-end, (3) time for the back-end to fetch the desired content, and (4) the RTT from the client to the back-end. Figure 4.25 shows that both client-side processing and back-end processing add little delay to requests. Instead, the majority of delay comes from fetching content, and the RTT from clients to the back-end cloud. Interestingly, Fig. 4.26 reveals that the average processing time of an outbound packet is longer than that of an inbound packet, although outbound packets are usually smaller than inbound packets. This is because the client-side filtering of malicious links and ads is the major source of client-side latency penalty.

In the worst-case scenario, we see that TrafficGuard does add significant latency to user requests. If we conservatively assume that clients can fetch content with the same latency distribution as Baidu's servers, then TrafficGuard adds 131 ms of latency in the median case and 474 ms of latency in the average case. However, if we take into account the three mitigating factors listed at the beginning of this section (which all reduce latency), the median latency penalty across all traffic is reduced to merely 53 ms, and the average is reduced to 282 ms.

Fig. 4.25 Latency for each phase content processing and retrieval (Reprinted with permission from [14])

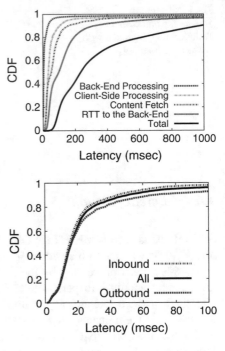

Fig. 4.26 Latency for clients' processing data packets (Reprinted with permission from [14])

4.7   Conclusion

Traffic optimization is a common desire of today's cellular users, carriers, and service developers. Although several existing systems can optimize the cellular traffic for specific apps (typically web browsers), cross-app systems are much rarer and have not been comprehensively studied. In this chapter, we share our design approach and implementation experiences in building and maintaining TrafficGuard, a real-world cross-app cellular traffic optimization system used by 10 million users.

To design TrafficGuard, we took a measurement-driven methodology to select optimization strategies that are not only high impact (i.e., they significantly reduce traffic) but also efficient, easy to implement and compatible with heterogenous apps. This methodology led to some surprising findings, including the relative ineffectiveness of text compression. Real-world performance together with trace-driven experiments indicates that our system meets its stated goal of reducing traffic (by 36% on average), while also being efficient (23 commodity servers are able to handle the entire workload). In the future, we plan to approach cellular carriers about integrating TrafficGuard into their networks, since this will substantially decrease latency penalties for users and simplify the overall design of the system.

References

1. Cisco Visual Networking Index: Global Mobile Data Traffic Forecast Update 2014-2019 White Paper. http://www.cisco.com/c/en/us/solutions/collateral/service-provider/visual-networking-index-vni/white_paper_c11-520862.html
2. Isaacman S, Martonosi M (2011) Low-infrastructure methods to improve internet access for mobile users in emerging regions. In: Proceedings of the 20th international world wide web conference (WWW), pp 473–482
3. Johnson D, Pejovic V, Belding E, van Stam G (2011) Traffic characterization and internet usage in Rural Africa. In: Proceedings of the 20th international world wide web conference (WWW), pp 493–502
4. Li Z, Wilson C, Xu T, Liu Y, Lu Z, Wang Y (2015) Offline downloading in China: a comparative study. In: Proceedings of the 15th ACM internet measurement conference (IMC), pp 473–486
5. Google to websites: be mobile-friendly or get buried in search results. http://mashable.com/2015/04/21/google-mobile-search-2/#UbuurRKFaPqU
6. The State of Digital Experience Delivery (2015). https://www.forrester.com/The+State+Of+Digital+Experience+Delivery+2015/fulltext/-/E-RES120070
7. Agababov V, Buettner M, Chudnovsky V, Cogan M, Greenstein B, McDaniel S, Piatek M, Scott C, Welsh M, Yin B (2015) Flywheel: Google's data compression proxy for the mobile web. In: Proceedings of the 12th USENIX symposium on networked systems design and implementation (NSDI), pp 367–380
8. Li Z, Huang Y, Liu G, Wang F, Zhang ZL, Dai Y (2012) Cloud transcoder: bridging the format and resolution gap between internet videos and mobile devices. In: Proceedings of the 22nd SIGMM workshop on network and operating systems support for digital audio and video (NOSSDAV), pp 33–38
9. Li Z, Jin C, Xu T, Wilson C, Liu Y, Cheng L, Liu Y, Dai Y, Zhang ZL (2014) Towards network-level efficiency for cloud storage services. In: Proceedings of the 14th ACM internet measurement conference (IMC), pp 115–128
10. Woo S, Jeong E, Park S, Lee J, Ihm S, Park K (2013) Comparison of caching strategies in modern cellular backhaul networks. In: Proceedings of the 11th ACM International Conference on Mobile Systems, Applications, and Services (MobiSys), pp 319–332
11. Naylor D, Schomp K, Varvello M, Leontiadis I, Blackburn J, Lopez D, Papagiannaki K, Rodriguez P, Steenkiste P (2015) Multi-context TLS (mcTLS): enabling secure in-network functionality in TLS. In: Proceedings of the 2015 ACM Conference on Special Interest Group on Data Communication (SIGCOMM), pp 199–212
12. Rao A, Kakhki A, Razaghpanah A, Tang A, Wang S, Sherry J, Gill P, Krishnamurthy A, Legout A, Mislove A, Choffnes D (2013) Using the Middle to Meddle with Mobile. Technical report NEU-CCS-2013-12-10, CCIS, Northeastern University
13. Sherry J, Lan C, Popa R, Ratnasamy S (2015) BlindBox: deep packet inspection over encrypted traffic. In: Proceedings of the 2015 ACM conference on special interest group on data communication (SIGCOMM), pp 213–226
14. Li Z, Wang W, Xu T, Zhong X, Li, X.Y., Wilson C, Zhao BY (2016) Exploring cross-application cellular traffic optimization with Baidu TrafficGuard. In: Proceedings of the 13th USENIX symposium on networked systems design and implementation (NSDI), pp 61–76
15. Aucinas A, Vallina-Rodriguez N, Grunenberger Y, Erramilli V, Papagiannaki K, Crowcroft J, Wetherall, D (2013) Staying online while mobile: the hidden costs. In: Proceedings of the 9th ACM conference on emerging networking experiments and technologies (CoNEXT), pp 315–320
16. Falaki H, Lymberopoulos D, Mahajan R, Kandula S, Estrin D (2010) A first look at traffic on smartphones. In: Proceedings of the 10th ACM internet measurement conference (IMC), pp 281–287

17. Huang J, Qian F, Mao Z, Sen S, Spatscheck O (2012) Screen-off traffic characterization and optimization in 3G/4G networks. In: Proceedings of the 12th ACM internet measurement conference (IMC), pp 357–364
18. Lumezanu C, Guo K, Spring N, Bhattacharjee B (2010) The effect of packet loss on redundancy elimination in cellular wireless networks. In: Proceedings of the 10th ACM internet measurement conference (IMC), pp 294–300
19. Qian F, Wang Z, Gao Y, Huang J, Gerber A, Mao Z, Sen S, Spatscheck O (2012) Periodic transfers in mobile applications: network-wide origin, impact, and optimization. In: Proceedings of the 21th international world wide web conference (WWW), pp 51–60
20. Android OS background data increase since 4.4.4 update. http://forums.androidcentral.com/moto-g-2013/422075-android-os-background-data-increase-since-4-4-4-update-please-help.html
21. Android OS is continuously downloading something in the background. http://android.stackexchange.com/questions/28100/android-os-is-continuously-downloading-something-in-the-background-how-can-i
22. How to Minimize Your Android Data Usage and Avoid Overage Charges. http://www.howtogeek.com/140261/how-to-minimize-your-android-data-usage-and-avoid-overage-charges
23. Vergara E, Sanjuan J, Nadjm-Tehrani S (2013) Kernel level energy-efficient 3G background traffic shaper for android smartphones. In: Proceedings of the 9th IEEE international wireless communications and mobile computing conference (IWCMC), pp 443–449
24. Viennot N, Garcia E, Nieh J (2014) A measurement study of google play. ACM SIGMETRICS Perform Eval Rev 42(1):221–233
25. Adblock Plus EasyList for ad blocking. http://easylist.adblockplus.org
26. Qian F, Sen S, Spatscheck O (2014) Characterizing resource usage for mobile web browsing. In: Proceedings of the 12th ACM international conference on mobile systems, applications, and services (MobiSys), pp 218–231
27. Spring N, Wetherall D (2000) A protocol-independent technique for eliminating redundant network traffic. In: Proceedings of the 2000 ACM conference on special interest group on data communication (SIGCOMM), pp 87–95
28. Qian F, Quah K, Huang J, Erman J, Gerber A, Mao Z, Sen S, Spatscheck O (2012) Web caching on smartphones: ideal vs. reality. In: Proceedings of the 10th ACM international conference on mobile systems, applications, and services (MobiSys), pp 127–140
29. Rhea S, Liang K, Brewer E (2003) Value-based web caching. In: Proceedings of the 12th international world wide web conference (WWW), pp 619–628
30. Wang Z, Bovik A, Sheikh H, Simoncelli E (2004) Image quality assessment: from error visibility to structural similarity. IEEE Trans Image Process 13(4):600–612
31. Rabin M (1981) Fingerprinting by random polynomials. Technical report TR-15-81, Center for Research in Computing Technology, Harvard University
32. Pucha H, Andersen D, Kaminsky M (2007) Exploiting similarity for multi-source downloads using file handprints. In: Proceedings of the 4th USENIX conference on networked systems design and implementation (NSDI), pp 2–2
33. Carroll A, Heiser G (2010) An analysis of power consumption in a smartphone. In: Proceedings of the 2010 USENIX annual technical conference (ATC), pp 21–21
34. Liu Y, Xiao M, Zhang M, Li X, Dong M, Ma Z, Li Z, Chen S (2016) GoCAD: GPU-assisted online content adaptive display power saving for mobile devices in internet streaming. In: Proceedings of the 25th international world wide web conference (WWW), pp 1329–1338

Chapter 5
Boosting Mobile Virtual Network Operator

Abstract Recent years have witnessed the rapid growth of mobile virtual network operators (MVNOs), which operate on top of the existing cellular infrastructures of base carriers, while offering cheaper or more flexible data plans compared to those of the base carriers. In this chapter, we present a nearly two-year measurement study toward understanding various key aspects of today's MVNO ecosystem, including its architecture, performance, economics, customers, and the complex interplay with the base carrier. Our study focuses on a large commercial MVNO with about 1 million customers, operating atop a nationwide base carrier. Our measurements clarify several key concerns raised by MVNO customers, such as inaccurate billing and potential performance discrimination with the base carrier. We also leverage big data analytics and machine learning to optimize an MVNO's key businesses such as data plan reselling and customer churn mitigation. Our proposed techniques can help achieve higher revenues and improved services for commercial MVNOs.

Keywords Mobile virtual network operator · Mobile carrier · Mobile ISP

5.1 Introduction

As propelled by the increasing market demand, mobile virtual network operators (MVNOs) have quickly gained popularity and commercial success in recent years [1]. The global MVNO market revenue has reached about $60.5 billion in 2018 [2] and is predicted to grow to $103 billion in 2023 [3]. Also, the number of MVNOs worldwide has exceeded 1000 [4]. MVNOs operate on top of the existing cellular infrastructures of *base carriers*, while offering cheaper or more flexible data and voice/SMS plans compared to those of the base carriers. In addition, MVNOs can enhance the utilization of base carriers' infrastructures. They may also promote the competition in the telecommunication market and prevent potential monopoly to some extent. Furthermore, MVNOs are expected to play a critical role in the 5G era [5]. MVNOs that obtain sliced radio access network resources from base carriers would act as a forerunner in mobile network slicing, which is a crucial technology in the revolution toward 5G cellular wireless networks.

Despite the unprecedented growth of MVNOs, end customers are still subject to manifold concerns when switching to MVNOs. For example, severe overcharge problems have been reported with regard to MVNO users [6]. Also, some base carriers may deliver MVNO users' data with lower priorities, leading to inferior performance experienced [7–9]. All above concerns may impede the reputation of MVNOs and hinder their development.

Due to the very few studies in the public literature, the research community lacks a thorough understanding of the MVNO ecosystem, including its architecture, performance, economics, customers, and the complex interplay between an MVNO and its base carrier. In this chapter, we present a nearly two-year measurement study toward understanding the above aspects. Our study focuses on Xiaomi Mobile (V-Mobile for short), a large commercial MVNO in China. It has $\sim$1M users and fully operates on top of China Telecom (B-Mobile for short), a nationwide base carrier in China that has 300M+ users. V-Mobile is a representative *light* MVNO (Sect. 5.2), the most popular type of MVNOs that fully rely on the base carrier's cellular infrastructure [1] while having the capability of designing their own data plans independently of the base carriers. In other words, V-Mobile resells data plans purchased from B-Mobile to its users. In order to attract customers while gaining profits, V-Mobile has to: (1) strategically design its own data plans and (2) judiciously purchase data plans from B-Mobile to fulfill the data plans selected by V-Mobile customers, based on estimating their monthly data usage.

Studying the MVNO ecosystem is challenging, as it involves multiple stakeholders (MVNO customers, the MVNO carrier, and the base carrier) that incur complex interplay, as well as components that are not present in traditional MNOs (Mobile Network Operators) such as data plan reselling. To enable our large-scale measurement, we collaborate with V-Mobile and collect five datasets (Sect. 5.3): (1) BBSDataset, which consists of about 12,000 posts from the Bulletin Board System (BBS) maintained by V-Mobile (2) UserDataset, which includes all customers' basic information, such as the gender, birthday, and the date of joining/leaving V-Mobile (3) MonthlyDataset, which refers to each user's monthly data plan, payment, data usage, and account balance information (4) PerfDataset, which comprises the network performance statistics of 342 V-Mobile users and 250 B-Mobile users that opted in to help us collect detailed network performance data (5) SURDataset, which is the set of two types of state update reports (SURs) that are collected from V-Mobile's accounting center (AC) These datasets include customers' demographic information, selected data plans, monthly data usage, traffic characteristics, network performance, and billing events. Jointly examining these datasets helps reveal a comprehensive landscape of the MVNO ecosystem. Specifically, we perform detailed studies of the following aspects:

- **Data Plan and Usage Characterization (Sect. 5.4).** We find that V-Mobile customers are sensitive to prices in that almost half of the customers prefer the data plan with the lowest cost per GB ($2.84/GB). Also, the customers' demographics are different from those of a regular MNO: there are significantly more female users (58.3%) than male users (41.7%), and V-Mobile customers are dominated by users younger than 30. Regarding the actual data usage, V-Mobile users typically considerably under-utilize their data plans. Besides, users' actual data usage is weakly correlated with their subscribed data plans. The above findings suggest that V-Mobile users' data plan selection is oftentimes economically suboptimal, while such suboptimality is a key reason why operating an MVNO can be profitable.

- **Network Performance Characterization (Sect. 5.5).** By analyzing PerfDataset, we find no noticeable network performance difference between B-Mobile and V-Mobile. This is distinct from previous reports where MVNO users may suffer from performance degradations compared to the base carrier users [7–9]. Our results indicate that the performance degradation reported by prior studies is very likely a (man-manipulated) policy-level result by the base barrier rather than a technical necessity.

- **Monthly Data Usage Prediction (Sect. 5.6.1)** plays a critical role in the operation of an MVNO. We demonstrate that by strategically applying off-the-shelf machine learning algorithms enhanced with domain-specific data preprocessing, we can achieve an average prediction accuracy of 86.75%. In addition to performing monthly data usage prediction on a per-user basis, we also holistically examine the entire user base by conducting *uncertainty modeling*, which establishes a global statistical distribution for the prediction accuracy. Doing so facilitates the prediction for new V-Mobile users with insufficient training samples.

- **Data Reselling Optimization (Sect. 5.6.2).** We develop a framework that leverages our data usage prediction technique to optimize V-Mobile's reselling profit, i.e., intelligently selecting the data plans to be purchased from B-Mobile in order to maximize the overall profit for V-Mobile. When applied to the 0.7 million active users in our dataset, our machine learning technique increases V-Mobile's profit rate by 17.1% compared to V-Mobile's current approach. Applying the uncertainty modeling further improves the profit rate by 34.1% an overall improvement of 57.1%.

- **Customer Churn Profiling and Mitigation (Sect. 5.7).** Customer churn refers to when a customer cancels or "drops out" her subscribed cellular service. We mine our dataset to reveal key factors that indicate a user's forthcoming service cancelation. We then use them to proactively predict customers' churn and manage to achieve both high precision (95.52%) and recall (94.45%). We further collaborate with V-Mobile to conduct a field trial. By sending to 1% of the customers with high churn probabilities (based on our prediction), a small gift card of $1.44, V-Mobile can reduce the customers' churn rate from 0.83% to 0.32%.

- **Understanding Inaccurate Billing Issues (Sect. 5.8).** We systematically investigate V-Mobile users' complaints on billing issues, such as their unexpectedly high monthly charges. We find that most billing issues are caused by the excessive propagation delay of the control-plane billing state update reports (SUR). The overall delay often reaches several minutes, causing billing inconsistency between B-Mobile and V-Mobile.

To our knowledge, this is so far the most comprehensive study of a large commercial MVNO. Our high-level contributions are multifold. From an end user's perspective, our study demystifies the MVNO ecosystem and clarifies several key concerns raised by customers. From an MVNO's perspective, we leverage statistical modeling, big data analytics, and machine learning to optimize an MVNO's key businesses such as data usage prediction, data plan reselling, and customer churn mitigation. Our study also exposes to the community new research topics, with intra-disciplinary nature, in the context of MVNO and its interplay with the base carrier.

5.2 Background

A base carrier typically owns a legal license to exclusively use certain frequencies of the radio spectrum in a country. This can often lead to market monopoly, service degradation, or under-utilization of radio resources. To address these problems, numerous MVNOs have emerged in recent years. An MVNO fully or partially leverages one or multiple base carriers' licensed radio spectrum and facilities.

According to their degrees of dependence on base carriers, today's MVNOs can be classified into three categories [1, 10]: *skinny MVNOs*, *light MVNOs*, and *thick MVNOs*. Skinny and light MVNOs do not have their own radio infrastructures; the former are mainly devoted to marketing and sales and are thus also known as "branded resellers," while the latter further have the ability to design specialized data plans independently of the base carriers. In some countries such as China, MVNOs have emerged and flourished for only several years, and they have not been allowed to set up their own infrastructures so far. In fact, light MVNOs act more as a transitional paradigm between the skinny MVNOs and the thick MVNOs. In contrast, thick MVNOs have their own infrastructures to exert more control over their offerings, which however are not permitted in many countries. Among the three categories, light MVNOs are the most common and are permitted in most countries [1]. In this work, our studied V-Mobile is a typical light MVNO.

Data Plan Reselling As a light MVNO, V-Mobile resells data plans purchased from B-Mobile to its users. However, V-Mobile does not have a wholesale (discounted) price from B-Mobile, nor is it allowed to buy a single data plan from B-Mobile to serve multiple users. Therefore, in order to attract customers while gaining profits, V-Mobile has to strategically design its own data plans. Specifically, let P_V be a data plan that V-Mobile offers its customers; let P_B be the same plan offered by B-Mobile; let P_V' be the corresponding plan that V-Mobile purchases from B-Mobile to fulfill P_V. Ideally, P_V needs to be cheaper than P_B; otherwise, customers have no incentives to switch to V-Mobile; P_V' should be inferior to (and thus cheaper than) P_V; otherwise, operating V-Mobile is not profitable.

Consider a concrete example. B-Mobile has a monthly plan of "$7.23 for 2 GB plus $0.01/MB overdraft" ($P_B$). To attract customers, V-Mobile lowers the price by offering "\$7.09 for 2 GB plus \$0.01/MB overdraft" (P_V). To fulfill P_V, V-Mobile can purchase from B-Mobile an inferior plan of "\$5.78 for 1 GB plus \$0.01/MB overdraft" (P_V'). The assumption here is that, despite having a 2 GB data plan, many users' actual monthly usages are much lower. In this example, the reselling is profitable if a V-Mobile user's monthly usage is lower than $1000 + (7.09 - 5.78)/0.01 = 1131$ MB. This example also illustrates the importance for V-Mobile to *accurately predict a user's monthly data usage*.

Billing As the base carrier of V-Mobile, B-Mobile has tens of millions of customers and over a million base stations across the country. Since V-Mobile is a light MVNO, all its SIM cards are issued by B-Mobile while possessing special phone numbers (MSISDN) that can be identified as MVNO numbers. Therefore, all the data traffic, voice calls, and SMS messages of V-Mobile users are delivered by the radio infrastructure of B-Mobile. Moreover, since V-Mobile establishes its own data plans, it needs to handle customers' billing, which is processed at the AC, by itself. In order for V-Mobile to generate bills in an accurate and timely fashion, the SURs, which contain users' up-to-date data usage information, need to be properly delivered to V-Mobile's AC. This can be achieved in two ways. The major way is shown in the upper branch in Fig. 5.1. Per the agreement between V-Mobile and B-Mobile, they establish a control-plane channel between their ACs, allowing B-Mobile to forward V-Mobile users' SURs, which we call B-Mobile-SURs, to V-Mobile. In B-Mobile, B-Mobile-SURs are gathered and propagated by its base stations. Another way of delivering SURs is illustrated in the bottom branch in Fig. 5.1. V-Mobile customers can optionally install an app developed by V-Mobile. When the app is running, it keeps monitoring the client device's data usage and uploading SURs, which we call App-SURs, directly to V-Mobile's AC.

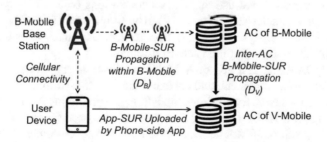

Fig. 5.1 Interactions among V-Mobile, its customers, and B-Mobile (Reprinted with permission from [11])

5.3   Measurement Data Collection

To enable our large-scale measurement of a typical MVNO, we collect multiple datasets from various sources. Correlating these datasets focusing on different aspects helps reveal a complete landscape of the MVNO ecosystem. We next describe our datasets in detail. Note that all users from whom we collected the data were presented with informed consent, and all customers' identities were fully anonymized before any analysis was conducted:

(1) **BBSDataset**. V-Mobile maintains a BBS (Bulletin Board System) website from which we gathered about 12,000 posts from the BBS users, who belonged to either the current or prospective users of V-Mobile. We then manually examine all the posts to understand the users' concerns. The content of the posts can roughly be classified into four categories. 25.4% of the posts concern with the network performance such as whether V-Mobile can provide performance that is as good as that offered by B-Mobile; 5.2% of the posts express users' doubts on their received bills and request for auditing; 37.9% of the posts involve specific complaints with regard to billing state update delay, e.g., notifications of data overdraft oftentimes arrive late, causing unexpected overdraft expense. We will revisit its root cause in Sect. 5.8. The remaining 31.5% of the posts are non-technical concerns, e.g., the appearance of V-Mobile's SIM cards, and the purchase, repair, and refund instructions.

(2) **UserDataset**. We obtain from V-Mobile a database containing each customer's basic information, including the gender, birthday, the date of joining V-Mobile, and the date of canceling the service (for dropout users). Our dataset was captured in Oct. 2017, involving a total of 908,548 users since Jan. 2016. In this "snapshot," 168,853 users terminated their contracts with V-Mobile and thus are excluded. We use this dataset for various types of analyses such as data usage characterization (Sect. 5.4), data usage prediction (Sect. 5.6.1), and customer churn analysis (Sect. 5.7). Hereafter, unless otherwise noted, we apply our analysis to the 0.7 million active customers.

(3) **MonthlyDataset**. The AC of V-Mobile archives every user's monthly data plan, data usage, payment, and account balance information. They provide an essential data source for profiling, modeling, and predicting each user's monthly data usage (Sects. 5.4 and 5.6.1). The data are also used for optimizing the data reselling profit of V-Mobile (Sect. 5.6.2), as well as customer churn profiling and mitigation (Sect. 5.7). Our studied **MonthlyDataset** here covers 22 billed months, i.e., from January 2016 to October 2017.

(4) **PerfDataset**. A challenge we face is to monitor V-Mobile users' network performance. We take a crowd-sourcing-based approach where we invite users of both V-Mobile and B-Mobile to voluntarily participate in a data collection campaign by installing an app developed by V-Mobile and turning on the "sampling performance" option for a whole month. The app we leverage for the campaign only works on Android (not iOS), so it is likely to introduce some bias to the measurement results. The app passively measures key performance

metrics such as RTT and throughput of users' traffic (we detail the measurement methodologies in Sect. 5.5). The collected statistics are securely uploaded to a remote server when users' devices are idle, and no actual content payload was collected or uploaded. Overall, 342 V-Mobile users and 250 B-Mobile users from 269 cities in the country voluntarily participated in our study for 30 days, forming a decently large dataset consisting of 1 TB TCP flows' statistics. We leverage this unique dataset to characterize the performance of B-Mobile and V-Mobile in Sect. 5.5.

(5) **SURDataset.** Recall from Sect. 5.2 (Fig. 5.1) that there are two types of SURs: B-Mobile-SURs and App-SURs. We collect both types of SURs at V-Mobile's AC and use this data to investigate the billing issues in Sect. 5.8. An SUR consists of a timestamp, a device ID, and the user's data usage in bytes. The two types of SURs can be correlated by counting the data bytes consumed by a customer.

5.4   Data Usage Characterization

We characterize V-Mobile customers in three aspects: data plan selection, actual data usage, and the relationship between them. Whenever possible, we also compare V-Mobile with B-Mobile to unravel the differences between an MVNO and its base carrier.

Data Plan Selection Recall from Sect. 5.2 that V-Mobile makes its data plans cheaper than those (counterparts) of B-Mobile to attract customers. Table 5.1 and Table 5.2 compare the specific data plans offered by both carriers, from which we find that V-Mobile customers can actually save a small portion (1.1–2.4%) of money. Although the economic incentives seem weak, V-Mobile also provides "soft" value-added services to its customers in terms of billing, state update, customer service, and so on. Furthermore, V-Mobile can operate on more than one base carrier and is expected to support the cross-carrier portability of users' phone numbers in the near future. Table 5.1 also shows the percentage of users subscribing to each of the V-Mobile's data plans, as obtained from the UserDataset. As shown in Table 5.1, V-Mobile users are price conscious: the 3 GB data plan attracts most (47.37%) of the users because it has the lowest cost per GB ($2.84/GB), followed by the 1 GB plan that has the lowest subscription cost. In contrast, the 4 GB plan has the fewest (6.32%) users, very likely because of its highest subscription cost as well as a large subscription cost increase from 3 to 4 GB.

V-Mobile's data plans are designed according to its current commercial contract with its base carrier. Using one B-Mobile plan to serve multiple V-Mobile users is not allowed; this restriction stems from business strategies rather than technical reasons. This restriction is generalizable to the other MVNOs in China such as Snail Mobile and Suning Mobile, but not the MVNOs in the USA or Europe. As time goes by, it is likely to be canceled or mitigated through business negotiation or even

118   5   Boosting Mobile Virtual Network Operator

Table 5.1 V-Mobile's data plans and their percentage of users

Monthly data	Subscription fee	Overdraft fee	Percentage of users
1 GB	5.64	$0.01/MB	35.79%
2 GB	7.09	$0.01/MB	10.52%
3 GB	8.53	$0.01/MB	47.37%
4 GB	12.87	$0.01/MB	6.32%

(Reprinted with permission from [11])

Table 5.2 B-Mobile's data plans (selected)

Monthly data	Subscription fee	Overdraft fee
500 MB	$3.62	$0.01/MB
1 GB	$5.78	$0.01/MB
2 GB	$7.23	$0.01/MB
3 GB	$8.68	$0.01/MB
4 GB	$13.01	$0.01/MB
6 GB	$27.47	$0.01/MB

(Reprinted with permission from [11])

Fig. 5.2 Gender distribution for V-Mobile's data plans (Reprinted with permission from [11])

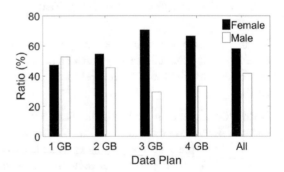

lawsuits in court. On the other hand, V-Mobile is allowed to adjust the threshold and price of each data plan without asking for B-Mobile's permission.

We also make several interesting observations regarding V-Mobile users' demographic distributions. As shown in Fig. 5.2, there are significantly more female users (58.3%) than male users (41.7%) in particular for large (3 and 4 GB) plans. Women tend to prefer V-Mobile to B-Mobile, only 45% of whose customers are female. Furthermore, by analyzing UserDataset, we notice that the ratio of female users increased by 1% in one year (from 2016 to 2017). Regarding the age distribution, as shown in Fig. 5.3, most of the V-Mobile customers are younger than 30, with the exception where the 4 GB data plan holders are dominated by people between 30 and 39 who are presumably more financially sound. From 2016 to 2017, the ratio of users younger than 30 increased by 1.7%, and the ratio of users older than 50 increased by 1%; on the contrary, the other users between 30 and 49 decreased by 2.7%. In other words, V-Mobile's penetrations have gradually increased as for children and seniors. The above observations can be leveraged by MVNOs for developing demographic-targeted products and promotions.

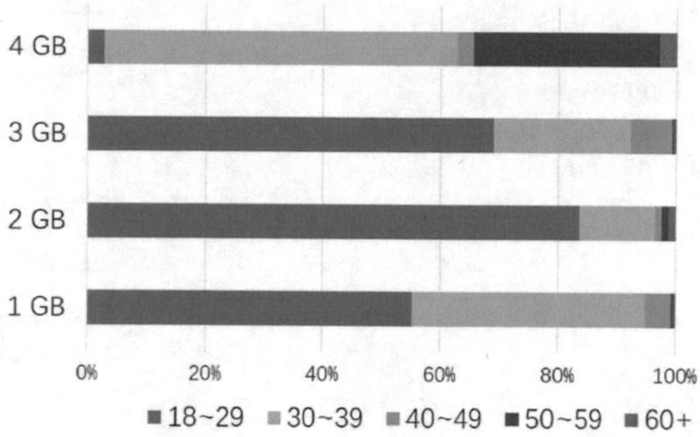

Fig. 5.3 Age distribution for V-Mobile's data plans (Reprinted with permission from [11])

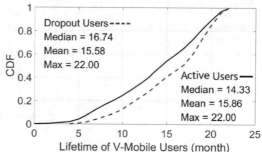

Fig. 5.4 Lifetime of V-Mobile users (active and dropout, as of 10/2017) (Reprinted with permission from [11])

Figure 5.4 plots the distribution of V-Mobile users' lifetime, which is defined as the time span from when the user joined V-Mobile to T_{end}. T_{end} is either the time when the user dropped out (canceled the V-Mobile service), or October 2017 which is the time when the data was collected if the user was still active at that time. We plot the lifetime for dropout and active users separately. As shown, active users' lifetime ranges from 0 to 22 months and averages at nearly 16 months. Note that the 22-month cap exists because V-Mobile started its business 22 months before Oct. 2017. For dropout users, their lifetime is statistically even longer. Overall, although the absolute lifetime of V-Mobile users is significantly shorter than that of typical MNO users (ranging from 0 to 138 months and averaging at 52 months [12]), most V-Mobile users tend to have a relatively long lifetime compared to the lifetime of V-Mobile itself. This implies that most users appear to be satisfactory with are willing to keep using V-Mobile's services.

Actual Data Usage We next study the data usage characteristics of V-Mobile users. Figure 5.5 plots the distribution of their monthly data usage across all of their billed months. It ranges between 0 and 6018 MB with a mean (median) being 1743 MB (1950 MB). We make two observations from Fig. 5.5. First, the tail indicates that overdraft may indeed occur in a non-trivial fraction of billed months, as to be quantified shortly. This brings potential obstacles for MVNOs toward making profits (Sect. 5.2). Second, more surprisingly, we see the other extreme for about 20% of the billed months in which a user consumes little data—we call this the *intermittent presences* of some users. In particular, some new users have just been enrolled for

Fig. 5.5 Distribution of
V-Mobile active users'
monthly data usage
(Reprinted with permission
from [11])

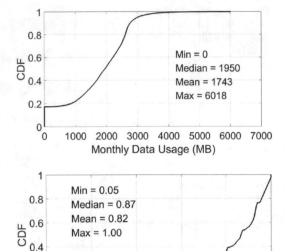

Fig. 5.6 Distribution of
V-Mobile active users'
presence ratios (Reprinted
with permission from [11])

less than one month, which obviously have no monthly data usage. Suppose a user
has been a V-Mobile customer for n full months, while she barely used her data
plan in m out of n months. We empirically define a "bare usage" as consuming no
more than 50 MB of data in a month with only full months being considered. We
then compute the *presence ratio* of the customer as $(n - m)/n$ to quantify how
often she uses the V-Mobile service. Figure 5.6 plots the presence ratio distribution
across users whose lifetimes are at least one full month. As shown, the presence ratio
ranges from 0.05 to 1 and averages at 0.82. About 23% of the users have a presence
ratio lower than 0.75. For the users with low presence ratios, V-Mobile made a
survey with them randomly via telephone interviews, which reveal the reason—
such low presence ratios are oftentimes from users who hold more than one SIM
card and use V-Mobile as a "backup" one that is used infrequently. These users can
bring high profits if V-Mobile can accurately predict their non-presence.

We next investigate how users' demographics affect the data usage. Figure 5.7
plots the distributions of the males' and females' monthly data usage across all
billed months. It shows the monthly data usages of users whose lifetimes are at
least one month. As shown, compared to males whose median (mean) monthly
usage is 892 MB (1423 MB), females tend to use much more data, with their median
(mean) usage being 2004 MB (2172 MB). The results echo our finding about the
relationship between gender and data plan selection in Fig. 5.2. They are also in line
with a recent study showing females tend to be heavier smartphone users compared
to males [13]. Figure 5.8 depicts the statistics (mean and standard deviation) of
each age group's monthly data usage. We observe a clear trend where young people

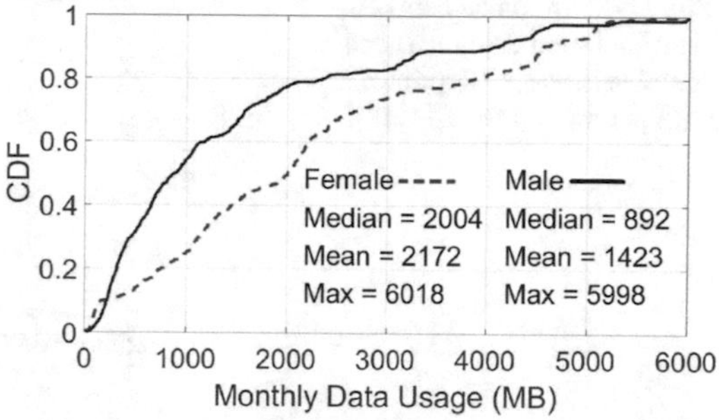

Fig. 5.7 Distributions of male and female active users' monthly data usage (Reprinted with permission from [11])

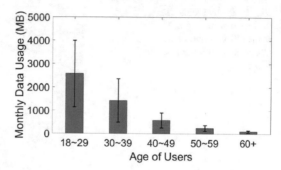

Fig. 5.8 Relationship between users' age and their monthly data usage (Reprinted with permission from [11])

consume considerably more cellular data than older people: on average teenagers and the twenties consume 80% more data compared to people in their thirties, and $20\times$ more compared to senior citizens (60+).

Data Plan vs. Actual Usage   To better understand the relationship between users' selected data plan and users' monthly actual usage, we plot the distribution of their difference in Fig. 5.9 across all billed months, where a positive value indicates under-utilizing the data plan, and a negative value corresponds to overdraft. Figure 5.10 further shows the statistics of actually consumed, under-utilized, and overdraft bytes for all billed months of each type of data plan. As shown, customers typically under-utilize their data plans (in 82.59% of all billed months). An average user under-utilizes her data plan by as much as 893 MB. This indicates that most users are conservative with their data usage, in particular given that cellular data usage monitoring and limiting tools have been incorporated into today's mobile OSes [14].

We also make a surprising observation from Fig. 5.10 that users' actual data usage is weakly correlated with their subscribed data plans: the average usage of the 2 GB plan is similar to that of the 3 GB plan, and the usage of the 4 GB plan is even less than 2 and 3 GB plans. This implies that *MVNO customers' data plan selection is oftentimes economically suboptimal* (especially for older customers who prefer larger data plans), while such suboptimality is a key reason why operating an MVNO can be profitable.

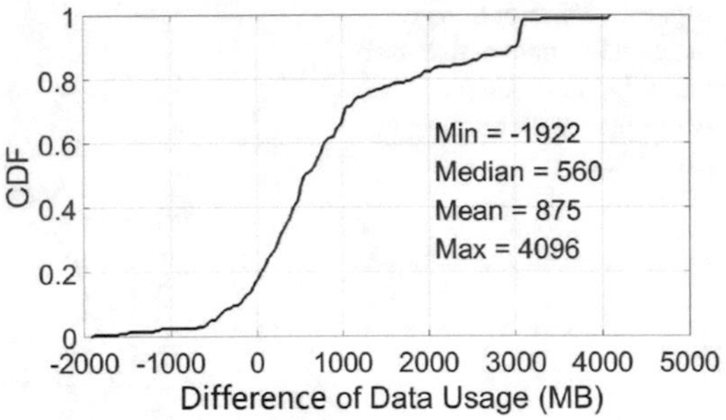

Fig. 5.9 Difference between users' selected data plans and actual data usage (Reprinted with permission from [11])

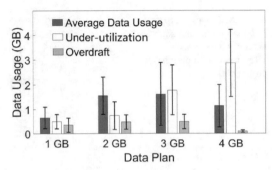

Fig. 5.10 Avg. data usage, under-utilization, and overdraft for each plan (Reprinted with permission from [11])

5.5   Network Performance

We now shift our focus to the network performance characterization by analyzing the PerfDataset, which, recall from Sect. 5.3, was collected from about 600 V-Mobile and B-Mobile users from an Android app. Once the "sampling performance" option is turned on, the app leverages libpcap to passively monitor the client device's traffic (only the TCP/IP headers) and compute several key performance metrics: (1) TCP handshake RTT, (2) TCP flow size, i.e., the total number of payload bytes within a flow, (3) TCP flow duration, i.e., the time span between the first and last packet of a flow, (4) TCP flow rate, i.e., the ratio between flow size and duration, with uplink and downlink measured separately, and (5) TCP uplink packet retransmission rate, i.e., the ratio between retransmitted uplink data packets and the total number of uplink data packets within a flow (note that we are unable to measure the downlink retransmission rate). In our subsequent analysis, for flow rate calculation, following similar methodologies of prior studies [15, 16], we only consider flows that are at least 100 ms and at least 1MB; for uplink retransmission rate, we only examine flows containing at least 10 uplink packets, to make the metric meaningful.

The above are known to be the key metrics quantifying the network performance [15]. Compared to prior characterizations of commercial cellular network performance (e.g., 3GTest in 2009 [17], 4GTest in 2011 [18], SpeedTest in 2011 [19], and an LTE study in 2012 [16]), our study focuses on both MVNO and MNO and provides more up-to-date statistics that can benefit other work on, for

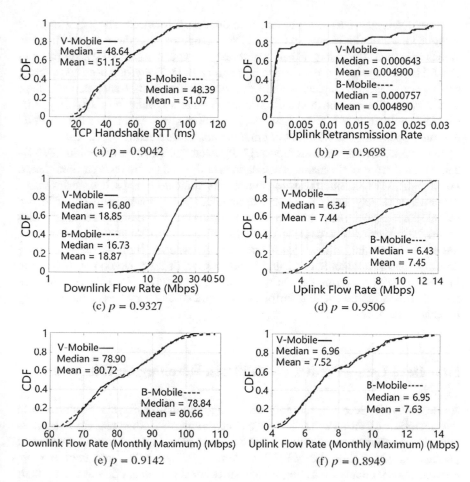

Fig. 5.11 Network performance characterization of crowd-sourced V-Mobile and B-Mobile users (Reprinted with permission from [11])

example, synthetic cellular traffic generation and cellular performance modeling. Our measurement results are shown in Fig. 5.11's six subplots. We plot the statistics for B-Mobile and V-Mobile separately. Each CDF in subplots (a)–(d) is across all eligible TCP flows; subplots (e) and (f) show the monthly maximum flow rates across all users' billed months, to reveal the maximum capacity that today's cellular networks can offer.

From the BBSDataset, we learn that many V-Mobile users have concerns that B-Mobile may potentially deliver their traffic at a lower priority. Surprisingly, our results in all plots of Fig. 5.11 disprove this by showing that statistically, there is no noticeable performance difference between V-Mobile and B-Mobile in all six metrics. Since we collect the samples from a small number of users, we further use the paired samples T-test [20] to compare their performances. The T-test result is a confidence (p-value) between 0 and 1. We accept the hypothesis that their mean values are equal if p is larger than α, a threshold typically set to 0.05. As listed in Fig. 5.11, all the values of p are much bigger than 0.05. Therefore, even considering the impact of small samples, we still find no significant difference between their performances. We ascribe this to the non-discriminatory packet routing policy of B-Mobile in delivering V-Mobile users' data, recalling that V-Mobile is a light MVNO that fully operates on B-Mobile's communication infrastructure (Sect. 5.2).

In contrast, several previous reports [7–9] noted that the users of certain MVNOs had suffered from performance degradations compared to the base carriers' users. For a light MVNO, our measurement results indicate that such a performance degradation is very likely a (man-manipulated) policy-level result rather than a technical necessity. The policy-level result means that it is the commercial policies of the base carrier that degrade the light MVNO users' network performance, rather than technical difficulties. Consequently, when a light MVNO can have desirable business negotiations with its base carrier, its users would not suffer from inferior network performance. On the contrary, for a full MVNO that has its own wireless infrastructure, such a performance degradation might be (partially) owing to technical reasons.

5.6   Data Usage Prediction and Data Reselling Optimization

As described in Sect. 5.2, monthly data usage prediction plays a pivotal role in the operation of an MVNO. It also enables numerous other use cases such as data plan recommendation, cellular infrastructure planning, and cost-aware content prefetching [21]. For the MVNO customers, it can help them choose more appropriate data plans for saving money since most customers do not use up their monthly data plans (see Fig. 5.9). For the base carrier, data usage prediction can help it design more appropriate data plans to fit more users' appetites. Additionally, our customer churn prediction can also benefit from data usage prediction to better retain customers (Sect. 5.7). In this section, we first describe the challenges and solutions for large-scale monthly data usage prediction (Sect. 5.6.1) and then detail how an MVNO can leverage it to optimize the reselling profit (Sect. 5.6.2).

5.6.1   Data Usage Prediction and Modeling

Monthly data usage prediction is a typical *time series forecasting* problem, which utilizes a model to predict a variable's future value(s) based on its previously observed values. In our scenario, for each user, we have a time series $X = \{X_1, X_2, \ldots, X_n\}$, where X_i is the user's data usage in the i-th month. Our objective is to predict X_{n+1}, the data usage of the $(n + 1)$-th month. The prediction of each user is independently performed. For a given user, we define the prediction accuracy as

$$\text{Accuracy} = 1 - \frac{|\text{predicted\_usage} - \text{actual\_usage}|}{max(\text{predicted\_usage, actual\_usage})}. \tag{5.1}$$

From a carrier's perspective, performing data usage prediction faces several challenges. First, customers' usage randomness makes an accurate prediction of *every* user's data usage impossible. We thus aim at achieving statistically good prediction results for the whole user base. Second, as the prediction is conducted on a per-month basis, each user only has a limited amount of historical data. Recall from Sect. 5.4 that an average V-Mobile user's lifetime is only 16 months. Third, as the carrier needs to perform the prediction for millions of users, we prefer an algorithm that is as lightweight as possible. In the literature, although there exist many studies on (typically short-term) traffic volume prediction, few studies, if any, specifically focus on long-term, large-scale monthly cellular data usage prediction with limited historical data. This is partially due to a lack of real cellular usage datasets.

Methodology We apply mainstream machine learning techniques for a user's monthly data usage prediction, including SVR (Support Vector Regression [22]), RBFNN (Radial Basis Function Neural Network [23]), BPNN (Back Propagation Neural Network [24]), and ULR (Unary Linear Regression [25]). Each user is trained and tested separately. We empirically select the algorithms' parameters as follows. As for SVR, it uses the RBF (Radial Basis Function) kernel with the kernel parameter of 0.01 and the regularization parameter of 100. As for RBFNN, we set the spread of radial basis function to 0.1 and the number of neurons that are added between displays to 100. Meanwhile, we limit the maximum number of neurons to 400. BPNN uses "tansig" and "purelin" for hidden layers and output layers. The maximum number of iterations is set to 100. Parameter settings are actually complex in our prediction algorithms because different datasets have their specific characteristics. However, the algorithms are fixed, and thus only the parameters need to be tuned to fit the datasets.

Another decision we need to make is to determine n, the window length of the time series X. It poses a tradeoff: a large n reduces the number of valid training samples and may cause potential overfitting, while a small n makes the training data less expressive. Specifically, our model is trained in the form of sliding windows on each user's historical data usage, where each user's historical data usage constitutes a time series. We test different values of n with comprehensive experiments on our collected big data and empirically choose $n = 3$ to balance the above tradeoff.

Furthermore, in order to filter out outliers and to avoid potential overfitting, we perform preprocessing on each user's entire historical data usage using k-means clustering in both training and testing. Specifically, we set $k = 2$ and only retain the larger cluster by removing the smaller cluster and concatenating the remaining samples in a chronological order. We empirically observe that such a simple preprocessing step reasonably handles the intermittent presence problem of most users (Sect. 5.4) as the infrequent low-usage months can typically be filtered out. As a matter of fact, at the beginning (after data cleaning), we did not filter out outliers and the results turned out not good enough. Thus, we explored various possible ways to improve the accuracy of data usage prediction, and we found that filtering out outliers was the most effective to achieve our goal. In detail, quite a few "abnormal" factors such as users' travel and death may degrade the prediction accuracy of users' data usage. Nonetheless, we need to focus on the general trends of users' data usage by eliminating those extreme or accidental situations, so as to figure out a proper prediction model with a sufficiently high accuracy. Our methodology inevitably introduces some bias, which however is acceptable according to our experiences.

Results For each user whose lifetime is l months, since we pick $n = 3$, we use $\{s_1, s_2, s_3 \rightarrow s_4\}, ..., \{s_{l-3}, s_{l-2}, s_{l-1} \rightarrow s_l\}$ to train a model, where s_i is the data usage of the i-th month obtained from the MonthlyDataset, using each of the aforementioned machine learning algorithms ("$\rightarrow$" separates the features and label). In the prediction phase, we employ the model to predict s_{l+1} based on $\{s_{l-2}, s_{l-1}, s_l\}$. To evaluate our approach, we compute the prediction accuracy, defined in Eq. (5.1), for each user, and compare the average accuracy of the five algorithms in Fig. 5.12. In fact, V-Mobile itself adopts a quite simple method to predict each user's monthly data usage by calculating the average value in previous months. However, it does not work well since the prediction accuracy is merely 68.67%. Among all these methods, our method achieves an overall prediction accuracy of up to 86.75% across users (using SVR with RBF kernel with outlier filtering). The outlier filtering improves the best accuracy across all algorithms from 80.35 to 86.75%.

We observe that users with a longer lifetime tend to exhibit a higher prediction accuracy because more historical data is available. This is illustrated in Fig. 5.13, which plots the average prediction accuracy for users with different lifetimes (using SVR with RBF kernel and outlier filtering). Moreover, SVR with RBF kernel, SVR with linear kernel, and ULR are very computationally efficient in that the total running time for all the 0.7 million active users is less than 20 min including both training and testing on a server with Intel E5-Xeon Broadwell (V4) CPU and 16 GB memory. RBFNN and BPNN take a longer yet still acceptable time of 11 h to train

Fig. 5.12 Average prediction accuracy of different ML techniques (Reprinted with permission from [11])

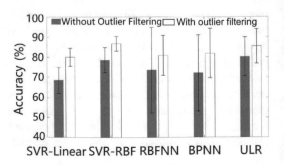

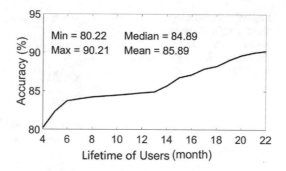

Fig. 5.13 Average prediction accuracy increases with the lifetime of users (Reprinted with permission from [11])

and test the whole dataset. We had also tried to use more attributes for data usage prediction, such as user information, plan type, and phone model. Unfortunately, this did not essentially improve the prediction accuracy, and using some attributes even degraded the accuracy. However, it is an interesting direction to explore how to further improve the accuracy, probably by considering other key attributes that we have not noticed yet.

Statistical Uncertainty Modeling Despite the overall good results, Fig. 5.12 indicates the high variation of the prediction accuracy across individual users. In particular, for users with a short lifetime, their data usage prediction is inherently difficult due to a lack of training samples. This motivates us to further holistically examine the entire user base by performing *uncertainty modeling*, which establishes statistical distributions for the prediction accuracy. As to be shown in Sect. 5.6.2, the uncertainty modeling helps users with insufficient training data; it also provides a building block for deriving a generic cost-aware optimization framework.

In metrology, all measurements are subject to uncertainty—a measurement result is complete only when it is accompanied by a statement of the associated uncertainty [26]. In our case, the way to reveal uncertainty is to understand the probability distribution of the prediction accuracy in the face of a large user base. We exemplify our modeling approach using the prediction results produced by SVR-RBF with outlier filtering, which yields the highest accuracy as shown in Fig. 5.12. Other prediction methods' results can be modeled in a conceptually similar manner (the actual distribution may differ though). For SVR-RBF, we make a key observation that the ratio between a user's actual monthly data usage and predicted usage follows a normal distribution, as illustrated in Fig. 5.14. Quantitatively, let k be the predicted data usage of a V-Mobile user, and k' be the actual usage in a billed month. Then the random variable $\frac{k'}{k}$ follows the normal distribution $N(1, \sigma^2)$, and its probability density function is

$$h\left(\frac{k'}{k}\right) = \frac{1}{\sqrt{2\pi}\sigma}e^{-\frac{\left(\frac{k'}{k}-1\right)^2}{2\sigma^2}}.$$
(5.2)

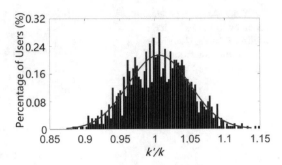

Fig. 5.14 The random variable k'/k follows a normal distribution (Reprinted with permission from [11])

Thereby, the probability density function of the actual data usage (k') can be derived as

$$g(x) = \frac{1}{\sqrt{2\pi}k\sigma}e^{-\frac{\left(\frac{x}{k}-1\right)^2}{2\sigma^2}}. \tag{5.3}$$

We next perform a hypothesis test to confirm our observation. We adopt the *Kolmogorov–Smirnov (K–S) test* [27], which is a nonparametric test that compares an empirical distribution of a set of samples with a reference probability distribution (in our case, the normal distribution). Suppose we have independently and identically distributed samples $\{X_1, \cdots, X_n\}$ with some unknown distribution $\mathbb{P}$, and we want to decide between the following hypotheses:

$$H_0 : \mathbb{P} = N(1, \sigma^2), \quad H_1 : \mathbb{P} \neq N(1, \sigma^2). \tag{5.4}$$

For the random variable $\frac{k'}{k}$, we run the K–S test on our data. The test result is a confidence (p-value) between 0 and 1. We accept H_0 if the p-value is larger than α, and a threshold typically set to 0.05. The numerical results indicate this is indeed the case, as the p-value is calculated to be $0.7949 \gg 0.05 = \alpha$. We note that for several other prediction algorithms such as ULR and RBFNN, their $\frac{k'}{k}$ also follows a normal distribution with $p > 0.05$ (e.g., $p = 0.7655$ for ULR). However, this may not hold for algorithms with a lower prediction accuracy such as BPNN and SVR-Linear, whose prediction results may conform to other types of statistical distributions.

5.6.2 Data Reselling Optimization

We now consider an important application of our data usage prediction: data reselling optimization. Recall that a V-Mobile user oftentimes does not use up her subscribed data plan P_V, so V-Mobile can purchase an inferior plan, P'_V, from B-Mobile to fulfill P_V, and utilize the price difference to make profits. Our goal here is to make the selection of P'_V more intelligent to increase the profit for V-Mobile. This process is transparent to V-Mobile users.

Since our data usage prediction may not be accurate for a specific user, we are unable to guarantee that every individual user's reselling profit is maximized. Instead, we aim at maximizing the *expected* data reselling profit across all users. We now describe our formulation and solution. Let there be a group of m customers with their predicted data usage $\{k_1, k_2, \cdots, k_m\}$, and a collection of the base carrier's data plans $\{P_1, P_2, \cdots, P_n\}$. Consider any given user, say user j whose predicted usage is k_j. Let $p_i(k_j)$ be the *expected* expense, which includes the monthly subscription fee and the overdraft cost, that V-Mobile pays B-Mobile if V-Mobile selects P_i as the underlying plan to fulfill this user's subscription. Since each user is handled independently by V-Mobile, the minimum total expense that V-Mobile pays B-Mobile is

$$\sum_{j=1}^{m} min_{1 \le i \le n}\{p_i(k_j)\}. \tag{5.5}$$

To calculate Eq. (5.5), we need to first calculate $p_i(k_j)$

$$p_i(k_j) = \int_0^{+\infty} f(x)g(x)dx, \tag{5.6}$$

where x is the independent variable of the customer's data usage, $g(x)$ is the probability density function of the user's actual data usage derived through uncertainty modeling (e.g., Eq. (5.3) for SVR-RBF), and $f(x)$ is the payment function of x under data plan P_i. For example, $f(x)$ for "\$3.62 for 500 MB plus \$0.01/MB overdraft" is defined as $f(x) = 3.62$ for $0 \le x \le 500$, and $f(x) = \frac{x}{100} - 1.38$ for $x > 500$.

Based on our modeling results in Sect. 5.6.1, $\frac{k_j'}{k_j}$ follows a certain distribution. Assume we use SVR-RBF or ULR whose prediction results follow a normal distribution $N(1, \sigma^2)$. In this case, the maximum likelihood estimation $\hat{\sigma}^2$ is

$$\hat{\sigma}^2 = \frac{1}{m} \sum_{j=1}^{m} \left(\frac{k_j'}{k_j}\right)^2 - 1. \tag{5.7}$$

From the historical data of V-Mobile, we calculate $\hat{\sigma}$ to be 0.04 for SVR-RBF and 0.22 for ULR.

To calculate Eq. (5.6), we first rewrite it as a sum of two integrations $\int_0^S f(x)g(x)dx + \int_S^{\infty} f(x)g(x)dx$, where S is the data plan size (e.g., 500 MB in the above example), due to the piecewise nature of $f(x)$. We then apply the rectangle method [28] to numerically calculate each integration.

Evaluation. To assess the effectiveness of the above method, we apply it to the historical usage data of V-Mobile users between January 2016 and October 2017 (obtained from the MonthlyDataset), to optimize the reselling profit for the billing cycle of November 2017. The key evaluation metric, *profit rate (PR)*, is defined as

$PR = (m_1 - m_2)/m_2$, where m_1 is the total expense that customers pay V-Mobile, and m_2 is the cost that V-Mobile pays B-Mobile. A higher PR is always preferred by V-Mobile. Note that a PR may be negative. We compare four optimization methods as follows:

- **The Current Approach** employed by V-Mobile, learned by us based on our communication with the company, works as follows: in each month, V-Mobile estimates each user's usage in the next month simply by calculating the arithmetic mean of all historical months' usage. V-Mobile then purchases the cheapest data plan (with the overdraft cost taken into account) from B-Mobile based on this rough usage estimation. We apply this method to our data and calculate the overall PR to be 3.5%.
- **Machine Learning Only.** For each customer, V-Mobile employs machine learning (SVR-RBF with outlier filtering, see Sect. 5.6.1) to predict next month's data usage and then determines the data plan to be purchased from B-Mobile accordingly. This approach yields an overall PR of 4.1%.
- **Machine Learning with Uncertainty Estimation.** We apply the full method in Sects. 5.6.1 and 5.6.2 that combines the machine learning (SVR-RBF) and statistical uncertainty estimation. This approach leads to an overall PR of 5.5%, which is 57.1% higher than V-Mobile's current approach and 34.1% higher than the ML-only approach. We find that the significant increase of PR is attributed to better selections of B-Mobile's data plans for customers with a short lifetime. For such customers with insufficient training samples, per-user machine learning is oftentimes ineffective. Instead, the cross-user prediction accuracy modeling (Sect. 5.6.1) can provide a more reasonable estimation of the expected expense ($p_i(k_j)$) based on the "big data."
- **The Optimum.** To estimate the upper bound of the profit that V-Mobile can make, we use the ground-truth data, i.e., customers' actual data usage in Nov. 2017, to compute the optimal data plan selection. This leads to a PR of 6.2%, only 12.7% higher than our achieved PR of 5.5%.

5.7   Customer Churn Profiling and Mitigation

Customer churn refers to when a customer ceases her relationship with a company (in our case, canceling her cellular service or dropout). Its mitigation [29] is extremely important for both base carriers and MVNOs because of the high expense that a carrier needs to pay to recruit new customers.

Correlation Analysis We seek answers to the following key question: which properties (features) of customers are good indicators of their forthcoming service cancelation? Understanding this is a key prerequisite of performing effective churn management in order to retain customers. We take a data-driven approach to address this problem. Specifically, we first compile a set of 12 features that cover a wide range of properties of users' personal, data usage, and performance. Obtained from

UserDataset and MonthlyDataset, the 12 features are listed as follows: users' gender, age, lifetime, data plan, monthly data usage, monthly expense, monthly uplink bytes, monthly downlink bytes, roaming events, account balance, state update performance (Sect. 5.8), and device type. For each of a user's billed months, we generate a vector containing the 12 features, as well as obtain a binary label representing the churn state (whether the user has canceled her service) in the next month. To further enrich the feature set, we extend the features with numerical values by computing basic statistical functions such as mean(), median(), stdev(), and mean_diff() (mean of the first order difference) over the user's past months.

We next study the correlation between each of the features and the label (the churn state of the next month) across all customers' billed months. We compute the Spearman's rank correlation coefficient [30], a robust, nonparametric measure of the dependency between the rankings of two statistical variables. The coefficient ranges between −1.0 (negative correlation) and +1.0 (positive correlation). We include both the active and dropout users (about 1 million in total) in this study. Figure 5.15 lists the top 8 features that have the strongest correlations with the customer churn. We make several observations as detailed below. To help quantify our findings, we define a metric called *Dropout Contribution (DC)*, which is the percentage of dropout users with certain properties (e.g., having a specific lifetime range) among all dropout users. *DC* is calculated by examining each user's features associated with the month in which she dropped out.

- Figure 5.16 plots the relationship between users' lifetime and their *DC*. As shown, the *DC* increases as users stay longer. For example, 26.6% of all V-Mobile users have a lifetime between 18 and 22 months, but their *DC* is as high as 51%. In contrast, for the 8% users who have joined V-Mobile within half a year, their *DC* is only 2%. In today's MVNO industry, vendors usually pay much attention to attracting new users while oftentimes ignoring existing, and in particular, long-time loyal customers. This practice appears to be unwise according to our observation.
- Females account for a larger fraction (58%) in all V-Mobile customers but are less likely (*DC* = 0.45) to drop out compared to males (*DC* = 0.55). Besides, young people are more likely to cancel their services compared to older customers. As shown in Fig. 5.17, 28.4% users are between 18 and 29, while their *DC* is as high

Fig. 5.15 Top features ranked by the Spearman's rank correlation coefficient (Reprinted with permission from [11])

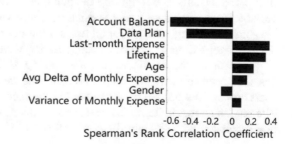

Spearman's Rank Correlation Coefficient

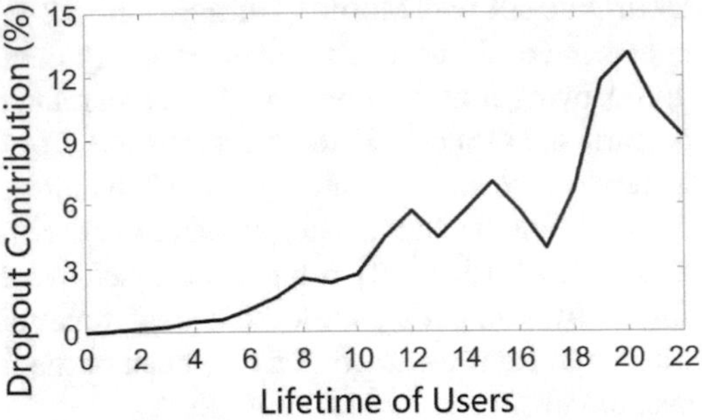

Fig. 5.16 V-Mobile users' lifetime vs. Dropout Contribution (DC) (Reprinted with permission from [11])

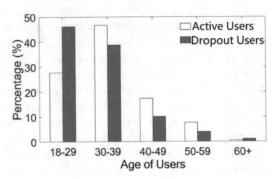

Fig. 5.17 V-Mobile users' age, for active and dropout users (Reprinted with permission from [11])

as 46.7%. These findings suggest the potential effectiveness of demographic-aware strategies for customer churn mitigation.

- A good indicator of a user's imminent dropout is her monthly expense being high and her account balance staying low. For example, if a user spends more than $57.8 in a month, while the account balance is lower than $1.5, then in 72.3% of such cases, she will drop out in the next month. This is likely due to the user's intent of using up her account balance, which will not be refunded when she drops out.

Customer Churn Prediction By jointly leveraging our identified features, we consider proactively predicting the customer churn. We apply off-the-shelf machine learning algorithms (Naive Bayes, SVM, Logistic Regression, RBF Neural Network, Decision Tree, and Random Forest) to the 8-dimensional feature vectors (Fig. 5.15). Details of configuring the machine learning algorithms are omitted for brevity. Unlike the data usage prediction where we build a per-user model, here we construct a single model for all users' monthly records, to capture the common behaviors regarding service cancelation among V-Mobile customers.

We evaluate the prediction accuracy using 10-fold cross-validation based on *users*. In each fold, we train a model using the monthly records from 90% of the users and use the trained model to predict the records of the remaining 10% users. The results shown in Table 5.3 indicate that the random forest model achieves the best precision (95.52%) and F1 score (0.95), as well a high recall rate (94.45%).

Table 5.3 Customer churn prediction results

ML model	Precision	Recall	F1 score
Naive Bayes	76.72%	50.54%	0.61
RBF neural network	81.52%	91.85%	0.86
SVM	78.79%	96.89%	0.87
Logistic regression	92.38%	85.02%	0.89
Decision tree	94.45%	94.10%	0.94
Random forest	95.52%	94.45%	0.95

(Reprinted with permission from [11])

Fig. 5.18 Churn probability distribution of V-Mobile users (Reprinted with permission from [11])

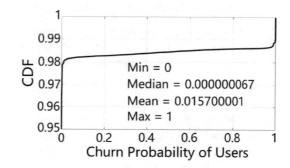

Real-World Churn Mitigation We collaborate with V-Mobile to conduct a field trial for churn mitigation in late October 2017. Specifically, we first apply the random forest model (trained using the data from 2/2016 to 9/2017) to predict whether each active user (as in 10/2017) will cancel her service in 11/2017. For each test sample, the random forest model outputs a probability indicating the likelihood of dropout. As shown in Fig. 5.18, the dropout probability exhibits a bimodal distribution where nearly 98% (1%) of the users have a churn probability near zero (one). Next, we select the top 1% of the users with the highest dropout probability and recommend V-Mobile to send to each of them via an SMS message a digital gift card containing a small amount ($1.44) of top-up fee (the gift card can only be activated next month). After conducting this churn mitigation campaign, V-Mobile observed that the churn rate, defined as the fraction of dropout users among all active users in the previous month, decreased significantly from 0.83% in October 2017 to 0.32% in November 2017. This indicates the potential effectiveness of our churn prediction approach.[1]

---

[1] To be more rigorous, ideally V-Mobile should also add a control group by distributing gift cards to 1% of users who are randomly chosen, in a different month. Unfortunately, V-Mobile was not able to conduct this due to non-technical reasons. Nevertheless, we feel it is still worthwhile to report our experiment and its results.

5.8   Inaccurate Billing in MVNO

Recall from Sect. 5.3 that based on our analysis of the BBSDataset, we find that more than 40% of the posts in the V-Mobile BBS concern inaccurate billing or delayed billing state notifications. These problems, if occur, are highly undesired because handling a billing issue requires considerable manual efforts from the customer service team, and problematic billing may also endanger the reputation of an MVNO. We manually examine the posts involving billing complaints in the BBSDataset and identify two issues:

Issue 1 *Termination of service despite a positive account balance.* A user suddenly loses her access to the cellular data service. Meanwhile, however, she still observes a positive account balance from the V-Mobile's app or website.

Issue 2 *Unexpectedly high monthly charge experienced by customers.* A user receives a monthly bill that substantially exceeds her expected cost. Typically, the user believes she has not yet used up her monthly data plan, but the received bill charges more than the data plan subscription cost.

In addition, we learn from V-Mobile that their internal billing sometimes also experiences inconsistencies:

Issue 3 *Unexpectedly high charge experienced by V-Mobile.* V-Mobile notices that for certain customers, the bill that it receives from B-Mobile appears to be higher than what it should be, based on its own data usage records of these customers. This does not affect V-Mobile customers' bills but causes V-Mobile to lose profit.

To understand the root causes of the above issues, we carefully analyze the SURDataset. Recall from Sect. 5.3 that it captures SURs delivered to V-Mobile's AC from two sources: users' apps (App-SURs) and B-Mobile's AC (B-Mobile-SURs) Our basic analysis methodology is to *correlate* the two types of SURs. For App-SURs, their delivery takes place in almost real time (typically less than 1 s), so their reception time can be largely regarded as a "ground-truth" of the time when the data is actually consumed. However, App-SURs are only used for troubleshooting purposes due to their low user coverage and the possibility of being tampered/spoofed. In contrast, B-Mobile-SURs are used for the actual billing. However, their delivery may experience high delays. To quantify that, as shown in Fig. 5.1, we use D_B to denote the B-Mobile-SUR propagation delay within B-Mobile and use D_V to denote the delivery latency from B-Mobile to V-Mobile. We can first calculate $D_B + D_V$ by taking the reception difference between a B-Mobile-SUR and its corresponding App-SUR and then calculate D_V as a delta between the timestamp field in the B-Mobile-SUR (denoting the time when it leaves B-Mobile's AC) and its reception time at V-Mobile's AC. D_B can thus be derived as $(D_B + D_V) - D_V$.

Figures 5.19 and 5.20 plot the distributions of D_B and D_V, respectively. As shown, D_B ranges from several seconds to 2.3 h and averages at nearly 16 min. D_V ranges from 1 s to 4.3 min, with an average of around 2 min.

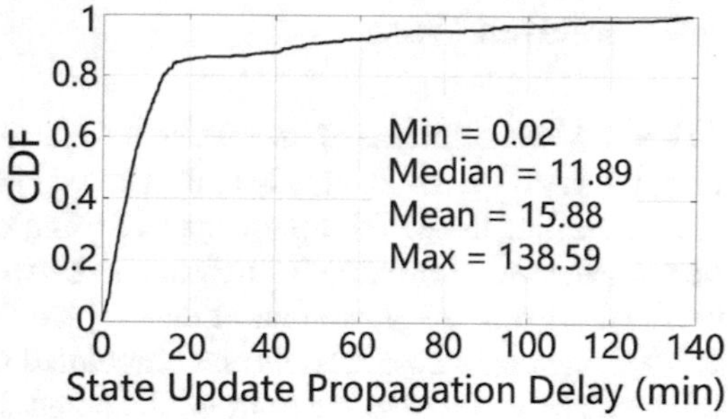

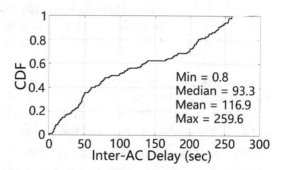

Fig. 5.19 B-Mobile-SUR propagation delay in B-Mobile (D_B) (Reprinted with permission from [11])

Fig. 5.20 Inter-AC B-Mobile-SUR propagation delay (D_V) (Reprinted with permission from [11])

Given the above finding, we can explain the root causes of the three aforementioned issues (Issues 1–3). For Issue 1, we find that the user-perceived account balance, despite being positive, was typically quite low when the user could not access the cellular service. In fact, at the time when the cellular service was terminated by the B-Mobile, the user's account balance had indeed decreased to zero or negative at B-Mobile's AC. However, the B-Mobile-SUR had not yet been propagated to V-Mobile's AC due to the high delay of D_V. Such a billing inconsistency is a unique issue in an MVNO.

For Issue 2, we find that in most cases the user actually had not used up her data plan of the current month. However, at the end of the *previous* month, due to the high propagation delay ($D_B + D_V$), a small portion of the B-Mobile-SURs arrived late at V-Mobile's AC, so V-Mobile was not able to add them to the previous month's bill. Instead, they were then added to the current month's bill, making it look unreasonable.

For Issue 3, we owe it to the excessive inter-AC delay (D_V). Specifically, after a V-Mobile user switches to a different data plan, the subscription is not always delivered from V-Mobile's AC to B-Mobile's AC in real time when the inter-AC channel is congested. As a result, before the new data plan actually takes effect at B-Mobile, the user's subscription will experience inconsistency between V-Mobile and B-Mobile. This inconsistency will be reflected on the next bill that B-Mobile sends to V-Mobile.

5.9   Related Work

MVNO Measurements There exist only a limited number of studies on commercial MVNOs. In 2014, Zarinni et al. [7] conducted a first study (based on their claim) of the MVNO performance using controlled experiments and noticed performance-wise differential treatments between some MVNOs and their base carriers. Also in 2014, Vallina et al. [1] studied the relationship between many MVNOs and their base carriers and pinpointed several potential issues for light and thick MVNOs. In 2016, Schmitt et al. noted that a packet may traverse a longer network path in an MVNO network than in the base carrier's network [8]. Recently, Oshiba studied how MVNOs affect bandwidth estimation algorithms [9]. Our study differs from theirs in several aspects: the study scale, the examined topics, and the findings.

Cellular Network Performance has been extensively studied in the literature. Several large-scale measurements include [16–19]. Our study in Sect. 5.5 focuses on an MVNO and its base carrier and provides more up-to-date performance statistics. We also compare our results with those in [16].

Traffic Prediction and MVNO Economics There exist a plethora of work on (typically short-term) network traffic prediction, such as [22, 31, 32], to name a few. However, it is unclear whether they are suitable for our long-term, large-scale data usage prediction with limited historical data. Researchers have also conducted analytical modeling and formulation on MVNO economics, such as market sharing between MVNOs and MNOs [33], leveraging users' feedback for pricing [34], and QoS-aware scheduling [35]. Compared to these theoretical studies, our reselling optimization takes a more practical and intuitive approach based on statistical modeling and machine learning. We also evaluate its effectiveness using real MVNO customers' data.

Customer Churn Mitigation has been widely studied in industries such as news media [36] and banking [37]. To predict dropout users, various techniques have been put forward [36, 38, 39]. We instead consider churn mitigation in the context of MVNO, which has a unique business model and customer churn characteristics.

5.10   Concluding Remarks

We conduct an in-depth investigation of V-Mobile, a large and representative light MVNO with about 1 million customers. Our findings shed light on various topics that are of the interests of the stakeholders: MVNO customers, the MVNO carrier, and the base carrier. At a high level, our study delivers several takeaway messages. First, MVNOs can leverage the unique demographics and usage patterns of their customers to promote and improve their services. Second, AI and big data can significantly boost the revenue and service quality for MVNOs. Third, the cross-layer and cross-entity interactions, in particular those between an MVNO and its base carrier, need to be better handled. Finally, we cannot quantify how generalizable our results are as to other MVNOs because we do not have their data. Qualitatively, we feel that the generalizability of our results depends mostly on the operating model of a different MVNO, rather than which country/area the different MVNO is operated in. We plan to perform deeper explorations in all above aspects in our future work.

References

1. Vallina-Rodriguez N, Sundaresan S, Kreibich C, Weaver N, Paxson V (2015) Beyond the radio: illuminating the higher layers of mobile networks. In: Proceedings of the 13th ACM international conference on mobile systems, applications, and services (MobiSys), pp 375–387
2. Statista. Size of the global MVNO market from 2012 to 2022. https://www.statista.com/statistics/671623/global-mvno-market-size/
3. Lanjudkar P, Bajaj S. Mobile virtual network operator (MVNO) market-global opportunity and forecasts, 2017–2023. https://www.alliedmarketresearch.com/mobile-virtual-network-operator-market
4. Morris A. Number of MVNOs exceeds 1,000 globally. https://www.fiercewireless.com/europe/report-number-mvnos-exceeds-1-000-globally
5. Nakao A, Du P, Kiriha Y, Granelli F, Gebremariam A, Taleb T, Bagaa M (2017) End-to-end network slicing for 5G mobile networks. J Inform Process 25:153–163
6. Ingram M. MVNOs: Phone companies without the equipment. https://www.theglobeandmail.com/technology/mvnos-phone-companies-without-the-equipment/article729367/
7. Zarinni F, Chakraborty A, Sekar V, Das SR, Gill P (2014) A first look at performance in mobile virtual network operators. In: Proceedings of the internet measurement conference (IMC), pp 165–172
8. Schmitt P, Vigil M, Belding E (2016) A study of MVNO data paths and performance. In: Proceedings of the 17th international conference on passive and active measurement (PAM), pp 83–94
9. Oshiba T (2018) Accurate available bandwidth estimation robust against traffic differentiation in operational MVNO networks. In: Proceedings of the 23rd IEEE symposium on computers and communications (ISCC), pp 694–700
10. Fiatal T. Mobile virtual network operator. US Patent 8,107,921
11. Xiao A, Liu Y, Li Y, Qian F, Li Z, Bai S, Liu Y, Xu T, Xin X (2019) An in-depth study of commercial MVNO: Measurement and optimization. In: Proceedings of ACM MobiSys, pp 457–468
12. Kapoor A. Churn in the telecom industry - identifying customers likely to churn and how to retain them. https://wp.nyu.edu/adityakapoor/2017/02/17/churn-in-the-telecom-industry-identifying-customers-likely-to-churn-and-how-to-retain-them/
13. Andone I, Błaszkiewicz K, Eibes M, Trendafilov B, Montag C, Markowetz A (2016) How age and gender affect smartphone usage. In: Proceedings of the 2016 ACM international joint conference on pervasive and ubiquitous computing (UbiComp), pp 9–12
14. Li Z, Wang W, Xu T, Zhong X, Li XY, Liu Y, Wilson C, Zhao BY (2016) Exploring cross-application cellular traffic optimization with Baidu TrafficGuard. In: Proceedings of the 13th USENIX symposium on networked systems design and implementation (NSDI), pp 61–76

15. Qian F, Gerber A, Mao ZM, Sen S, Spatscheck O, Willinger W (2009) TCP revisited: a fresh look at TCP in the wild. In: Proceedings of the internet measurement conference (IMC), pp 76–89
16. Huang J, Qian F, Guo Y, Zhou Y, Xu Q, Mao ZM, Sen S, Spatscheck O (2013) An in-depth study of LTE: Effect of network protocol and application behavior on performance. ACM SIGCOMM Comput Commun Rev 43(4), 363–374 (2013)
17. Huang J, Xu Q, Tiwana B, Mao ZM, Zhang M, Bahl P (2010) Anatomizing application performance differences on smartphones. In: Proceedings of the 8th ACM international conference on mobile systems, applications, and services (MobiSys), pp 165–178 (2010)
18. Huang J, Qian F, Gerber A, Mao ZM, Sen S, Spatscheck O (2012) A close examination of performance and power characteristics of 4G LTE networks. In: Proceedings of the 10th ACM international conference on mobile systems, applications, and services (MobiSys), pp 225–238
19. Sommers J, Barford P (2012) Cell vs. WiFi: On the performance of metro area mobile connections. In: Proceedings of the internet measurement conference (IMC), pp 301–314
20. Hsu H, Lachenbruch PA (2007) Paired T-test. Wiley encyclopedia of clinical trials pp 1–3
21. Ravindranath L, Agarwal S, Padhye J, Riederer C (2014) Procrastinator: pacing mobile apps' usage of the network. In: Proceedings of the 12th ACM international conference on mobile systems, applications, and services (MobiSys), pp. 232–244
22. Zhang L, Alharbe NR, Luo G, Yao Z, Li Y (2018) A hybrid forecasting framework based on support vector regression with a modified genetic algorithm and a random forest for traffic flow prediction. Tsinghua Sci Technol 23(4):479–492
23. Broomhead DS, Lowe D (1988) Radial basis functions, multi-variable functional interpolation and adaptive networks. Tech. rep., Royal Signals and Radar Establishment Malvern (United Kingdom)
24. Rumelhart D, Hinton G, Williams R (1986) Learning representations by back-propagating errors. Nature 323(6088):533
25. Bourennane H, King D, Couturier A (2000) Comparison of Kriging with external drift and simple linear regression for predicting soil horizon thickness with different sample densities. Geoderma 97(3–4):255–271 (2000)
26. González AG, Herrador MÁ (2007) A practical guide to analytical method validation, including measurement uncertainty and accuracy profiles. Trends Anal Chem 26(3), 227–238
27. Lopes RH (2011) Kolmogorov-Smirnov test. In: International encyclopedia of statistical science. Springer, Berlin, Heidelberg, pp 718–720
28. Davis PJ, Rabinowitz P (1984) Methods of numerical integration. In: Methods of numerical integration, 2nd edn. Academic Press, New York, pp 51–198
29. Bi W, Cai M, Liu M, Li G (2016) A big data clustering algorithm for mitigating the risk of customer churn. IEEE Trans Ind Inform 12(3), 1270–1281
30. Dodge Y (2004) Spearman rank correlation coefficient. In: The concise encyclopedia of statistics. Springer, New York, pp 502–505
31. Feng H, Shu Y (2005) Study on network traffic prediction techniques. In: Proceedings of the international conference on wireless communications, networking and mobile computing (WCNM), pp 1041–1044
32. Peyravi H, Sehgal R (2017) Link modeling and delay analysis in networks with disruptive links. ACM Trans Sensor Netw 13(4):31
33. Debbah M, Echabbi L, Hamlaoui C (2012) Market share analysis between MNO and MVNO under brand appeal based segmentation. In: Proceedings of the 6th international conference on network games, control and optimization (NetGCooP), pp 9–16
34. Meidanis C, Stiakogiannakis I, Papadopouli M (2014) Pricing for mobile virtual network operators: The contribution of U-map. In: Proceedings of the IEEE international symposium on dynamic spectrum access networks (DYSPAN), pp 133–136
35. Zhang T, Wu H, Liu X, Huang L (2016) Learning-aided scheduling for mobile virtual network operators with QoS constraints. In: Proceedings of the 14th international symposium on modeling and optimization in mobile, ad hoc, and wireless networks (WiOpt), pp 1–8

36. Coussement K, Van den Poel D (2008) Churn prediction in subscription services: an application of support vector machines while comparing two parameter-selection techniques. Expert Syst Appl 34(1):313–327
37. Popović D, Bašić B (2009) Churn prediction model in retail banking using fuzzy C-means algorithm. Informatica 33(2):243–247
38. Hung SY, Yen DC, Wang HY (2006) Applying data mining to telecom churn management. Expert Syst Appl 31(3):515–524
39. Owczarczuk M (2010) Churn models for prepaid customers in the cellular telecommunication industry using large data marts. Expert Syst Appl 37(6):4710–4712

Part IV
Metric 3 Reliability: Stay Connected All the Time

Chapter 6
Enhancing Nationwide Cellular Reliability

Abstract With recent advances on cellular technologies that push the boundary of cellular performance, cellular reliability has become a key concern of cellular technology adoption and deployment. However, this fundamental concern has never been addressed due to the challenges of measuring cellular reliability on mobile devices and the cost of conducting large-scale measurements. This chapter closes the knowledge gap by presenting the first large-scale, in-depth study on cellular reliability with 70M Android phones across 34 different hardware models. Our study identifies the critical factors that affect cellular reliability and clears up misleading intuitions indicated by common wisdom. In particular, our study pinpoints that software reliability defects are the main root cause of cellular data connection failures. Our work provides actionable insights for improving cellular reliability at scale. More importantly, we have built on our insights to develop enhancements that effectively address cellular reliability issues with remarkable real-world impact—our optimizations on Android's cellular implementations have reduced 40% cellular connection failures for 5G phones and 36% failure duration across all phones.

Keywords Cellular reliability · Cellular connection failure

6.1 Introduction

Cellular technologies have been the keystone of mobile systems and applications that empower our daily lives, all the way from wireless telephony and mobile Internet to emerging applications such as ultra-high-definition (UHD) video streaming and AR/VR. The rise of 5G technologies has started to realize even higher bandwidth and lower latency cellular networks, driving the grand vision of AI, IoT, and self-driving vehicles. Specifically, 5G cellular networks support up to 10 Gbps bandwidth (100× faster than 4G), 1 ms latency (cf. 30–50 ms for 4G), and connection density of 1 million devices per square kilometer (100× more than 4G) [1].

While we have been mainly focusing on the performance of cellular network technologies and the availability of cellular network services, the cellular reliability of mobile devices has been largely overlooked—without reliable cellular connections, performance would be a mirage. From a mobile device's perspective, cellular data connections can fail mostly in the following three ways (note that we use Android terminologies throughout the chapter):

- Data_Setup_Error [2]:[1] The mobile device can receive signals from a nearby base station (BS) but cannot establish a data connection with the BS.
- Out_of_Service [3]: The data connection has been established, but the mobile device cannot receive cellular data.
- Data_Stall [4]: The mobile device can receive cellular data, but the data connection abnormally stalls (for ≥ 1 min as suggested in Android).

However, cellular reliability is rarely studied or measured but constantly acts as an X-factor in discussion or decision-making [1, 5]. Certainly, understanding cellular reliability at large is challenging. First, as we will discuss in Sect. 6.2, existing mobile systems do not provide sufficient tracing and logging support for low-level cellular connection components, creating significant barriers to precisely capturing failure events and effectively diagnose their root causes. Second, it is difficult and expensive to conduct large-scale reliability measurements on real-world mobile devices; controlled lab studies could help but hardly yield representative characteristics [6].

To close the knowledge gap, we collaborate with a major Android phone vendor, Xiaomi Co. LTD, which serves hundreds of millions of mobile users in China, to conduct a large-scale, in-depth study on cellular reliability from the device perspective. Specifically, our goal is to measure the prevalence and severity of cellular reliability problems perceived by user devices and reveal the root causes of cellular (data connection) failures, including Data_Setup_Error, Out_of_Service, Data_Stall, and so forth. Interestingly, understanding cellular reliability turns out to be well aligned with the business need of Xiaomi, as cellular connection issues were a major contributor to their customer reports but had been elusive problems for Xiaomi engineers. Therefore, we have the common interests in understanding cellular failures and improving cellular reliability.

Measurement We build a continuous monitoring infrastructure on top of a customized Android system called Android-MOD, which records system-level traces (without requiring root privileges) upon the occurrence of suspicious cellular failure events. To extract true failure events and collect diagnostic information, we instrument relevant system services to record detailed device/network state information and carefully filter out false positives.

---

[1] Strictly speaking, some Data_Setup_Error events defined in Android are not true failures since they occur rationally due to BS overloading. Such false positives will be carefully removed in our study.

We invited all users of Xiaomi to participate in the measurement study by installing Android-MOD on their phones, and finally 70M users opted in and shared data with us for eight months (January–August 2020). The dataset involves 34 different models of Android phones, 3 mobile ISPs (ISP-A: China Mobile, ISP-B: China Telecom, and ISP-C: China Unicom), and 5.3M BSes. All the data were collected with informed consent of opt-in users, and no personally identifiable information (PII) was collected during the measurement.

Analysis Our measurement reveals that cellular failures are prevalent on all the 34 models of devices. For each model, 0.15–45% (averaging at 23%) of the devices have experienced at least one cellular failure. On average, as many as 33 failures occur to a device during the measurement, and a failure lasts for as long as 3.1 min. Newer OS versions (e.g., Android 10) and communication modules (e.g., 5G modules) substantially aggravate the situation, while better hardware does not seem to relieve the situation. In particular, our results indicate that cellular failures are mainly caused by software reliability defects rather than inexpensive hardware, e.g., the implementation that blindly prioritizes 5G connection in Android 10 greatly impairs the stability of cellular connections.

Moreover, we find that most (94%) failure duration is owing to Data_Stall failures. To recover a cellular connection from Data_Stall failures, Android implements a three-stage progressive mechanism which sequentially tries light (cleaning up and restarting the current connection), moderate (re-registering into the network), and heavy (restarting the radio component) recovery techniques based on one-minute probations. Our data show that for the majority of Data_Stall failures, either the user device can automatically fix them in less amount of time, or the user would manually reset the connection after ~30 s. Thus, the three-stage design is not efficient.

From the viewpoint of ISPs, cellular failures occur more prevalently (27.1%) on ISP-B users than on ISP-A users (20.1%) and ISP-C users (14.7%) due to the inferior signal coverage of ISP-B. Counter-intuitively, while both the number and overall signal coverage of 3G BSes are smaller than those of 2G or 4G BSes, the prevalence of failures on 3G BSes is lower than that on 2G or 4G BSes. This can be ascribed to the fact that 3G access is usually not preferred when 4G access is available and its signal coverage is worse than that of 2G when 4G access is unavailable and thus is confronted with less resource contention.

With respect to BSes, common wisdom suggests a positive correlation between cellular reliability and received signal strength (RSS). However, our measurement shows the opposite when there is excellent (level 5) RSS—failures are in fact more likely to happen in this case than when there is weaker (level-1 to level-4) RSS. We clear up the mystery—most of the excellent RSS failures come from densely deployed BSes around public transport hubs; while such BSes offer excellent RSS, they increase the control channel overhead of LTE mobility management [7, 8], causing frequent failures tagged with EMM_ACCESS_BARRED, INVALID_EMM_STATE, etc. [9].

Enhancements Our study provides insights to improve cellular reliability at scale (1) for mobile phone vendors to roll out 5G modules and new OS versions, (2) for mobile ISPs to make use of radio resources, e.g., utilizing "idle" 3G BSes and planning BS deployment density in public areas, and (3) for promoting cross-ISP infrastructure.

More importantly, some of our enhancements have been practically deployed with real-world impact. First, instead of aggressively pursuing the potential high data rate of 5G, we optimize the radio access technology (RAT) selection policy in Android 10 by judiciously considering the likelihood of cellular failures and utilizing the novel 4G/5G dual connectivity mechanism [10].

Second, we optimize the three-stage cellular connection recovery mechanism in Android by replacing its fixed-time trigger with a flexible and dynamic trigger based on a time-inhomogeneous Markov process [11] (TIMP). TIMP advances the traditional Markov process that can only model a stationary process, to model complex state transitions in a time-sensitive manner. The TIMP-based recovery helps most user devices to recover more quickly (the three probations are adaptively tuned as 21, 6, and 16 s, each being much shorter than one minute) and effectively with negligible overhead.

Since the release of the patched Android-MOD system with the above twofold optimizations (adopted by 40% of the 70M opt-in users in late Oct. 2020), we have successfully reduced 40% cellular failures for 5G phones (without sacrificing the data rate) and 38% Data_Stall duration (equivalent to 36% total failure duration) for all phones during Nov.–Dec. 2020.

Code Release The failure diagnosis and fixing code involved in the study is publicly available at https://CellularReliability.github.io.

6.2 Study Methodology

We conduct a large-scale measurement study on cellular failures based on continuously monitoring 70M opt-in user devices over eight months. The study is enabled by a customized Android system that provides lightweight, privacy-preserving tracing and analysis beyond the capability of vanilla Android.

6.2.1 Limitations of Vanilla Android

Cellular connection management exists as a system service in Android, where the life cycle of a cellular data connection is modeled by a state machine [12] as shown in Fig. 6.1: a total of five states are used to represent different stages of a cellular connection, including Inactive, Activating, Retrying, Active, and Disconnect. As one state changes to another, Android provides quite a few facilities to monitor various problems during the process, most of which are related to our targeted cellular failures.

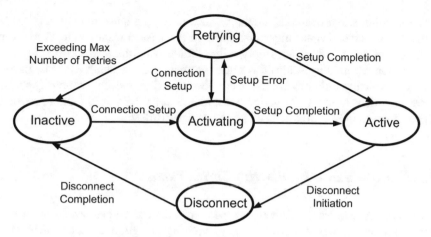

Fig. 6.1 The state machine that models the life cycle of a cellular data connection in Android (Reprinted with permission from [13])

First of all, if a user device fails to establish a data connection to a nearby base station (BS), a Data_Setup_Error [2] failure event will be reported to relevant system services (but not to user-space apps); then, a retry attempt will be initiated, trying to establish the connection again. Here the failure may occur at the physical layer (e.g., radio signal loss), the data link or MAC layer (e.g., device authentication failure), and/or the network layer (e.g., IP address allocation failure). Upon any failure, an error code will be generated by the underlying radio interface, based on either the received responses to the issued connection setup negotiation requests (if any) or the return values of the modem commands executed by the underlying radio interface.

Furthermore, if the data connection is successfully established but the user device still cannot access the cellular network, i.e., the user device cannot send/receive data to/from outside, Android will mark its current service state as Out_of_Service [3]. Worse still, even if data can be sent to or received from outside, sometimes the data connection can abnormally stall for a long time, incurring annoying user experience. This phenomenon is termed as Data_Stall [4] in Android. In detail, when there have been over 10 outbound TCP segments but not a single inbound TCP segment during the last minute (the statistics are made by the Linux kernel in its network protocol stack), a Data_Stall failure is reported to both relevant system services and user-space apps. In addition, there are other types of failures we do not elaborate here but will mention when necessary in the remaining parts.

For all the abovementioned failure events, Android currently provides basic notification interfaces with which the relevant system services can register themselves as the event listeners. Nevertheless, only a part of the interfaces (including the Data_Stall notifier and Out_of_Service checker) is exposed to user-space apps, and some interfaces are inaccessible even with root privileges. Therefore, we are unable to capture all the concerned failure events by simply developing an Android app. To make the matter worse, some of the abovementioned failure events are in fact not true failures. For example, a data connection setup request may be rejected by a nearby BS which is currently overloaded; in this case, a Data_Setup_Error event will be reported but does not imply a true failure. Additionally, the event-related information reported by Android is often insufficient for in-depth analysis. In fact, Android typically only reports the occurrence of a failure event without capturing other important in situ information, such as the desired BS information, received signal strength (RSS), protocol error code, and network state.

6.2.2   Continuous Monitoring Infrastructure

To practically address the above-described multifold challenges, we customize the vanilla Android system for continuously acquiring fine-grained system-level traces upon the occurrence of suspicious cellular failure events, which are otherwise impossible to obtain but are crucial to our study requirements. The resulting system is called Android-MOD, in which we focus on modifying the framework-layer programs. We do not make modifications to the hardware abstract layer (HAL) or the kernel layer—while HAL/kernel modifications can help us collect more underlying and detailed data, they can easily impair the system stability and robustness in practice (even with careful testing) [14].

At a high level, our modifications aim to realize three goals: (1) system service instrumentation, (2) concerned information logging, and (3) failure recovery monitoring. Specifically, we first instrument the Android system service of cellular connection management by registering our developed monitoring service as its event listener, so that all the occurrences of Data_Setup_Error, Out_of_Service, Data_Stall, and other concerned failure events can be captured in real time. It is worth noting that when instrumenting the service, we carefully rule out a variety of false failure events (a.k.a., false positives), such as connection disruption by incoming voice calls, service suspension due to insufficient account balance, and manual disconnection of the network.

Second, we need to record important radio- and BS-related information upon the occurrence of a cellular failure for in-depth analysis. Such information includes the current radio access technology (RAT, e.g., 4G LTE or 5G NR), received signal strength (RSS), access point names (APNs), and BS ID that consists of Mobile Country Code (MCC), Mobile Network Code (MNC), Location Area Code (LAC), and Cell Identity (CID):[2] All this information can be accessed via the APIs provided by the Android TelephonyManager and ServiceState services. Besides, we record the protocol error codes for Data_Setup_Error events to facilitate our uncovering the root causes and to rule out possible false positives like rational setup rejection due to BS overloading. In particular, we carefully analyze all the 344 cellular connection-

---

[2] For some CDMA BSes, System Identity (SID), Network Identity (NID), and Base Station Identity (BID) are recorded instead of MNC, LAC, and CID.

related error codes defined in Android [9] and recognize tens of error codes highly correlated with false positives as critical auxiliary information.

Third, we note that the existing Data_Stall detection mechanism in Android cannot provide an accurate measurement of a Data_Stall failure duration, given its fixed detection time (as long as one minute). According to our observations (detailed later in Sect. 6.3.1), in most (>80%) cases a Data_Stall failure lasts for <300 s, so the incurred measurement error is non-trivial relative to the Data_Stall duration. Also, detection results of this mechanism may contain false positives for lack of crucial knowledge regarding the current states of network stack and Internet connectivity.

To address these issues, we build a network state probing component in Android-MOD. Once a suspicious Data_Stall failure is detected, this component checks the states of network stack and Internet connectivity by simultaneously sending an ICMP message to the local IP address (127.0.0.1), as well as sending an ICMP message and a DNS query (for our dedicated test server's domain name) to each of the user device's assigned DNS server(s). If the ICMP message intended for the local IP address reaches a timeout (empirically configured as one second as suggested by the ICMP protocol [15]), we know that the problem lies at the system side rather than the network side (hence a false positive case). In practice, such false positives typically involve erroneous firewall configurations, problematic proxy settings, and modem driver failures. Otherwise, if all the DNS queries reach a timeout (empirically configured as five seconds as suggested by the DNS protocol [16]), we know the problem lies at the network side. However, if timeouts only occur to the DNS queries but not to the ICMP messages sent to the DNS servers, we figure out that the problem is induced by the unavailability of DNS resolution service (also a false positive case).

The above probing process needs at most five seconds, given the one-second timeout for the ICMP message deliveries and five-second timeout for the DNS queries. If the probing results indicate that Data_Stall has not been fixed, we will initiate a new probing process; otherwise, we add up the duration values recorded in all the previous probing processes (since the beginning of this Data_Stall failure) to approximate the actual duration of this Data_Stall failure. Thus, our measurement error is at most five seconds (<<1 min).

Furthermore, to avoid excessive network overhead, if a Data_Stall failure lasts for >1200 s (in less than 10% cases, as illustrated later in Sect. 6.3.1), we will multiplicatively increase the timeout values by a factor of two in the next probing process to balance the incurred error and overhead. Finally, if either timeout value grows to >1 min, we will revert to Android's original detection mechanism to estimate the Data_Stall duration.

All in all, our modifications to Android involve system-level information logging (primarily through existing interfaces) and lightweight network probing activities. For even a low-end Android phone at the moment, Android-MOD only incurs <2% CPU utilization, <40 KB of memory usage, and <100 KB of storage space; the network usage per month is <100 KB. Note that here the CPU utilization is measured by the portion of additional CPU overhead induced by our monitoring infrastructure within the duration of detected failures, rather than during the entire measurement process. As a matter of fact, in daily usages without cellular failures, our monitoring infrastructure is dormant at the client side and thus does not incur additional CPU overhead.

On the other hand, we do notice for a small fraction (<1%) of user devices, they experience as many as 40,000+ failures (as to a single user) in a month. Even so, the incurred CPU, memory, and storage overheads are still acceptable: <8% CPU utilization, <2 MB memory usage, and <20 MB storage space; the network usage per month can reach 20 MB, so the recorded data are uploaded to our backend server only when there is WiFi connectivity.

Finally, the network overhead incurred by our measurement is fairly low even in a cumulative sense. For all the 70M users who participated in our study, the aggregate network overhead per second on the entire cellular networks of the three involved ISPs was below 500 KB and thus had negligible influence on the studied cellular networks.

6.2.3 Large-Scale Deployment

With the continuous monitoring infrastructure, in December 2019, we invited all the users of Xiaomi to participate in our measurement study of cellular reliability by installing Android-MOD on their phones. Note that the installation is a lightweight update that will not affect their installed apps, existing data, and OS version. Eventually, 70,965,549 users opted in and collected data for us for eight months (January–August 2020). All data are compressed and uploaded to our backend server for centralized analysis.

Ethical Concerns All analysis tasks in this study comply with the agreement established between Xiaomi and its users. The users who participated in the study opted-in as volunteers with informed consent, the analysis was conducted under a well-established IRB, and no personally identifiable information (e.g., phone number, IMEI, and IMSI) was collected. We never (and have no way to) link collected information to users' true identities.

6.3 Measurement Results

In this section, we first present the general characteristics of our collected measurement data (Sect. 6.3.1). Then, to systematically describe cellular failures and their underlying causes in a more readable manner, we present our data analysis results from the viewpoints of Android phones (Sect. 6.3.2) and ISPs/BSes (Sect. 6.3.3), respectively.

6.3.1 General Statistics

With the crowdsourcing help from 70,965,549 Android-MOD user devices with 34 different phone models (as listed in Table 6.1), we record the system-level traces with regard to 2,315,314,213 cellular failures, involving 16,183,145 user devices, 3 mobile ISPs, and 5,273,972 base stations. To our knowledge, this is so far the largest dataset regarding cellular failures in the wild.

First of all, we are concerned with the *prevalence* and *frequency* of cellular failures: the former denotes the fraction of devices that experience at least one cellular failure, and the latter is the average number of cellular failures experienced per phone. Our measurement results reveal that cellular failures occur prevalently on all the 34 studied phone models. As indicated in Table 6.1 and Fig. 6.2, on different models of phones, the prevalence varies from 0.15% to 45% and averages at 23%. More notably, as many as 33 cellular failures occur to a phone on average during our 8-month measurement (see Fig. 6.3), and the average number of cellular failures happening to a specific model varies from 2.3 to 90.2 (see Table 6.1). In a nutshell, while the majority (77%) of phones do not report cellular failures during the measurement, the maximum number of cellular failures happening to a single phone can reach 198,228 (see Fig. 6.3).

Also, we are concerned with the duration of cellular failures. As shown in Fig. 6.4, the average duration of cellular failures is as long as 188 s (=3.1 min). This is an astonishing value in case of emergency, considering that a victim user is expected to be out of contact for 3.1 min. In detail, the duration distribution is highly skewed—while 70.8% cellular failures last for less than 30 s, the maximum duration can reach 91,770 s (=25.5 h). Closer examination reveals that such long-duration failures typically occur in remote regions such as mountain and offshore areas, where the BSes have been long neglected and in disrepair.

Among the 2.32 billion collected cellular failures, the vast majority (>99%) include Data_Setup_Error, Out_of_Service, and Data_Stall events. The remainder (<1%) are mainly related to the traditional short message and voice call services that are less frequently used today (e.g., short message sending failure tagged by Android as RIL_SMS_SEND_FAIL_RETRY [17]), whose functions and enabling techniques have been stable for nearly 20 years. As depicted in Fig. 6.3, an average of 16 Data_Setup_Error, 14 Data_Stall, and 3 Out_of_Service events occur to a single phone in our study. While most (95%) phones do not experience Out_of_Service events, the maximum number of Out_of_Service events on a single phone is as large as 102,696. In particular, Data_Stall failures lead to the vast majority of (94%) cellular failure duration among all the collected cellular failure events, which will be explained in Sect. 6.3.2 and practically mitigated in Sect. 6.4.2.

Table 6.1 Hardware configurations of our studied 34 phone models, generally ordered from low end to high end. The rightmost five columns correspond to the phone's 5G capability (5G), Android version (Version), user percentage (Users), fraction of devices that experience at least one cellular failure (Prevalence), and the average number of cellular failures experienced per phone (Frequency) during our measurement, respectively

Model	CPU	Memory	Storage	5G support	Version	Users	Prevalence	Frequency
1	1.8 GHz	2 GB	16 GB	–	10.0	2.71%	28%	35.9
2	1.95 GHz	2 GB	16 GB	–	9.0	3.02%	13%	23.8
3	2 GHz	2 GB	16 GB	–	9.0	7.31%	10%	13.8
4	2 GHz	3 GB	32 GB	–	9.0	3.90%	19%	22.4
5	2 GHz	3 GB	32 GB	–	9.0	2.85%	21%	28.2
6	2 GHz	3 GB	32 GB	–	10.0	4.33%	4%	5.3
7	2 GHz	3 GB	32 GB	–	10.0	1.44%	5%	6.4
8	2 GHz	3 GB	32 GB	–	9.0	4.07%	0.15%	2.3
9	2 GHz	3 GB	32 GB	–	10.0	5.47%	2%	2.6
10	2.2 GHz	4 GB	32 GB	–	9.0	5.78%	27%	36.8
11	1.8 GHz	4 GB	64 GB	–	10.0	1.18%	25%	28.5
12	2 GHz	4 GB	64 GB	–	10.0	1.44%	33%	43.5
13	2.05 GHz	6 GB	64 GB	–	10.0	5.39%	26%	18.7
14	2.2 GHz	6 GB	64 GB	–	9.0	2.98%	15%	17.9
15	2.2 GHz	4 GB	128 GB	–	10.0	3.98%	25%	26.7
16	2.2 GHz	4 GB	128 GB	–	10.0	3.02%	19%	28.0
17	2.2 GHz	6 GB	64 GB	–	10.0	1.09%	28%	48.4
18	2.2 GHz	6 GB	64 GB	–	10.0	0.26%	13%	38.8
19	2.2 GHz	6 GB	64 GB	–	10.0	1.31%	24%	44.8
20	2.2 GHz	6 GB	64 GB	–	10.0	0.57%	21%	33.0
21	2.2 GHz	6 GB	64 GB	–	10.0	2.80%	36%	46.6
22	2.2 GHz	6 GB	128 GB	–	9.0	0.44%	38%	61.1
23	2.4 GHz	6 GB	64 GB	YES	10.0	0.84%	44%	49.6
24	2.4 GHz	6 GB	128 GB	YES	10.0	3.25%	37%	38.0
25	2.45 GHz	6 GB	64 GB	–	9.0	4.99%	14%	19.6
26	2.45 GHz	6 GB	64 GB	–	9.0	2.15%	17%	24.6
27	2.8 GHz	6 GB	64 GB	–	10.0	1.84%	22%	54.2
28	2.8 GHz	6 GB	64 GB	–	10.0	7.14%	28%	58.1
29	2.8 GHz	6 GB	64 GB	–	10.0	1.31%	30%	65.1
30	2.8 GHz	6 GB	128 GB	–	10.0	1.01%	30%	90.2
31	2.84 GHz	6 GB	64 GB	–	10.0	1.88%	28%	61.7
32	2.84 GHz	6 GB	64 GB	–	10.0	3.63%	29%	57.8
33	2.84 GHz	8 GB	128 GB	YES	10.0	4.78%	32%	70.9
34	2.84 GHz	8 GB	256 GB	YES	10.0	1.84%	25%	79.3

(Reprinted with permission from [13])

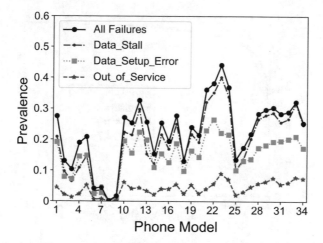

Fig. 6.2 Prevalence of cellular failures on each model of phones (Reprinted with permission from [13])

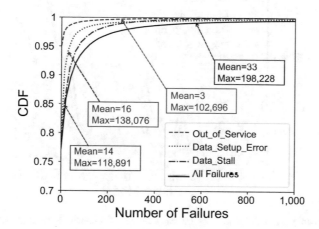

Fig. 6.3 Number of cellular failures happening to a single phone (Reprinted with permission from [13])

6.3.2   Android Phone Landscape

In this part, we go deeper into the internals of user devices with respect to their hardware, software, and OS components that may pose impact on cellular failures, especially those with regard to the emerging technologies.

Hardware Configuration Intuitively, using higher end cell phones should help to mitigate cellular failures as they usually imply the adoption of more reliable and/or powerful hardware components. However, our measurement results generally

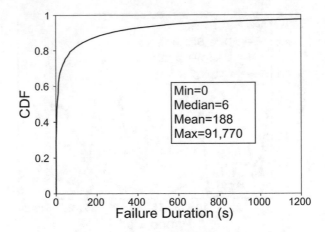

Fig. 6.4 Duration of our recorded cellular failures (Reprinted with permission from [13])

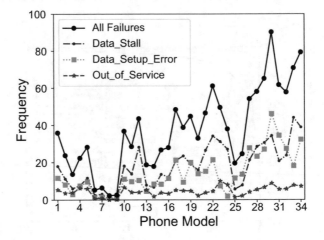

Fig. 6.5 Frequency of cellular failures on each model of phones (Reprinted with permission from [13])

indicate the opposite: as shown in Figs. 6.2 and 6.5, both the prevalence and frequency of cellular failures tend to increase with better hardware configurations. To demystify this, we examine the correlation between each feature (in Table 6.1) and the prevalence/frequency of cellular failures, finding that two features, i.e., 5G capability and Android version, have significant influence on the occurrence of cellular failures.

Four out of the 34 phone models are equipped with 5G modems, in which Models 23 and 24 have typical hardware configurations at the moment while Models 33 and 34 have the best. As illustrated in Figs. 6.6 and 6.7, both the prevalence and frequency of cellular failures on 5G phones are higher than those on non-5G phones.

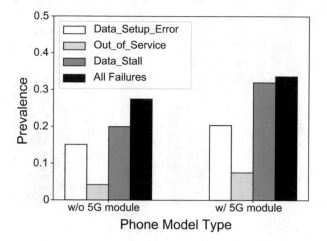

Fig. 6.6 Prevalence of cellular failures on models w and w/o the 5G module (Reprinted with permission from [13])

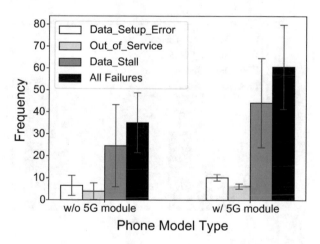

Fig. 6.7 Frequency of cellular failures on models w and w/o the 5G module (Reprinted with permission from [13])

This suggests that the emerging 5G communication modules have negative impact on the reliability of cellular connections, probably due to the high workload they inflict on the network stack and system kernel of Android for processing large volumes of inbound/outbound data in short time, as well as their relatively immature production state.

Android Version The studied 34 phone models use either Android 9 or Android 10, which are released in August 2018 and September 2019, respectively. Android 11 was recently released in September 2020 and thus was not covered in our study (from January to August 2020). We note that as Android evolves from

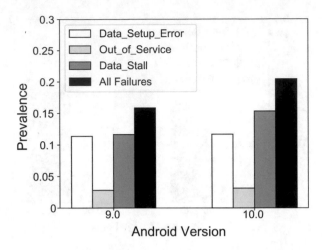

Fig. 6.8 Prevalence of cellular failures for different Android versions (Reprinted with permission from [13])

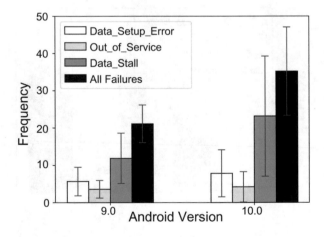

Fig. 6.9 Frequency of cellular failures for different Android versions (Reprinted with permission from [13])

version 9 to 10, a number of new functions and performance improvements have been implemented [18]. Although these updates are supposed to benefit users, we unexpectedly find that both the prevalence and frequency of cellular failures on Android 10 phones are higher than those on Android 9 phones, as demonstrated in Figs. 6.8 and 6.9. We attribute this primarily to the better stability and robustness of Android 9, as Android 10 was still undergoing constant fixes and patches during our measurement.

Adapting to the emerging 5G techniques, Android 10 added considerable dedicated services, network functions, and programming APIs [19]. While these novelties can enable various high-demanding applications such as UHD video streaming and AR/VR, they inevitably bring defects, risks, and vulnerabilities to the cellular connection management modules of Android from the perspective of software engineering.

In particular, we note that in the RAT (radio access technology) selection policy of Android 10, 5G is blindly preferred to the other RATs, probably aiming to maximize the potential benefit of 5G, especially its remarkably higher peak bandwidth. Nevertheless, this policy could incur severe cellular failures. For example, when a user device can establish either a 5G connection with low received signal strength (RSS) or a 4G connection with high RSS, the preferred usage of 5G might bring rather unstable cellular performance and even cellular failures, although the co-existing 4G connection might have better cellular performance. Worse still, this example is not a rare case but happens frequently in our everyday life, thus leading to a great number of cellular failures on 5G phones.

Data_Setup_Error Decomposition When a data connection setup fails, an error code will be generated by the radio interface to describe the reasons of the Data_Setup_Error failure, based on the responses to the issued setup requests (if any) or the return values of executed modem commands. In Android, a total of 344 error codes are defined. In Table 6.2, we list the top 10 most common error codes (after removing false positives) and their corresponding meanings and percentages. As shown, the top 10 codes account for nearly half (46.7%) of the

Table 6.2 Brief description and percentage of top 10 most common Data_Setup_Error error codes in Android

Error code	Brief description	Percentage
GPRS_REGISTRATION_FAIL	Failures due to unsuccessful GPRS registration	12.8%
SIGNAL_LOST	Failures due to network/modem disconnection	7.2%
NO_SERVICE	No service during connection setup	6.5%
INVALID_EMM_STATE	Invalid state of EPS Mobility Management in LTE	4.9%
UNPREFERRED_RAT	Current RAT is no longer the preferred RAT	4.3%
PPP_TIMEOUT	Failures at the Peer-to-Peer Protocol setup stage due to a timeout	3.5%
NO_HYBRID_HDR_SERVICE	No hybrid High-Data-Rate service	2.2%
PDP_LOWERLAYER_ERROR	Packet Data Protocol error due to radio resource control failures or a forbidden PLMN	1.9%
MAX_ACCESS_PROBE	Exceeding maximum number of access probes	1.8%
IRAT_HANDOVER_FAILED	Unsuccessful transfer of data call during an Inter-RAT handover	1.6%

(Reprinted with permission from [13])

Data_Setup_Error failures. In addition, we find that these error codes and their related causes are quite diverse, covering cellular failures occurring at the physical layer (e.g., SIGNAL_LOST and IRAT_HANDOVER_FAILED), the data link or MAC layer (e.g., PPP_TIMEOUT), and the network layer (e.g., INVALID_EMM_STATE).

Data_Stall Recovery Recall that in Android, when there have been over 10 outbound TCP segments but not a single inbound TCP segment during the last minute, a Data_Stall event happens [4]. According to our measurement, ~40% of the cellular failures are Data_Stall events, which however account for 94% duration of all cellular failures, thus posing broad and disruptive impact on user experiences. To tackle the problem, when a Data_Stall event is detected, Android launches the *three-stage progressive mechanism* that sequentially tries light (cleaning up and restarting the current connection), moderate (re-registering into the network), and heavy (restarting the radio component) recovery techniques. Before carrying out each of the above operations, Android would wait for one minute to watch whether the problem has already been fixed (by constantly examining whether Data_Stall still exists).

In practice, we observe that this mechanism is quite effective—once executed, even the first-stage lightweight operation (cleaning up the current connection) can fix the problem in 75% cases. Nevertheless, our measurement shows that this mechanism is overly conservative and thus rather time-consuming. In fact, for the majority of Data_Stall events, the user device can automatically recover them in less time, as illustrated in Fig. 6.10. For example, 60% of Data_Stall failures are automatically fixed in just 10 s. Also, we notice that the victim user would manually reset the data connection within ~30 s (according to our sampling user survey). Therefore, the one-minute "probation" adopted by Android is unnecessarily

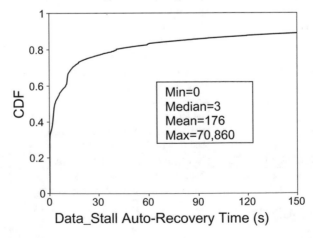

Fig. 6.10 Most Data_Stall failures are automatically fixed in a few seconds (Reprinted with permission from [13])

long, rendering the recovery mechanism to be neither efficient nor user-friendly in practice.

6.3.3   ISP and Base Station Landscape

In this part, we look at cellular failures from the viewpoint of ISPs and BSes, by considering the geographic locations, ISP discrepancies, radio access technologies, and signal strengths.

Geographic Location By ranking the involved BSes with their experienced number of cellular failures (in descending order), we observe a Zipf-like [20] skewed distribution as depicted in Fig. 6.11 (where $a = 0.82$ and $b = 17.12$). The median and average numbers are 1 and 444, respectively, while the maximum number reaches 8,941,860. We then delve into the 10,000 top ranking BSes and find that they are mostly located in crowded urban areas. Hence, they are confronted with essentially more ambient interferences and heavier cellular access workloads, both of which aggravate the problems.

ISP Discrepancy The BSes involved in our study belong to three mobile ISPs, referred to as ISP-A, ISP-B, and ISP-C. Specifically, 44.8%, 29.4%, and 25.8% BSes belong to ISP-A, ISP-B, and ISP-C, respectively. From Fig. 6.12, we can see that cellular failures occur more prevalently (27.1%) on ISP-B's users than on ISP-A's (20.1%) and ISP-C's (14.7%), mainly due to the inferior signal coverage of ISP-B's BSes. In detail, while ISP-B's BSes are a bit more than ISP-C's, to our knowledge, most of ISP-B's BSes have a smaller signal coverage because they usually use a higher radio frequency. The situation is similar in terms of frequency, as shown in Fig. 6.13.

Radio Access Technology (RAT) Among the involved BSes, 23.4%, 10.2%, 65.2%, and 7.3% support 2G, 3G, 4G, and 5G access, respectively. Here the four

Fig. 6.11 BS Ranking by the experienced number of cellular failures (Reprinted with permission from [13])

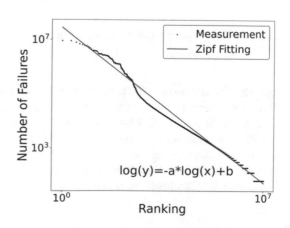

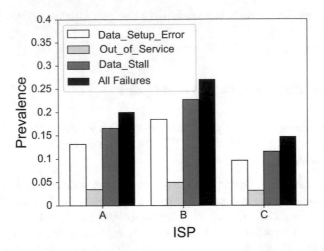

Fig. 6.12 Prevalence of cellular failures for different ISPs' users (Reprinted with permission from [13])

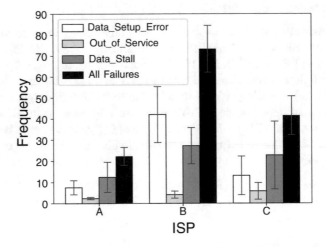

Fig. 6.13 Frequency of cellular failures for different ISPs' users (Reprinted with permission from [13])

percentages add up to $> 100\%$ because some BSes simultaneously support multiple RATs. While both the number and overall signal coverage of 3G BSes are smaller than those of 2G or 4G BSes, we observe that the prevalence of cellular failures on 3G BSes is lower than that on 2G or 4G BSes, as indicated in Fig. 6.14. This is probably because 3G access is usually not favored by user devices when 4G access is available, and the signal coverage of 3G is much worse than that of 2G when 4G access is unavailable. In other words, 3G networks currently face less resource

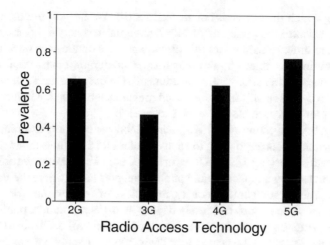

Fig. 6.14 Prevalence of cellular failures on 2G, 3G, 4G and 5G BSes (Reprinted with permission from [13])

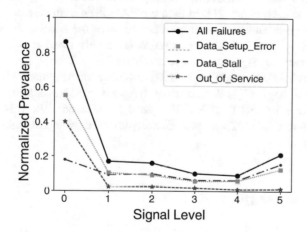

Fig. 6.15 Normalized prevalence (or simply likelihood) of cellular failures for different signal levels (Reprinted with permission from [13])

contention from the users (i.e., relatively "idle") and thus manifest fewer cellular failures.

Received Signal Strength (RSS) In common sense, RSS is a key factor that impacts the reliability of cellular service, and a higher RSS level (or simply signal level) is usually expected to come with better service reliability. However, our measurement results in Fig. 6.15 refute this common understanding by revealing that excellent RSS seems to increase the likelihood of cellular failures. As the signal level increases from 0 (the worst) to 4 (good), the *normalized prevalence* of cellular failures monotonously decreases. Here the "normalized" prevalence denotes the regular prevalence (as explained and computed in Table 6.1) divided by the total time during which the device is connected to a BS. We have to use the normalized prevalence because the durations of different signal levels can differ greatly from each other; in order to account for this discrepancy, we divide each prevalence by its average duration to achieve a fair comparison (the duration data are also provided by Xiaomi based on a nationwide measurement). On the other hand, when the signal level goes to 5 (excellent), the normalized prevalence of cellular failures suddenly grows to larger than each case of level-1 to level-4.

To demystify this counter-intuitive phenomenon, we carefully examine a series of in situ information corresponding to such excellent RSS cellular failures, including the BS location, serving ISP, RAT, error code, etc. As a result, we find that this phenomenon usually happens around public transport hubs, where the nearby BSes tend to be problematic simultaneously, regardless of the serving ISPs and RATs. Actually, ISPs often choose to densely deploy their BSes around a public transport hub so as to better cope with the large volume of human traffic. Owing to this special BS deployment strategy, the nearby user devices can typically have excellent (level 5) RSS.

On the other hand, such densely deployed BSes could bring non-trivial signal interferences to each other [21]. In fact, the three ISPs' radio frequency bands are fairly close to one another (more specifically, with the median frequency being ISP-B's > ISP-C's > ISP-A's) and even occasionally overlap one another, thus leading to potentially significant adjacent-channel interference. More importantly, dense BS deployment could make LTE mobility management highly complicated and challenging [7, 22], causing frequent cellular failures tagged with EMM_ACCESS_BARRED, INVALID_EMM_STATE, etc. [9]. This is especially the case when multiple ISPs adopt similar deployment strategies without coordinations.

6.4   Enhancements

Our multifold findings in Sect. 6.3 drive us to rethink the current techniques widely employed by cell phones, mobile OSes, and ISPs with respect to their influence on the reliability of cellular connections. Accordingly, in this section we provide insightful guidance for addressing various cellular failures at scale (Sect. 6.4.1), as well as practical enhancements that have registered large-scale deployment and yielded real-world impact (Sect. 6.4.2).

6.4.1   Guidelines in Principle

In Sect. 6.3, we have revealed a variety of technical and business issues that could lead to or aggravate cellular failures. As elucidated in Sect. 6.3.2, cellular failures on 5G phones are more prevalent and frequent than the other phones (without

5G capability), most probably owing to the high network workload and immature production state of today's 5G communication modules. Thus, we suggest that mobile phone vendors be cautious when incorporating 5G modules to their products; more specifically, we encourage the vendors to comprehensively validate the new 5G modules' coordination and compatibility with existing hardware/software, so as to produce more reliable phone models in terms of cellular communication.

Also in Sect. 6.3.2, we note that Android 10 phones are more subject to cellular failures than Android 9 phones, due to the typically worse stability and robustness of newly released OSes, in particular the blindly prioritized usage of 5G connection over 4G/3G/2G connections. We have reported the discovered problems of Android 10 to its official development team but have not got useful feedback. Hence, we propose that for the vendors, sufficient testing for new characteristics (e.g., the 4G/5G switching policy) should be carried out before pushing a new OS to certain phone models.

For mobile ISPs, we unravel in Sect. 6.3.3 that due to less workload and radio resource contention from user devices, 3G BSes are less subject to cellular failures than 2G and 4G BSes. Thereby, ISPs may consider making better use of these relatively "idle" infrastructure components to alleviate the burdens on busy 2G/4G BSes. Furthermore, our in-depth investigation into the correlation between signal level (or RSS) and cellular failures uncovers that due to ISPs' dense BS deployment around public transport hubs, cellular failures can be rather severe despite very high signal levels, for reasons of intensive signal interferences and highly complex mobility management requirements. Therefore, we advise ISPs to carefully control their BS deployment density in such areas. Finally, we advocate the recent campaign of cross-ISP infrastructure sharing [23], which aims to coordinate the BS deployment among different ISPs for more efficient utilization of radio infrastructure resources and thus can help mitigate cellular failures.

6.4.2 Real-World Practices

Apart from the above heuristic guidelines for the broad community, by collaborating with Xiaomi, we have practically explored optimization opportunities with respect to the aggressive 5G usage policy (cf. Sect. 6.3.2) during RAT transition and the conservative Data_Stall recovery mechanism (cf. Sect. 6.3.2) in vanilla Android. Based on critical insights obtained from our measurement study, below we first devise a stability-compatible RAT transition mechanism to make cellular connections more reliable and then leverage the time-inhomogeneous Markov process (TIMP) model to accelerate the Data_Stall recovery. Both efforts have been put into practice and produced promising results.

Stability-Compatible RAT Transition As introduced in Sect. 6.3.2, we observe that Android 10 adopts a quite aggressive strategy to prioritize the usage of 5G connections during RAT transition, which pays little attention to the cellular network

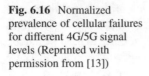

Fig. 6.16 Normalized
prevalence of cellular failures
for different 4G/5G signal
levels (Reprinted with
permission from [13])

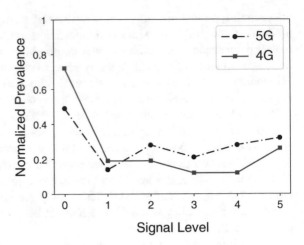

status (e.g., signal level) and thus leads to a large number of cellular failures. In fact, as shown in Fig. 6.16, the normalized prevalence (or simply likelihood) of cellular failures varies significantly across different signal levels under 4G/5G networks. More specifically, as depicted in Fig. 6.17f, four cases of RAT transitions (including 4G level-1 → 5G level-0, 4G level-2 → 5G level-0, 4G level-3 → 5G level-0, and 4G level-4 → 5G level-0) drastically increase the likelihood of cellular failures and thus should be avoided if no side effect is incurred.

Here the side effect mainly lies in the potential data rate increase if we allow such 4G→5G RAT transitions. Nonetheless, given that in all the four cases the 5G access is coupled with level-0 signal strength (and thus can hardly provide a high data rate), the "potential" increase in data rate brought by these RAT transitions can scarcely happen in principle. To check this practically, we conduct small-scale benchmark experiments using four different 5G phones as listed in Table 6.1, finding that these RAT transitions almost always (>95%) decrease the data rate. Consequently, we conclude that in general the four undesirable cases of RAT transitions can be safely avoided to preserve the stability of cellular connections.

In addition, to achieve more smooth RAT transition, we integrate the novel 4G/5G dual connectivity mechanism advocated by 3GPP [10] on compatible devices (including all the four 5G models in Table 6.1). It allows a device to establish and maintain control-plane cellular connections with a 4G BS and a 5G BS simultaneously, where the master connection is also responsible for data plane packet transfer while the slave connection is not. Then, when a RAT transition is decided, the transition process can be effectively shortened and thus would incur less disturbance to user experience.

Apart from the major case of 4G→5G transition, Fig. 6.17 also depicts the increase of normalized prevalence of cellular failures for the other RAT transition cases. Similar as in the 4G→5G transition, for all the RATs, we can observe "undesirable" transition cases where the prevalence of cellular failures is largely increased. A common pattern of such cases is that failures tend to occur when

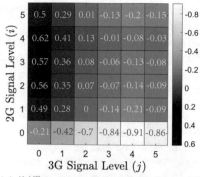

(a) RAT transition from 2G level-i to 3G level-j.

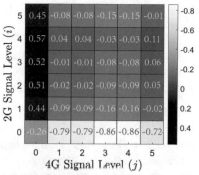

(b) RAT transition from 2G level-i to 4G level-j.

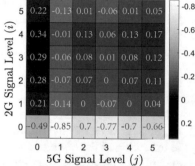

(c) RAT transition from 2G level-i to 5G level-j

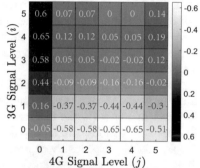

(d) RAT transition from 3G level-i to 4G level-j.

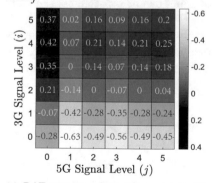

(e) RAT transition from 3G level-i to 5G level-j.

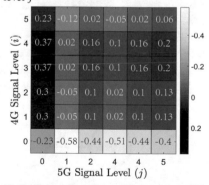

(f) RAT transition from 4G level-i to 5G level-j.

Fig. 6.17 Increase of normalized prevalence of cellular failures for different RAT transitions (e.g., from 4G level-i to 5G level-j). Deeper color represents larger increase. For example, the dark cell in (**f**) ($i = 4$ and $j = 0$) means that when a cell phone switches from 4G level-4 signal access to 5G level-0 signal access, the normalized prevalence of cellular failures will sharply increase by 0.37, implying that this RAT transition will significantly increase the likelihood of cellular failures (Reprinted with permission from [13])

there is level-0 RSS after transition. This can be intuitively explained by the highest prevalence of cellular failures with regard to level-0 RSS, as shown in Fig. 6.15. Therefore, we suggest OS developers to carefully avoid these cases so as to improve cellular reliability. Meanwhile, avoiding these problematic cases should not negatively impact the devices' data rates, as the RSS is extremely weak after transition and thus can hardly provide better cellular performance.

TIMP-based Flexible Data_Stall Recovery Recall in Sect. 6.3.2 that to address Data_Stall failures, Android has implemented a *three-stage progressive recovery mechanism* that attempts to repair the user device's cellular connection with three operations: (1) cleaning up current connections, (2) re-registering into the network, and (3) restarting the device's radio component. Before entering each stage (including the first stage), Android would passively monitor the existence of Data_Stall for one minute (which we call the "probation") in case that the previous (more lightweight) operation has already fixed the problem. Although the three recovery operations can be quite effective when executed, as discussed in Sect. 6.3.2, in practice we notice that the fixed-time recovery trigger is usually lagging and not user-friendly.

To figure out an appropriate trigger, our key insight is that the conceptual three-stage progressive recovery in Android is essentially a state transition process. As depicted in Fig. 6.18, the process includes five states: S_0, S_1, S_2, S_3, and $S_e = S_4$. Here S_0 denotes the start point (when Data_Stall is detected by Android), S_1, S_2, and S_3, respectively, represent starting the execution of the aforementioned three recovery operations, and S_e marks the end of the process. According to our measurement, the state transition from S_i to the next state is basically only dependent on S_i and other stochastic events and thus can be modeled by a Markov process [11].

With the above understanding, we can formalize the expected overall recovery time ($T_{recovery}$) so as to calculate more suitable triggers that are able to minimize $T_{recovery}$. However, the traditional Markov process can only model a stationary process where the state transition probability is not affected by the elapsed time

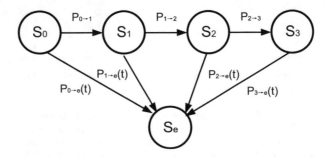

Fig. 6.18 The time-inhomogeneous Markov process (TIMP) that models the Data_Stall recovery process in Android, where the transition probabilities among the five states are also impacted by the elapsed time (t) (Reprinted with permission from [13])

t and thus is not applicable to our scenario where the state transition probability also depends on t, as indicated in Fig. 6.10 (the user device can automatically fix the problem as time goes by).

Thus, using our dataset, we build a *time-inhomogeneous Markov process* [11] (TIMP) to model the complex state transitions during the Data_Stall recovery process in a time-sensitive manner, by incorporating recovery probabilities within different time windows. Specifically, after entering S_i, the user device either automatically recovers from Data_Stall within the time window $[S_i, S_{i+1}]$ (referred to as Case-1) or enters the next state after Pro_i seconds (referred to as Case-2), where Pro_i denotes the probation time for leaving S_i. For any elapsed time t within the time window, we denote the probability of the device's recovering from Data_Stall as $\mathbb{P}_{i \to e}(t)$. Thereby, the probability of its not recovering (thus entering S_{i+1}) is $\mathbb{P}_{i \to i+1} = 1 - \mathbb{P}_{i \to e}(\sigma Pro_i)$, where $\sigma Pro_i = \sum_{k=0}^{i} Pro_k$ is the elapsed time from S_0 to S_{i+1}.

At this point, we can formalize the expected recovery time after entering state S_i (denoted as T_i) as the sum of three parts:

$$T_i = \int_{\sigma Pro_{i-1}}^{\sigma Pro_i} \mathbb{P}_{i \to e}(t)dt + \mathbb{P}_{i \to i+1} \cdot T_{i+1} + O_i. \tag{6.1}$$

The first part is the integral of $\mathbb{P}_{i \to e}(t)$ over the time window $[S_i, S_{i+1}]$, i.e., $\int_{\sigma Pro_{i-1}}^{\sigma Pro_i} \mathbb{P}_{i \to e}(t)dt$, representing that Case-1 occurs. The second part is the probability of the device's entering the next state ($\mathbb{P}_{i \to i+1}$) multiplying the expected recovery time (T_{i+1}) after entering the next state, i.e., $\mathbb{P}_{i \to i+1} \cdot T_{i+1}$, representing that Case-2 occurs. Finally, the third part is the time overhead for executing each recovery operation, denoted as O_1, O_2, and O_3, where $O_1 < O_2 < O_3$ given the progressive nature of the three recovery operations.

In detail, we can obtain the approximate values of $\mathbb{P}_{i \to e}$ and O_i using our duration measurement data of Data_Stall failures. Specially, when $i = 0$, $O_i = 0$ since no recovery operation is executed at this stage; when $i = 3$, $T_3 = \int_{\sigma Pro_2}^{t_m} \mathbb{P}_{3 \to e}(t)dt + O_3$, where t_m is the maximum duration of Data_Stall failures. Thus, we know that the expected overall recovery time $T_{recovery} = T_0$ is essentially determined by the three probations Pro_0, Pro_1, and Pro_2.

Our optimization objective is then to minimize $T_{recovery}$ for different possible values of Pro_0, Pro_1, and Pro_2. To this end, we use the annealing algorithm [24] to search for the global minimum, thus knowing that $T_{recovery}$ is minimized when $Pro_0 = 21\,\text{s}$, $Pro_1 = 6\,\text{s}$, and $Pro_2 = 16\,\text{s}$. Consequently, the desired $T_{recovery} = 27.8\,\text{s}$, which is smaller than a normal user's tolerance of Data_Stall duration ($\sim 30\,\text{s}$, cf. Sect. 6.3.2). In contrast, using the default probations ($Pro_0' = Pro_1' = Pro_2' = 60\,\text{s}$) in the original recovery mechanism of Android, the expected recovery time is $38\,\text{s}$, indicating that our designed trigger clearly outperforms the original one in Android.

6.4.3 Deployment and Evaluation

In order to validate the real-world effect of our design, we patched the above twofold mechanisms to Android-MOD and invited the original 70M opt-in users in late October 2020 to participate in our evaluation of the optimization mechanisms (Sect. 6.4.2). This time, 40% of the 70M users opted-in and upgraded to our patched system. The evaluation has been conducted for two months (November and December 2020).

As shown in Figs. 6.19 and 6.20, thanks to our Stability-Compatible RAT Transition mechanism, cellular failures occur 10% less prevalently and 40.3%

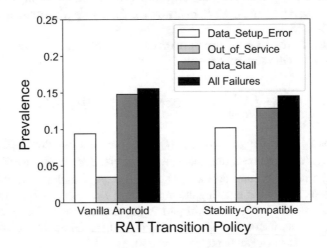

Fig. 6.19 Prevalence of cellular failures with the RAT transition policy of vanilla Android and our Stability-Compatible RAT Transition (Reprinted with permission from [13])

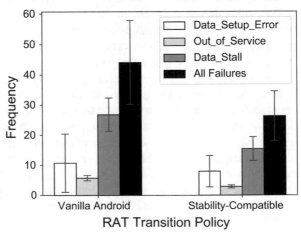

Fig. 6.20 Frequency of cellular failures with the RAT transition policy of vanilla Android and our Stability-Compatible RAT Transition (Reprinted with permission from [13])

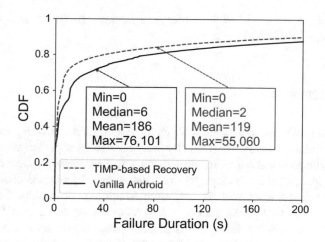

Min=0
Median=6
Mean=186
Max=76,101

Min=0
Median=2
Mean=119
Max=55,060

- - - - TIMP-based Recovery
———— Vanilla Android

Fig. 6.21 Duration of cellular failures with the Data_Stall recovery mechanism in vanilla Android and our TIMP-based Flexible Recovery (Reprinted with permission from [13])

less frequently on the participant 5G phones, without sacrificing the data rate (as explained in Sect. 6.4.2). In detail, for Data_Setup_Error, Data_Stall, and Out_of_Service failures, the decrease of prevalence (frequency) is −7% (25.72%), 13.45% (42.4%), and 5% (50.26%), respectively. Here the only exception lies in the prevalence of Data_Setup_Error failures, which slightly increases after our optimization is applied; however, given the occurrence frequency is significantly reduced by 25.72% by our optimization, we feel that the exception is most probably due to normal statistical fluctuation during the evaluation—after all, the measurement study and the evaluation study are conducted in two disjoint time periods.

Furthermore, as shown in Fig. 6.21, after our TIMP-based Flexible Data_Stall Recovery mechanism is put into practice, 38% reduction on the duration of Data_Stall failures is achieved on average, corresponding to 36% reduction on the total duration of all types of failures. More notably, the median duration of all failures is remarkably reduced by 67% (from 6 to 2 s). Most importantly, our TIMP-based recover mechanism works in a principled and flexible manner, so it will automatically adapt to the possible pattern changes of Android system behaviors and cellular reliability in the future.

To evaluate the overhead of our patched Android-MOD, we perform small-scale benchmark experiments using 34 different phones as in Table 6.1. The results demonstrate that our optimizations incur little overhead to a low-end Android phone: <3% CPU utilization, ~60 KB of memory usage, and <100 KB of storage space; the network usage is <100 KB per month. Even in the worst case where the monthly number of failures reaches 24,000+ on a single phone (as shown in Fig. 6.3), the incurred CPU, memory, and storage overheads are still acceptable:

<9% CPU utilization, ∼3 MB of memory usage, and <20 MB of storage space; the network usage is ∼20 MB per month.

6.5   Conclusion

This chapter presents our efforts toward understanding and combating the reliability issues in cellular networks. Despite prior focuses on cellular performance and availability, the fundamental reliability situations are still not clearly understood at scale. We close this critical knowledge gap by conducting a large-scale crowdsourcing-based measurement study with the help from 70 million opt-in users. Collaborating with a major Android phone vendor, we develop and deploy a continuous monitoring platform to collect fine-grained in situ system traces, leveraging which we reveal the nationwide prevalence and frequency of cellular failures for the first time. More in depth, we uncover severe reliability problems in the cellular connection management of Android, as well as the BS utilization and deployment strategies of mobile ISPs. Driven by the study insights, we provide useful guidelines to help tackle a variety of cellular failures. Most importantly, some of our solutions have been adopted by 28 million users, generating prominent realistic impacts.

References

1. Duffy C. The big differences between 4G and 5G. https://www.cnn.com/2020/01/17/tech/5g-technical-explainer/index.html
2. Android.org. Data setup error in android. https://android.googlesource.com/platform/frameworks/opt/telephony/+/refs/heads/master/src/java/com/android/internal/telephony/dataconnection/DcTracker.java
3. Android.org. State out of service in android. https://developer.android.com/reference/android/telephony/ServiceState
4. Android.org. Data stall report in android. https://developer.android.com/reference/android/net/ConnectivityDiagnosticsManager.DataStallReport
5. Mathias CJ. Opinion: how not to build more reliable cellular networks. https://www.computerworld.com/article/2537774/opinion--how-not-to-build-more-reliable-cellular-networks.html
6. Zhang G, Quek TQ, Huang A, Shan H (2015) Delay and reliability tradeoffs in heterogeneous cellular networks. IEEE Trans Wirel Commun 15(2):1101–1113
7. Deng H, Peng C, Fida A, Meng J, Hu YC (2018) Mobility support in cellular networks: a measurement study on its configurations and implications. In: Proc. of ACM IMC, pp 147–160
8. Li Y, Li Q, Zhang Z, Baig G, Qiu L, Lu S (2020) Beyond 5G: reliable extreme mobility management. In: Proc. of ACM SIGCOMM, pp 344–358
9. Android.org. Data fail cause in android. https://android.googlesource.com/platform/frameworks/base/+/master/telephony/java/android/telephony/DataFailCause.java
10. v15.0.0, G.T. (2018) 3rd generation partnership project; NR; technical specification group radio access network; multi-connectivity; overall description; stage-2 (release 15), vol 15. 3GPP
11. Winkler G (2012) Image analysis, random fields and Markov chain Monte Carlo methods: a mathematical introduction, vol 27. Springer, Berlin

12. Android.org. Data connection management in android. https://android.googlesource. com/platform/frameworks/opt/telephony/+/master/src/java/com/android/internal/telephony/ dataconnection/DataConnection.java
13. Li Y, Lin H, Li Z, Liu Y, Qian F, Gong L, Xin X, Xu T (2021) A nationwide study on cellular reliability: measurement, analysis, and enhancements. In: Proceedings of ACM SIGCOMM, pp 597–609
14. Horn J. Mitigations are attack surface, too. https://googleprojectzero.blogspot.com/2020/02/ mitigations-are-attack-surface-too.html
15. Srisuresh P, Ford B, Sivakumar S, Guha S et al. (2009) NAT behavioral requirements for ICMP. Tech. rep., Apr. 2009, RFC 5508
16. Kumar A, Postel J, Neuman C, Danzig P, Miller S (1993) Common DNS implementation errors and suggested fixes. Tech. rep., Oct. 1993, RFC 1536
17. Android.org. SMS manager in android. https://developer.android.com/reference/android/ telephony/SmsManager
18. Android.org. Android 10 highlights. https://developer.android.com/about/versions/10/ highlights
19. Android.org. Enhance your apps with 5G. https://developer.android.com/training/connectivity/ 5g/enhance-with-5g
20. Zipf GK (1949) Human behavior and the principle of least effort: an introd. to human ecology. Addison-Wesley Press, Reading
21. Sheng J, Tang Z, Wu C, Ai B, Wang Y (2020) Game theory-based multi-objective optimization interference alignment algorithm for HSR 5G heterogeneous ultra-dense network. IEEE Trans Veh Technol 69(11):13371–13382
22. Müller MK, Taranetz M, Rupp M (2015) Providing current and future cellular services to high speed trains. IEEE Commun Mag 53(10):96–101
23. Cano L, Capone A, Carello G, Cesana M, Passacantando M (2017) On optimal infrastructure sharing strategies in mobile radio networks. IEEE Trans Wirel Commun 16(5):3003–3016
24. Otten RH, van Ginneken LP (2012) The annealing algorithm, vol 72. Springer, Berlin

Chapter 7
Legal Internet Access Under Extreme Censorship

Abstract Internet censorship is pervasive across the world. However, in some countries like China, even *legal*, nonpolitical services (e.g., Google Scholar) are *incidentally* blocked by extreme censorship machinery. Therefore, properly accessing legal Internet services under extreme censorship becomes a critical problem. In this chapter, we conduct a case study on how scholars from a major university of China access Google Scholar through a variety of middleware. We characterize the common solutions (including VPN, Tor, and Shadowsocks) by measuring and analyzing their performance, overhead, and robustness to censorship. Guided by the study, we deploy a novel solution (called ScholarCloud) to help Chinese scholars access Google Scholar with high performance, ease of use, and low overhead. This work provides an insider's view of China's Internet censorship and offers a legal avenue for coexistence with censorship.

Keywords Internet censorship · Great Firewall · VPN

7.1 Introduction

Internet censorship, despite being highly controversial, is pervasive across the world mainly for political reasons. Some countries such as China, Iran, Russia, and Thailand wield extreme Internet censorship that even block *legal*, nonpolitical Internet services [1–4], e.g., Google Scholar. In these countries, easily accessing legal Internet services under extreme censorship becomes a critical problem.

As one of the largest research and education communities in the world, China's scholars unfortunately cannot access Google Scholar—the world's largest academic search engine. This creates enormous obstacles to their academic activities. Google Scholar is blocked by China's national-scale censorship firewall, known as the Great Firewall (GFW), as it is under the *google.com* domain.[1] Over the past decade, the

---

[1] Internet services under the Google domain have been blocked in China since 2010, including Search, Gmail, Maps, Docs, Drive, Google+, Sites, and Picasa [5].

GFW has become the most extensive and advanced Internet surveillance and control system in the world, adopting methods including IP blocking, DNS poisoning, URL filtering, packet filtering based on deep packet identification (DPI) and active probing [1, 6–20].

Unfortunately, Google Scholar is *incidentally* blocked in China: in fact, Google Scholar is principally considered a legal service by the relevant governmental regulators of China [21–23] but suffers from collateral damage of the GFW. The GFW is only responsible for technical blocking in China's complex Internet censorship system; non-technical policy and regulation are operated by government agencies, mainly including MIIT, TCA, MPS, and MSS (Sect. 7.2 explains the organizational structures of China's Internet censorship ecosystem in detail). The contradictory blocking of Google Scholar (and other ostensibly legal online services) stems from a critical fact that has been neglected in the literature: *the behavior of the GFW is not always consistent with the policies of the Chinese government (and both evolve over time)*.

To understand the above issue, we conduct a case study on how scholars (including 371 faculty members and students) at Tsinghua University, one of the top academic institutions in China, bypass the GFW to access Google Scholar through a variety of middleware. Interestingly, despite Google Scholar being blocked by the GFW, 26% of scholars in our survey are able to regularly bypass the GFW to access Google Scholar. We study the common bypass solutions: VPN (including both native VPN and OpenVPN), Tor, and Shadowsocks, by measuring their performance, overhead, and robustness against censorship. Our major findings are summarized as follows:

- Native VPN based on layer-2 tunneling protocols (PPTP and L2TP) is supported by most OSes. Our measurements show that it is currently robust to the GFW with a low packet loss rate (0.21% in average).[2] Unfortunately, since it forwards all traffic to remote VPN servers outside China, it significantly increases access latency to domestic Internet services. Hence, users have to frequently and manually reconfigure their network connections.
- OpenVPN implements both layer-2 and layer-3 VPN tunnels with multiple customizations for security and resilience (e.g., traffic redirection). Its performance is similar to that of native VPN when accessing Google Scholar. However, OpenVPN requires users to install extra client software and go through complicated configurations, considerably decreasing its usability.
- Tor requires the installation of a Tor client which directs browser traffic through a free, volunteer network of relays and bridges. Consequently, we find that it suffers from large client-side overhead and the longest first-time page load time (PLT) between 13 and 20 s (= seconds). Still worse, even when using the latest

---

[2] The GFW's censorship toward VPNs has changed significantly over the years. During 2012–2015, VPNs were extensively blocked by the GFW [24, 25]. Starting from 2015, registered VPN services have become legal and pervasive in China [26, 27]. In contrast, unregistered VPN services are considered illegal and many of them have been shut down by the government agencies [28].

meek obfuscation protocol, Tor is severely censored by the GFW, indicated by the high packet loss rate (4.4% in average).

- Shadowsocks [29] sets up an encrypted connection between a local proxy client and a remote proxy server on top of the layer-4 TLS protocol. The project was banned in China in 2015, but the software has been widely spread since 2012. We find Shadowsocks suffers from the longest average PLT (3.7 s) because it imposes an extra TCP connection for user/password authentication into each HTTP session. We also find that it is vulnerable to the GFW [30, 31], with an average packet loss rate of 0.77%.

Our study shows that none of the common solutions have provided satisfactory user experiences for accessing Google Scholar. Note that most scholar users do not have a background of computer science or engineering; it is unrealistic to expect these users to manage advanced software setups and configurations. To effectively help scholars in China access Google Scholar, we deploy a novel solution, ScholarCloud, with high performance, ease of use, and low overhead. This is achieved by the following endeavors:

- ScholarCloud uses a **split-proxy architecture** that encapsulates complicated proxy configuration and software installation (required by OpenVPN and Shadowsocks) into an easy-to-use domestic proxy.
- We implement **message blinding** that obfuscates the encrypted messages by encoding them into formats that are not recognized by the GFW. This achieves a low packet loss rate (0.22% in average) and short PLT (1.3 s in average).
- We focus on helping users access legal services that are incidentally blocked by the GFW. Therefore, we have **legalized ScholarCloud** through registration at government agencies with a *visible* whitelist of services.

We describe the ScholarCloud system in more detail in Sect. 7.3. It was launched in January 2016 and has served more than 2000 users, with 700 users online every day at present. The service can be accessed via http://scholar.thucloud.com. The system is hosted on top of two regular VM (virtual machine) servers; its daily operational cost is merely 2.2 USD. This work provides an insider's view of China's Internet censorship (Sect. 7.2), which is mostly missed or even misunderstood in prior work. Most importantly, ScholarCloud offers a legal avenue for accessing Internet content under extreme censorship. Despite its limitations (Sect. 7.6), it is currently the most practical and sustainable solution built inside the wall.

7.2   Extreme Internet Censorship

China's Internet censorship ecosystem is bilateral—it consists of the GFW for technical blocking and the relevant government agencies for non-technical regulation. To the best of our knowledge, these two components do not operate synchronously; inconsistencies are often observed (e.g., whether or not to prohibit access to Google

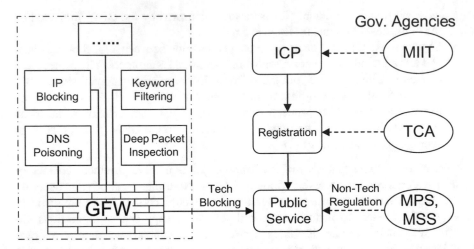

Fig. 7.1 The bilateral ecosystem of China's Internet censorship: the GFW for technical blocking and the relevant government agencies for non-technical regulation (Reprinted with permission from [32])

Scholar). Figure 7.1 depicts the relationship between the two components. Most of the prior work studies the GFW in terms of its censorship techniques; however, little correctly understand the government agencies and their regulation polices. This section focuses on their organizational structure and respective roles.

At present, there are mainly four government agencies collaboratively regulating public Internet services in China: the Ministry of Industry and Information Technology (MIIT), the Ministry of Public Security (MPS), the Ministry of State Security (MSS), and the Telecommunication Administration (TCA) agencies located in each city [33–35]. Specifically, any organization or company who attempts to deliver digital content across the Internet in China is termed an Internet Content Provider (ICP), such as Alibaba, Baidu, and Tencent. Any ICP who intends to provide public services is required to *register* the service at the TCA agencies in the corresponding city. MIIT is responsible for formulating legislation, guiding the TCA agencies, and maintaining a centralized database of registered ICPs, hosted at http://www.miitbeian.gov.cn.

Registration is a manual process. It involves recording and subsequently verifying the ICP's service name, service type, domain name, responsible person, and other critical information (which typically takes weeks to months) [33, 36, 37]. If a registered ICP is considered illegal (providing illegal Internet services), the MPS and MSS are responsible for quickly shutting down the service by blocking the domain name and even arresting the responsible person.

Different from the GFW's aggressive technical blocking, MPS and MSS adopt a relatively *conservative* approach to regulating Internet services (i.e., they usually block an Internet service after extensive investigation and evidence collection). This is partially because non-technical regulations are difficult to automate and thus take time to apply in practice. For example, many ICPs that provide VPN services do not register at the TCA agencies. Although *in theory* the MPS and MSS have the right to shut down any Internet services provided by an unregistered ICP, detecting, identifying, and localizing them is not an easy job given the open and distributed nature of the Internet. In reality, a number of transnational corporations have their branches in China and they often provide unregistered VPN services to their employees [38]. In this case, if the MPS or MSS were to simply block all VPN services, this would create disputes and hinder economic development [1].

In this work, we demonstrate using ScholarCloud that it is possible and feasible to provide high-performance, usable services to access legal Internet content, even under extreme censorship. On the one hand, the service needs to bypass the technical blocking of the GFW, and on the other hand, the service has to adhere to the policies and regulations enforced by government agencies.

7.3   The ScholarCloud System

ScholarCloud provides a platform to help Chinese scholars access legal Internet services incidentally blocked by the GFW. It is designed for scholar users who may not have a technical background and does not require any software installation. ScholarCloud works transparently to its users—they only need to configure their browsers using a proxy auto-config (PAC [39]) file generated by our system. All of the underlying connection tunneling is then automatically handled and the users do not even notice the existence of our system. The PAC file only diverts traffic for a small whitelist of legal (but incidentally blocked) domains to our proxy; all other traffic is routed to the Internet normally. Figure 7.2 illustrates the architectural difference between ScholarCloud and four other solutions. ScholarCloud achieves high performance and usability, as well as low overhead by the following main endeavors.

Split-Proxy Architecture and Configuration Automation Our ScholarCloud system adopts a split-proxy architecture—a domestic proxy located inside China and a remote proxy outside China. This design is inspired by Shadowsocks which also has a dual-proxy architecture. However, Shadowsocks places a local proxy on every client device (which requires software installation and extensive configuration). In contrast, ScholarCloud encapsulates the per-client proxies into a logically centralized, domestic proxy server that automates the vast majority of configuration. Users simply need to change one setting in their browser to use a PAC file supplied by ScholarCloud to begin using the service.

Message Blinding ScholarCloud aims to bypass the GFW in a robust and efficient way. Prior work has shown that the GFW is able to identify and block traffic using well-known encryption and obfuscation schemes (e.g., HTTPS, AES, and *meek*) [8, 30]. To address this issue, ScholarCloud blinds the messages between the domestic proxy and the remote proxy by adopting a custom encoding approach

Fig. 7.2 Architectural overview of the studied solutions (Reprinted with permission from [32])

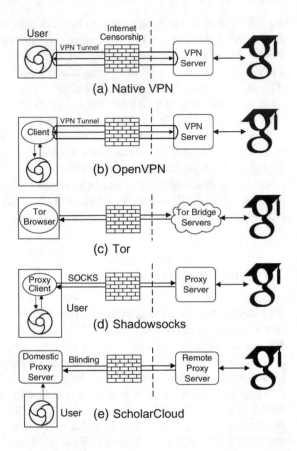

which is confidential and not recognized by the GFW. There are a number of encoding approaches that can potentially meet our requirements [40, 41]. In our experiments, we notice that even using a simple but non-public algorithm like byte mapping ($f : [0, 2^8) \rightarrow [0, 2^8)$) can successfully blind the encrypted messages from the GFW's inspection, thus bypassing the GFW. Therefore, by making the encrypted messages blind to the GFW, we give our system high resistance to the Internet censorship.

Since we control both the domestic and remote proxy, we can change our blinding mechanism at any time without impacting users. This gives ScholarCloud the ability to adapt to GFW's reactions to our blinding scheme, i.e., we are agile against future changes in the GFW. In contrast, Tor cannot easily do this because it would require many independent relays to upgrade; similarly, Shadowsocks can only adapt if users upgrade their client software.

Data Security and Privacy During the three phases in Fig. 7.2e (i.e., User ↔ Domestic Proxy, Domestic Proxy ↔ Remote Proxy, and Remote Proxy ↔ Target Web Server), if a message is already encrypted with HTTPS (by the user's browser and the target web server), ScholarCloud will not encrypt it again; otherwise,

ScholarCloud creates an encrypted tunnel between the domestic and remote proxy using HTTPS. Note that there is a potential privacy risk when using ScholarCloud, as it can observe the content of unencrypted packets. However, this risk also exists with VPN services, Tor exit nodes, and Shadowsocks proxies; ScholarCloud does not increase the privacy risks to users.

Service Legalization We focus on helping users access legal services that are incidentally blocked by the GFW. Therefore, we have legalized ScholarCloud by registering it with the relevant government agencies (with China's ICP Reg. #15063437). Specifically, besides providing a series of information about our service (as mentioned in Sect. 7.2), we start a company as the business entity of our ScholarCloud service and register at the responsible TCA agency. The registration requires the following documents: (1) biometric document of the legal representative of the company and (2) documentation of the ScholarCloud service with text, screenshots, and real-world usage videos, as well as a workable user guide.

In addition, ScholarCloud only redirects those user traffic corresponding to a *visible* whitelist of legal services (which are incidentally blocked). Only when a service (domain) appears in the whitelist, ScholarCloud redirects the traffic to bypass the GFW; otherwise, it does not modify the traffic at all. Therefore, government agencies can examine which legal services are defined by us and request that we alter the whitelist on demand.

7.4 Measurement Study

In this section, we first introduce our user survey results to understand the common practices of accessing Google Scholar in China. Next, we present our methodology for comparing different GFW circumvention techniques. Finally, we report the measurement results as well as our analysis and insights.

7.4.1 Common Practices

To understand how Chinese scholars access Google Scholar, we posted a survey through the bulletin board system (BBS) of Tsinghua University in July 2015 and received 371 results from faculty members and students. Most of the participants were not from the departments of computer science or engineering. Note that ScholarCloud had not been deployed in 2015 and thus was not an option at the time of the survey. Figure 7.3 shows the distribution of methods for accessing Google Scholar reported by the participants. 26% of the scholars reported bypassing the GFW and accessing Google Scholar. Among them, 43% reported utilizing VPNs (93% using native VPN and 7% using OpenVPN), 2% used Tor, 21% used Shadowsocks, and the remaining 34% adopted other solutions (e.g., other web

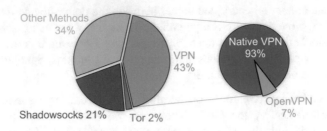

Fig. 7.3 Distribution of methods for accessing Google Scholar adopted by scholars in Tsinghua University (Reprinted with permission from [32])

proxies such as Free Gate [42] or modifying their system's hosts file). Therefore, our measurements focus on the four most common solutions, as well as ScholarCloud (cf., Fig. 7.2).

7.4.2   Methodology

To comparatively study the performance of the five access methods in a fair manner, we conduct controlled benchmark experiments during February–April, 2017. In all the experiments, the client is a common laptop (ThinkPad T440s) located at Tsinghua University (Beijing, China) inside CERNET (China Education and Research Network). The client uses 64-bit Windows 8.1. Except for Tor, which requires the dedicated Tor browser (version 6.5), we use the Chrome web browser (version 56.0, 64 bit) to access Google Scholar. In all cases, we automate the web browser to send HTTP requests for the home page of Google Scholar every 60 s (hence two consecutive accesses do not overlap) and each experiment lasts for a whole day.

On the server side, except for Tor where the remote servers are assigned by the Tor network, we employ a VM server rented from Aliyun ECS located at San Mateo, CA, USA. The server has a single-core Intel Xeon CPU (2.3 GHz), 1 GB DDR3 memory, 50 GB HDD disk storage, and an auto-scale Internet connection (with maximum bandwidth of 100 Mbps). The server OS is 64-bit Ubuntu 14.04. For ScholarCloud, we rent another VM to function as the domestic proxy located in Tsinghua University with the same configuration.

In our experiments, different access methods exploit different communication and encryption protocols. For native VPN, we use the PPTP protocol based on pptpd.[3] For OpenVPN, we adopt the layer-3 implementation and use the Easy-RSA tool to create the PKI certificates and keys. For Tor, we employ the latest *meek* obfuscation protocol for connecting to bridge servers. For Shadowsocks, we encrypt the data connection between the proxy client and the proxy server based on the AES-256-CFB implementation. Finally, for ScholarCloud, we blind the messages using our custom scheme, so as to maximize its robustness to the censorship of the GFW.

7.4.3   Measurement Results

We report measurement results from the perspectives of performance, robustness to blocking, and overhead. Specifically, we examine the following metrics:

- *Page load time* (PLT) denoting user-perceived web experience
- *Round-trip time* (RTT) representing network-level efficiency
- *Packet loss rate* (PLT) indicating robustness to censorship
- *Client-side overhead*: network traffic, CPU, and memory usages
- *Scalability* illustrating how many requests a solution can simultaneously support without obvious performance degradation

To facilitate the analysis of measurement results, we plot in Fig. 7.4 the interactions between the client and the server in the whole HTTP session for an access to Google Scholar.

Page Load Time (PLT) As shown in Fig. 7.5a, PLTs can be dramatically different when the page is loaded for the *first time* and *subsequent* accesses. The former is much longer than the latter for three main reasons. First, there is no local DNS cache when accessing a web page for the first time, so the DNS resolution procedure must be performed. Second, there is no local content cache for the web page, so the web client has to setup required data connections to all the involved web servers to fetch corresponding content. Third, the Google Scholar server needs to record the client's IP address and Google account, as demonstrated by the fourth TCP connection (TCP 4) in Fig. 7.4.

Tor has the largest initial PLT, since its connection setup process involves interactions with multiple bridges and relays. The first-time PLT (15 s) is 5.4 times longer than the normal PLT (2.8 s) on average. In the worst case, the first-time PLT is close to 20 s.

Native VPN and OpenVPN have similar normal PLTs between 1.2 and 1.5 s, while Shadowsocks has much longer PLT (3.7 s on average). In order to understand the root cause, we delve into the implementation of Shadowsocks at the source-code level [29]. We find that Shadowsocks imposes an extra TCP connection for

---

[3] We also tested with other VPN protocols (L2TP and IPSec) based on implementations of xl2tpd, openswan, and ppp and observed similar performance to PPTP.

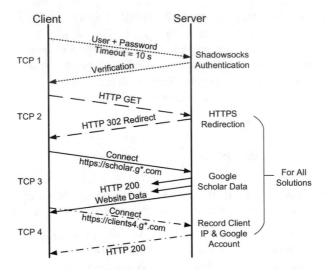

Fig. 7.4 Detailed client–server interactions during the whole HTTP session to access Google Scholar of the studied methods. Note that the four TCP connections (TCP 1–4) are *not* present in all cases: TCP-1 (for user/password authentication) is only set up by Shadowsocks, TCP-2 (for HTTPS redirection) only appears when the client sends an HTTP request rather than an HTTPS request, and TCP-4 (for recording the client's IP and Google account) only appears when the client accesses Google Scholar for the first time. TCP-3 (for real Google Scholar data exchange) appears in all cases (Reprinted with permission from [32])

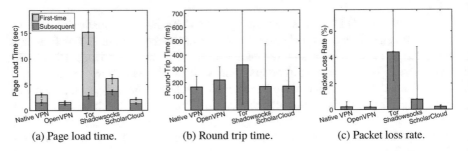

(a) Page load time.　　　(b) Round trip time.　　　(c) Packet loss rate.

Fig. 7.5 Performance and robustness of different access methods. The error bars show the max and min values observed (Reprinted with permission from [32])

user/password authentication in the beginning of each HTTP session, as demonstrated by TCP 1 in Fig. 7.4. Additionally, the default configuration of keep-alive timeout in Shadowsocks is 10 s, i.e., Shadowsocks reinitializes the authentication procedure if there is no request passing through the connection in 10 s. This makes the communication more secure but considerably prolongs PLT.

Although ScholarCloud and Shadowsocks adopt a similar dual-proxy architecture, the former's PLTs (first time 2.1 s and subsequent 1.3 s on average) are remarkably shorter than the latter's for two main reasons. First, ScholarCloud does not impose an extra TCP connection for user/password authentication in each HTTP session. Second, ScholarCloud's message blinding mechanism greatly reduces the packet loss rate (see Fig. 7.5c), which also influences the PLT. As a result, ScholarCloud achieves short PLTs.

Round-Trip Time (RTT)   It is known that RTT is correlated to PLT. In this section, we quantify the impact of RTT on PLT. According to Fig. 7.5b, RTT has stronger correlations with the first-time PLT than the normal PLT. For example, Tor bears the longest first-time PLT (15 s in average) as well as the longest RTT (330 ms in average). This can be explained by the fact that the first-time access to a web page requires more round trips than subsequent accesses, thus making RTT have larger influence on the first-time PLT.

Packet Loss Rate (PLR)   As explained in Sect. 7.1, the GFW exploits a variety of techniques for Internet censorship, including IP blocking, DNS poisoning, URL filtering, packet filtering, and so forth. Many of these techniques result in packet losses over the end-to-end connection. Therefore, we use PLR as a key indicator of robustness against the censorship of the GFW.

As illustrated in Fig. 7.5c, Tor is severely impacted by the censorship of the GFW, with the highest PLR (4.4%) on average. Shadowsocks is also vulnerable to the censorship of the GFW with the average PLR being 0.77%. In comparison, when using Tor or Shadowsocks in the USA to access Google Scholar, we observe that the PLR usually stays below 0.1%. Over the past few years, a number of techniques specific to Tor and Shadowsocks have been added into the GFW, such as deep packet inspection and active probing [7, 10, 43]. Therefore, we do not use these methods as the building blocks of ScholarCloud.

Both native VPN and OpenVPN are robust to the censorship of the GFW, with low PLR being around 0.2% on average, similar to the PLR of accessing non-blocked US websites (e.g., Amazon) from a web client in China. We do not build ScholarCloud upon VPN because the government policies toward VPN keep changing in China [28, 38]. On the other hand, ScholarCloud's message blinding achieves a similar PLR (0.22% on average) compared with VPN.

Client-Side Overhead   Figure 7.6 illustrates the client-side overhead of different access methods in terms of network traffic, CPU, and memory, respectively. Compared with accessing non-blocked web sites, bypassing GFW requires extra network traffic for tunneling, encrypting, or obfuscating the exchanged data. As indicated in Fig. 7.6a, during a direct access to Google Scholar from a web browser in the USA, the network traffic amounts to 19 KB on average (the dotted line). When bypassing the GFW to access Google Scholar, OpenVPN adds the least traffic overhead (8 KB) while native VPN adds the most (14 KB). In general, none of the solutions, including ScholarCloud, exhibit significant traffic overhead.

The CPU utilizations of the web browser and the extra client software (if there is any) are listed in Fig. 7.6b. Native VPN increases CPU utilization the least (3.07%) while Tor increases it the most (3.62%). However, the increase percentage (18%)

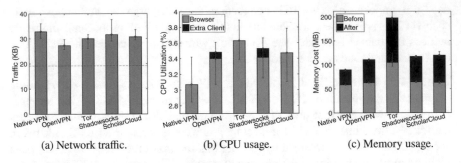

(a) Network traffic.   (b) CPU usage.   (c) Memory usage.

Fig. 7.6 Client-side overhead of different access methods. The error bars show the max and min values observed (Reprinted with permission from [32])

from 3.07% to 3.62% is not remarkable. Also, the extra CPU cost brought by the extra client software of OpenVPN and Shadowsocks is trivial.

For memory usage, as shown in Fig. 7.6c, when the web browser is running but not being really used to access those blocked web content ("Before"), the Tor browser consumes nearly 70% more memory than Chrome. Also, when the web browser is actually used to access Google Scholar ("After"), native VPN consumes the least extra memory usage (30 MB) while Tor consumes the most (90 MB). The two observations consistently show that the complication of Tor leads to obviously larger memory consumption.

Scalability Figure 7.7 shows the scalability of native VPN, OpenVPN, Shadowsocks, and ScholarCloud. We do not measure the scalability of Tor because we are unable to control the Tor bridge servers. Specifically, we use the average page load time (PLT) as the major indicator of scalability as the number of concurrent clients increases, because PLT is the most important user-perceived web experience. We observer that Shadowsocks bears the worst scalability because its PLT sharply grows when the number of concurrent clients exceeds 60. In contrast, the PLTs

Fig. 7.7 Scalability of each access method in terms of PLT (Reprinted with permission from [32])

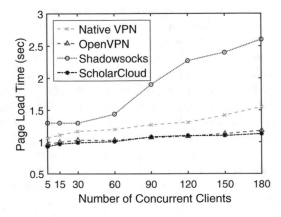

of native VPN, OpenVPN, and ScholarCloud exhibit linear growth when there are more concurrent clients. Among the three linear cases, OpenVPN and ScholarCloud possess the best scalability with their PLTs growing gently.

7.5 Related Work

After launching since 2000, the GFW has raised significant concerns. There has been extensive work that attempts to understand the blocking techniques adopted by the GFW and circumvent its censorship. As revealed by previous work, the GFW has deployed at least four types of techniques to restrict the activities of Internet users in China [13]: IP blocking [6, 20], DNS poisoning/hijacking [17–19], keyword filtering [12, 14], and deep packet inspection [8, 30, 31]. It is reported that 99% of the blocking behavior of the GFW occurs at the border routers between China and the USA [12, 18], which motivates the split-proxy architecture of ScholarCloud.

The deployment of Internet censorship systems has led to an everlasting arms race between blocking techniques and circumvention approaches [40, 41, 44–52]. Many circumvention approaches that were once effective at bypassing the GFW are currently impaired by the GFW's new blocking techniques. One such example is Tor, which has become less effective after the GFW's deployed Deep Packet Inspection [7, 9, 10, 15, 43, 53–55]. In our survey (Sect. 7.4.1), Tor is only used by 2% of surveyed users.

Our work is complementary to the aforementioned work. We focus on helping users to access legal Internet services rather than complete censorship circumvention. In China, many valuable and beneficial Internet resources (e.g., Google Scholar) are incidentally blocked. However, there has been little work on accessing these legal Internet services along with censorship.

7.6 Limitation and Discussion

Despite its real-world deployment and sound performance, ScholarCloud has its limitations. Its user group is mainly composed of China's scholars, mostly faculties and students in certain universities. Also, it is used for whitelisted websites rather than all blocked websites by the GFW. Hence, its proxy servers receive less traffic and interact with fewer content providers compared with VPN, Tor, and Shadowsocks. In addition, ScholarCloud is a web-based proxy solution, so it cannot help the users to access those non-HTTP(S) content. Essentially, the web-based design strategy is a double-edge sword—it greatly simplifies the configurations imposed on users, while it inevitably restricts the application scenarios.

ScholarCloud demonstrates a practical and sustainable approach to help users access legal Internet services with the existence of extreme censorship, complementary to the solutions that rely on external services outside China. In addition, we hope that this chapter can help the community better understand China's Internet censorship ecosystem, which provides opportunities for designing circumstance solutions to benefit a massive population of end users.

References

1. Anderson D (2012) Splinternet behind the great firewall of China. ACM Queue 10(11):1–10
2. Aryan S, Aryan H, Halderman JA (2013) Internet censorship in Iran: a first look. In: Proc. of USENIX FOCI
3. Verkamp JP, Gupta M (2012) Inferring mechanics of web censorship around the world. In: Proc. of USENIX FOCI
4. Gebhart G, Author A, Kohno T (2017) Internet censorship in Thailand: user practices and potential threats. In: Proc. of the 2nd IEEE European symposium on security and privacy (EuroS&P)
5. Drummond D. A new approach to China: an update. https://googleblog.blogspot.com/2010/03/new-approach-to-china-update.html. The Official Google Blog. Retrieved March 24, 2010
6. Clayton R, Murdoch SJ, Watson RN (2006) Ignoring the great firewall of China. In: Proc. of the 6th workshop on privacy enhancing technologies (PETS)
7. Ensafi R, Fifield D, Winter P, Feamster N, Weaver N, Paxson V (2015) Examining how the great firewall discovers hidden circumvention servers. In: Proc. of ACM IMC
8. Wang L, Dyer KP, Akella A, Ristenpart T, Shrimpton T (2015) Seeing through network-protocol obfuscation. In: Proc. of ACM CCS
9. Ensafi R, Winter P, Mueen A, Crandall JR (2015) Analyzing the great firewall of China over space and time. In: Proc. of the 15th privacy enhancing technologies symposium (PETS)
10. Winter P, Lindskog S (2012) How the great firewall of China is blocking Tor. In: Proc. of USENIX FOCI
11. Nobori D, Shinjo Y (2014) VPN gate: a volunteer-organized public VPN relay system with blocking resistance for bypassing government censorship firewalls. In: Proc. of NSDI
12. Crandall JR, Zinn D, Byrd M, Barr E, East R (2007) ConceptDoppler: a weather tracker for internet censorship. In: Proc. of ACM CCS
13. Xu X, Mao ZM, Halderman JA (2011) Internet censorship in China: where does the filtering occur? In: Proc. of the 12th international conference on passive and active measurement (PAM)
14. Park JC, Crandall JR (2010) Empirical study of a national-scale distributed intrusion detection system: backbone-level filtering of HTML responses in China. In: Proc. of IEEE ICDCS
15. Winter P, Crandall JR (2012) The great firewall of China: how it blocks Tor and why it is hard to pinpoint. Login: Usenix Mag 37(6):42–50
16. Wright J (2012) Regional variation in chinese internet filtering. Tech. rep., Oxford Internet Institute, University of Oxford
17. Lowe G, Winters P, Marcus ML (2007) The great DNS wall of China. Tech. rep., New York University
18. Anonymous (2012) The collateral damage of internet censorship by DNS injection. ACM SIGCOMM Comput Commun Rev 42(3):22–27
19. Anonymous (2014) Towards a comprehensive picture of the great firewall's DNS censorship. In: Proc. of USENIX FOCI
20. Zittrain J, Edelman B (2003) Internet filtering in China. IEEE Internet Comput 7(2):70–77
21. Post SCM. Google Scholar may be Google's first service to return to China, Chinese lawmaker reveals. http://www.scmp.com/news/china/policies-politics/article/2078173/google-another-step-closer-being-unblocked-china
22. Mashable. Google scholar might finally be Google's way back into China. http://mashable.com/2017/03/13/google-scholar-in-china/#uQIB4xtjFSqB

23. TechWeb. Google scholar is likely to return China. http://www.techweb.com.cn/internet/2017-03-14/2499526.shtml
24. China News. China News: it is much harder for Chinese netizens to get across great Firewall since Nov 2012. http://news.creaders.net/china/2013/03/02/1238807.html
25. BBC News. BBC report: China blocks virtual private network. http://www.bbc.com/news/technology-30982198
26. Daily P. VPN services should be registered in China. http://legal.people.com.cn/n/2015/0128/c188502-26462092.html
27. Beijinger T. China ministry says foreign VPN operators must register. https://www.thebeijinger.com/blog/2015/01/28/china-ministry-says-foreign-vpn-operators-must-register
28. South China Morning Post. China tightens great firewall by declaring unauthorised VPN services illegal. http://www.scmp.com/news/china/policies-politics/article/2064587/chinas-move-clean-vpns-and-strengthen-great-firewall
29. Clowwindy. Shadowsocks project. https://github.com/shadowsocks
30. Cai X, Zhang XC, Joshi B, Johnson R (2012) Touching from a distance: website fingerprinting attacks and defenses. In: Proc. of ACM CCS
31. Chen W, Li C, Shen J, Zhang W, Yang G. Webpage fingerprint identification method aiming at specific website category. https://www.google.com/patents/CN105281973A?cl=en
32. Lu Z, Li Z, Yang J, Xu T, Zhai E, Liu Y, Wilson C (2017) Accessing Google scholar under extreme internet censorship: a legal avenue. In: Proceedings of The 18th ACM/IFIP/USENIX international middleware conference (Middleware), pp 8–14
33. State Council of China. Administrative measures on internet information services. http://www.gov.cn/gongbao/content/2000/content_60531.htm
34. State Council of China. Administrative measures for protection of the security of international internetworking of computer information networks. http://www.mps.gov.cn/n2254314/n2254409/n2254443/n2254451/c4113546/content.html
35. The State Council. Interim Provisions of the People's Republic of China Governing International Interconnection of Computer-based Information Networks. http://www.cac.gov.cn/1996-02/02/c_126468621.htm. Decree No. 218 of the State Council
36. The Ministry of Information Industry. Measures for the Administration of Record-Filing of Non-Profit-Making Internet Information Services. http://www.miit.gov.cn/n11293472/n11293877/n11301753/n11496139/11537734.html. Order No. 33 of the Ministry of Information Industry
37. The Ministry of Information Industry. Ministry of Industry and Information Technology: On the Further Implementation of the Site Record Information Authenticity Verification Program. http://www.miitbeian.gov.cn/state/outPortal/queryMutualityDownloadInfo.action?id=267. Order No. 64
38. China News. MIIT: Cleansing illegal VPN services will not affect normal operation of transnational corporations. http://www.chinanews.com/cj/2017/01-24/8134818.shtml
39. Netscape: Proxy auto-config (PAC) file. https://en.wikipedia.org/wiki/Proxy_auto-config
40. Dyer KP, Coull SE, Shrimpton T (2015) Marionette: a programmable network traffic obfuscation system. In: Proc. of the 24th USENIX Security Symposium
41. Luchaup D, Dyer KP, Jha S, Ristenpart T, Shrimpton T (2014) LibFTE: a toolkit for constructing practical, format-abiding encryption schemes. In: Proc. of the 23rd USENIX Security Symposium
42. Global Internet Freedom Consortium. Free gate web site. https://freegate.en.softonic.com/
43. McLachlan J, Hopper N (2009) On the risks of serving whenever you surf: vulnerabilities in Tor's blocking resistance design. In: Proc. of the 8th ACM workshop on privacy in the electronic society (WPES), pp 31–40
44. Fifield D, Lan C, Hynes R, Wegmann P, Paxson V (2015) Blocking-resistant communication through domain fronting. In: Proc. on privacy enhancing technologies (PETS)
45. Houmansadr A, Nguyen GT, Caesar M, Borisov N (2011) Cirripede: circumvention infrastructure using router redirection with plausible deniability. In: Proc. of ACM CCS

46. Karlin J, Ellard D, Jackson AW, Jones CE, Lauer G, Mankins D, Strayer WT (2011) Decoy routing: toward unblockable internet communication. In: Proc. of USENIX FOCI
47. Khattak S, Javed M, Anderson PD, Paxson V (2013) Towards illuminating a censorship monitor's model to facilitate evasion. In: Proc. of USENIX FOCI
48. Wustrow E, Wolchok S, Goldberg I, Halderman JA (2011) Telex: anticensorship in the network infrastructure. In: Proc. of USENIX security
49. Luo X, Zhou P, Chan EW, Lee W, Chang RKC, Perdisci R (2011) HTTPOS: sealing information leaks with browser-side obfuscation of encrypted flows. In: Proc. of NDSS
50. Dyer KP, Coull SE, Ristenpart T, Shrimpton T (2013) Protocol misidentification made easy with format-transforming encryption. In: Proc. of ACM CCS
51. Houmansadr A, Brubaker C, Shmatikov V (2013) The parrot is dead: observing unobservable network communications. In: Proc. of S&P
52. Weinberg Z, Wang J, Yegneswaran V, Briesemeister L, Cheung S, Wang F, Boneh D (2012) StegoTorus: a camouflage proxy for the Tor anonymity system. In: Proc. of ACM CCS
53. Ling Z, Luo J, Yu W, Yang M, Fu X (2012) Extensive analysis and large-scale empirical evaluation of Tor bridge discovery. In: Proc. of IEEE INFOCOM
54. Winter P, Pulls T, Fuss J (2013) ScrambleSuit: a polymorphic network protocol to circumvent censorship. In: Proc. of the 12th ACM workshop on privacy in the electronic society (WPES)
55. Mani A, Sherr M (2017) HisTorε: differentially private and robust statistics collection for Tor. In: Proc. of NDSS

Part V
Metric 4 Security: Do Not Relax Our Vigilance

Chapter 8
Combating Nationwide WiFi Security Threats

Abstract Carrying over 75% of the last-mile mobile Internet traffic, WiFi has inevitably become an enticing target for various security threats. In this work, we characterize a wide variety of real-world WiFi threats at an unprecedented scale, involving 19M WiFi APs mostly located in China, by deploying a crowdsourced security checking system on 14M mobile devices in the wild. Leveraging the collected data, we reveal the landscape of nationwide WiFi threats for the first time. We find that the prevalence, riskiness, and breakdown of WiFi threats deviate significantly from common understandings and prior studies. In particular, we detect attacks at around 4% of all WiFi APs, uncover that most WiFi attacks are driven by an underground economy, and provide strong evidence of web analytics platforms being the bottleneck of its monetization chain. Furthermore, we provide insightful guidance for defending against WiFi attacks at scale, and some of our efforts have already yielded real-world impact—effectively disrupted the WiFi attack ecosystem.

Keywords WiFi security · WiFi attack · WiFi access point

8.1 Introduction

More than 75% of the last-mile Internet traffic of today's mobile systems is delivered via WiFi [1], which thereby has also become an enticing target for various security threats. Criminals exploit security vulnerabilities of WiFi access points (APs) to eavesdrop on wireless traffic [2], to launch phishing attacks through DNS hijacking [3], and to directly generate profits through cryptojacking [4]. Adversaries not only compromise existing WiFi APs but also deploy malicious WiFi-based edge devices. WiFi-based attacks have become nationwide security threats, affecting hundreds of millions of users.

Census Methodology To comprehensively understand nationwide WiFi threats, we take a unique opportunity to collaborate with WiFiManager (actual name anonymized), a crowdsourcing-based WiFi discovery and management service used by 800+ million (M) Android devices across 200+ countries/regions. It helps

Android systems automatically discover accessible WiFi APs with Internet connectivity, by crowdsourcing the connectivity information and statistics contributed by the numerous live devices—each user device serves as a tester for a given WiFi AP. Leveraging this massive-scale crowdsourcing platform, we build a WiFi security checking system, which we call WiSC (WiFi Security Checker), integrated in WiFiManager as an optional function. WiSC enables us to measure a wide variety of real-world WiFi threats at an unprecedented scale.

Running on a massive number of heterogeneous mobile devices requires WiSC to address three challenges: (1) *no root privilege access*, as WiFiManager needs to be a pure user-space app to register wide deployment, (2) *achieving a good detection coverage while maintaining high precision*, both being crucial to a comprehensive and in-depth understanding of the WiFi threat ecosystem, and (3) *no long-term traffic monitoring* to avoid excessive resource consumption on mobile devices and to minimize users' privacy concerns.

To tackle these issues, we judiciously engineer our attack detection framework. Deployed atop a regular Android app, WiSC utilizes generic system APIs with limited system privileges to detect attacks on both LAN and WAN. As a result, our threat model targets attacks mainly occurring at upper layers, including ARP/DHCP spoofing in LAN and TCP/DNS hijacking in WAN; for other attacks operating at the MAC/PHY layer, we cannot detect them since WiSC has no privileged access to WiFi modem and other hardware.

To balance the detection accuracy and resource overhead, WiSC conducts the detection through a novel two-stage pipeline, by first capturing suspicious attacks in a fast and resource-efficient manner, followed by a more detailed scrutiny to rule out possible false positives. For LAN-side attacks, WiSC performs *cross-connection gateway-consistency detection* (Sect. 8.2.2) by leveraging a common usage scenario where user devices are repeatedly connected to the same AP; it overcomes limitations in traditional detection schemes [5, 6]. For WAN-side attacks, we develop a *cross-layer decoy-based detection* scheme (Sect. 8.2.3), where we instrument carefully crafted decoy packets to extensively trigger primary WAN attacks and analyze the attack risks by synthesizing cross-layer information. Combining the above efforts, WiSC manages to realize accurate attack detection on commodity Android devices within 5 s, incurring less than 10 KB of network traffic.

Under user consent and a well-established IRB, WiSC collected measurement data from 14M user devices upon 19M WiFi APs, over a period of six months (10/2018–04/2019). The data analysis enabled us to develop a holistic understanding of WiFi threats, with a number of novel insights.

Prevalence and Riskiness We detect attacks at 3.92% of the examined WiFi APs. The percentage is significantly higher than those (0.21–1.5%) reported by small-scale studies [7, 8]. A key reason is that prior studies omit attacks that are considered difficult to launch given today's seemingly strengthened mobile OS and network protocols. In particular, common sense suggests that given the increasing adoption of HTTPS, web content manipulation such as advertisement (ad) injection is unlikely to occur. Nevertheless, our findings indicate that the majority (55%)

of our detected attacks remain ad injections. We attribute this to the prevalent *misconfigurations of HTTPS* in the real world. We find (and confirm through controlled experiments) that ad injections can be successfully launched toward popular HTTPS-equipped content providers (e.g., TMall, BBC, and Shopify) due to improper HTTPS configurations. For example, a lack of HTTP Strict Transport Security (HSTS) allows an HTTPS session to fall back to HTTP, making SSL/TLS stripping attack and henceforth ad injection feasible. Worse still, even among equipped with HSTS, most do not properly configure the HSTS parameters (e.g., timeout threshold and preload list).

Counter-intuitively, we notice that ad injections are more likely to occur on better protected APs: 2.3% of the APs using strong encryption (WPA/WPA2) *vs.* 1% of the APs with no or weak encryption (WEP). We attribute this to the statistically better Internet connectivity of the APs with stronger encryption. The results indicate that common practices for enhancing WiFi security are not that effective when confronting today's sophisticated, mature cybercrime market.

Within the LAN, we identify both ARP and DHCP spoofings. While ARP spoofing has been reported before [9, 10], DHCP spoofing was mostly deemed as a hypothetical form of attack under WiFi environments due to the high cost of launching it [11, 12]. Nonetheless, our observation refutes this by revealing that DHCP spoofing is as feasible as other popular attacks in practice. We observe a considerable fraction (25%) of APs are subject to poor network connectivity with user devices, and such poor network conditions substantially increase the success rate of DHCP spoofing.

Economics Behind Next, we go beyond basic characterizations by revealing the economics behind WiFi threats: *what are attackers' key decisions for maximizing their profits?* A major finding is that APs under LAN attacks (ARP/DHCP spoofing) exhibit significant physical movements (median of 724 m) during our measurement; in comparison, APs under WAN attacks and benign APs are quite stationary (median of 31 m and 21 m, respectively). This can be explained by our observation that LAN attacks are more likely to succeed under poor LAN environments, which in turn can easily arouse network administrators' vigilance and defensive measures. Thus, adversaries need to strategically relocate to increase the success rate and evade detection. Notably, 10% of the APs under LAN attacks even manifest a clear pattern of shifting among several locations, forming one or multiple loops.

More surprisingly, we notice that most adversaries do not inject ads to every web page visited by a victim user. Instead, they opportunistically perform ad injections at a low probability of ~17%. The rationale for such "low-rate" attacks is that high-frequency ad injections are more likely to incur users' complaints and henceforth AP reset, AP firmware upgrade, or even AP disconnection, causing the attacker to lose the compromised AP. The attacker thus needs to tune the injection frequency to maximize the profit. We mathematically model the attacker's revenue and find that the modeling results well support our hypothesis—the maximum profit appears at an ad injection probability of 15%, close to the measurement observation (17% on average).

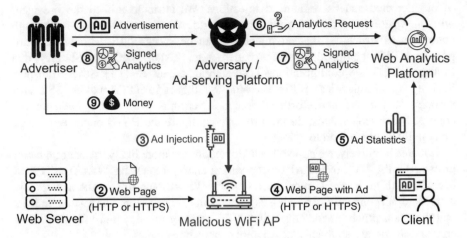

Fig. 8.1 The underground ecosystem of WiFi attacks uncovered by our census (Reprinted with permission from [13])

Furthermore, our end-to-end analysis on ad injection attack unravels its underground ecosystem centered around the monetization chain. As depicted in Fig. 8.1, adversaries first collect ad requirements from advertisers (①) and then distribute *visible* ads to victim users via compromised or maliciously deployed APs (②③④); after that, according to the ad-effect reports generated and signed by web analytics platforms (⑤⑥⑦⑧), adversaries get paid by the advertisers (⑨). Our key insight is that the legitimate web analytics platforms are abused by the attackers; however, they are also the bottlenecks (i.e., "cut points") in the monetization chain—almost all of the injected ads are monetized using only four web analytics platforms. We have reported our findings to the four platforms, leading to defensive intervention that effectively disrupted the WiFi attack ecosystem. For example, Baidu Analytics have responded to us and stopped serving 67% of the reported ad links, leading to 49.8% of decrease of ad injections as of August 2020.

Broader Impact Most of the WiFi APs in our study are located in China. It is worth mentioning that we also detect extensive WiFi attacks in many other countries where WiFiManager is widely used. In some countries (e.g., Burma and Russia), the fraction of malicious APs is even larger than 4%, as shown in Table 8.2. Hence, we feel that our study also provides valuable insights for combating WiFi security threats outside China. Owing to its prominent impact in understanding and mitigating WiFi threats in the wild, WiSC is now an official component of the production WiFiManager system.

8.2 Study Methodology

We first outline how the WiSC system works (Sect. 8.2.1). We then explain in detail our detection schemes for LAN (Sect. 8.2.2) and WAN (Sect. 8.2.3) attacks. Finally, we describe our large-scale deployment (Sect. 8.2.5).

8.2.1 WiSC System Overview

To address the three design challenges mentioned in Sect. 8.1, we develop a novel two-stage pipeline to detect the abovementioned LAN and WAN attacks. It first efficiently captures suspicious events and then scrutinizes them to remove false positives, thus ensuring a high detection accuracy and low resource footprint. WiSC's architecture is illustrated in Fig. 8.2.

On the UI (user interface) of WiFiManager, there is a "Security Checking" button; once clicked, WiSC starts the LAN attack detection (Sect. 8.2.2) by first retrieving (Step ①) and then examining (Step ②) related LAN information. To detect WAN attacks (Sect. 8.2.3), WiSC first performs a transport-layer detection (Step ③) by sending decoy IP packets to the connected AP to determine whether it is *suspicious*. For a suspicious AP, WiSC further launches the application-layer detection (Step ④) to rule out possible false positives, by checking DNS responses and modifications to an instrumented decoy web page from our own server. The detection results, along with the LAN information, received responses of sent

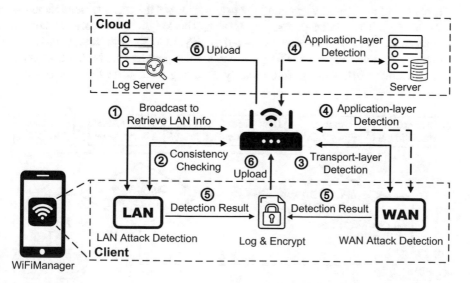

Fig. 8.2 Workflow of WiSC, which crowdsourced data from WiFiManager users for WiFi security checking (Reprinted with permission from [13])

decoys, and the device's location data collected via GPS or cellular base station localization, are then encrypted and uploaded via the connected AP to our log server (Step (5)(6)).

8.2.2 LAN Attack Detection

To detect LAN-side attacks, we develop a novel method called *cross-connection gateway-consistency detection*. Our scheme first broadcasts ARP Request messages to all the hosts within a subnet to retrieve the LAN information and configurations of the examined AP and then runs consistency checking with cross-connection and historic data to accurately detect the attacks. As to be detailed shortly, in real-world operational scenarios, such additional data help to rule out various false positives that traditional detection methods (e.g., ARP cache consistency checking [5]) may fall into.

ARP Spoofing Detection A user device leverages ARP to map the IP address of another device in the LAN to its corresponding MAC address. In ARP spoofing, a local network attacker broadcasts spoofed ARP Response messages that associate her own MAC address with the gateway's IP address [6]. If the user device accepts such messages, its future local network traffic will be directed to the attacker instead of the actual gateway.

Our detection is performed by examining changes in the gateway's (IP, MAC) address pair, a classic method for detecting ARP spoofing. As in Fig. 8.3, when a user device initially connects to an AP, the client of WiSC records the gateway's (IP, MAC) address pair by scanning the user device's ARP cache table, denoted as (IP_0, MAC_0). Then when performing security checking, we compare the current gateway's (IP, MAC) address pair, denoted as (IP_1, MAC_1), with the recorded one. However, this consistency checking is prone to false positives stemming from ARP cache eviction [14]. Thus, before security checking, we update the user device's

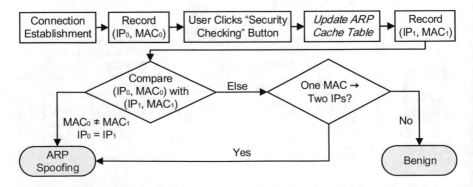

Fig. 8.3 Workflow of our ARP spoofing detection (Reprinted with permission from [13])

ARP cache table by querying for the corresponding MAC addresses of all the possible IP addresses in the subnet and then record each (IP, MAC) address pair when it is updated, so as to prevent ARP cache eviction from affecting our results. If the gateway's MAC address changes but the associated IP address remains ($MAC_0 \neq MAC_1$ and $IP_0 = IP_1$), we determine that the AP is under ARP spoofing.

It is worth noting that when the criterion above does not hold, it is still possible that the AP is under ARP spoofing—the AP may have already been compromised at the connection establishment (AP association) time (i.e., MAC_0 is already the attacker's MAC address and thus equal to MAC_1). In this case, the gateway's IP address and the attacker's own IP address should have been both mapped to the attacker's MAC address. Thus, if we find that there exists a MAC address mapped to two different IP addresses in the ARP cache table, we also conclude that the AP is under ARP spoofing.

DHCP Spoofing Detection When a user device connects to an AP, it first broadcasts DHCP Discovery messages within the LAN to acquire the gateway's IP address. In DHCP spoofing, upon receiving such messages, the attacker sends spoofed DHCP. The offer messages claiming that her own IP address is the gateway's IP address [15]. If the spoofed messages reach the user device earlier than the legitimate ones and are accepted, the attacker can intercept its future traffic. To detect DHCP spoofing, one direct solution is to examine changes in the gateway's IP address recorded by the user device [5]. However, this does not work in practice since in the design of DHCP, neither does the gateway periodically broadcast its IP address within the LAN, nor does the user device periodically query to check/update the gateway's IP address. Another solution proposed in prior work is to detect DHCP spoofing by continuously monitoring duplicate DHCP messages within the LAN [16], but this requires root privileges and incurs enormous overhead on the user device. To the best of our knowledge, there is no existing method that can detect DHCP spoofing without root privileges.

To address these, we design a novel *cross-connection* approach that compares the current gateway's address pair (IP_1, MAC_1) with the gateway's address pair (IP_0, MAC_0) recorded in the *last-time secure connection*, as depicted in Fig. 8.4. We define *last-time secure connection* as the user device's latest connection to the examined AP, i.e., with the same BSSID,[1] when the connection is determined by WiSC as *benign*; occasionally, if there are no benign connections recorded for the AP, we simply use the latest connection. Then, if the gateway's IP and MAC addresses have both changed ($MAC_0 \neq MAC_1$ and $IP_0 \neq IP_1$), we *suspect* that the examined AP is under DHCP spoofing. Note that switching to another WiFi network will not trigger this suspicious case, as the last-time secure connection ensures that the user device connects to the same network (i.e., with the same BSSID).

In the above suspicious case, it is possible that the gateway's changes in IP and MAC addresses are benign—such changes might be legitimately performed

---

[1] A BSSID (Basic Service Set Identifier) is derived from the AP's MAC address, and they are usually identical except when the AP supports multiple service sets [17].

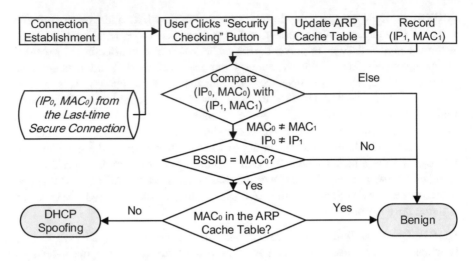

Fig. 8.4 Workflow of our DHCP spoofing detection (Reprinted with permission from [13])

by network administrators. To address this issue, we add additional logic shown in
Fig. 8.4. We check whether the AP was used as the gateway in the last-time secure
connection—this can be identified by checking whether the AP's BSSID equals the
gateway's MAC address (BSSID $=$ MAC$_0$). If this is true, it is certain that the AP's
MAC address is used as its BSSID (a common practice), and thus the AP's MAC
address is MAC$_0$. Since MAC$_0$ is the gateway's MAC address in the last-time secure
connection, we can then confirm that the AP was used as the gateway.

Provided that the AP was used as the gateway according to the above examination
and the gateway's changes (in IP and MAC addresses) are legitimate, the AP's IP
address should stay in the same subnet with the user device's IP address. This is
because the 802.11 standard declares that only one logical network segment (i.e.,
one IP subnet) can exist under a Basic Service Set (BSS, including all the devices
connected to the AP and the AP itself) [17]. Since the AP's IP address and the user
device's IP address are in the same subnet, and ARP cache table update is performed
at the beginning of our examination, MAC$_0$ should show up in the user device's
ARP cache table. On the other hand, if the gateway's changes are caused by DHCP
spoofing, this may not hold because a stealthy attacker often uses a different subnet
for her new gateway (otherwise address conflict will occur as the attacker does not
know which addresses have been allocated by the real gateway). Thus, if MAC$_0$ is
not in the user device's ARP cache table, we can rule out the possibility of legitimate
gateway changes and conclude that the AP is under DHCP spoofing.

8.2.3   WAN Attack Detection

For WAN attacks, we target the man-in-the-middle threat model where adversaries can easily launch TCP/DNS hijacking attacks and then *redirect* or *manipulate* traffic flows without users' knowledge. Under this threat model, even packets with *unreachable destination IP addresses* are highly likely to trigger the hijacking behavior since it is much easier to fabricate spoofed responses than to check the actual reachability of packets' destination IP addresses [18, 19]. Thus, we devise *cross-layer decoy-based detection* which starts with a transport-layer detection that sends decoy IP packets with unreachable destination IP addresses and uses the response rates to determine the suspicious APs in terms of TCP/DNS hijacking. For the suspicious APs, we then perform an application-layer detection to further rule out possible false positives. In this design, transport-layer detection acts as a quick filtering scheme of benign cases, so as to reduce the relatively high network overhead for performing application-layer scrutinizing. The flowchart of the detection process is shown in Fig. 8.5.

8.2.3.1   Transport-Layer Attack Detection

In the transport-layer detection step, we assemble several decoy IP packets with mostly unreachable destination IP addresses, which are randomly selected from an IP list that excludes easy-to-recognize IP addresses summarized in previous studies [20]. To make these decoys particularly attractive to attackers, we mimic

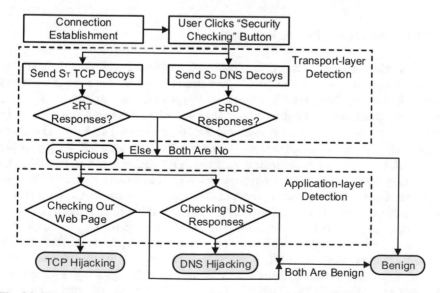

Fig. 8.5 Workflow of our WAN attack detection process (Reprinted with permission from [13])

web traffic by crafting TCP handshake segments with destination port 80 and DNS queries of domain names randomly selected from Alexa's list of popular websites (e.g., Baidu.com). This is because web traffic has been a major target of WiFi attacks due to its wide usage and richness in privacy data, making it an excellent "bait."

We then send out our decoys and monitor their responses in a 5-s time window (5 s is a typical user's tolerance of waiting according to the previous studies [21–23]). To mimic regular user behaviors, we send $S_T = 8$ TCP packets to the AP, which is the maximum number of parallel connections supported by common web browsers. We also emulate the timeout-retry process of DNS querying by sequentially sending $S_D = 3$ DNS packets, with a 2-s inter-packet delay, given the 5-s detection time window and the 2-s timeout value of the DNS protocol. We then determine the AP as *suspicious* for (1) TCP hijacking if at least R_T out of the S_T TCP packets have responses and (2) DNS hijacking if at least R_D out of the S_D DNS queries have responses. For these cases, we then apply application-layer detection to reduce false positives as detailed later in Sect. 8.2.3.3.

The above detection method is generally robust against deliberate evasion of knowledgeable adversaries for three reasons. First, our generated decoy packets are basically indistinguishable from normal ones, thereby preventing adversaries from identifying them without incurring high overheads on their sides. Second, our parameter settings for generating decoy packets are adjustable as the circumstances may require; the adjustment strategy is discussed in Sect. 8.2.3.2. Third, if an adversary alters her attack patterns (e.g., responding to much fewer packets) to largely evade our detection, her attack effectiveness and profits will be directly impaired.

8.2.3.2   Data-Driven Parameter Settings

In this section, we take a data-driven approach to systematically set R_T and R_D, the key parameters in our transport-layer detection. We list the related notations and definitions in Table 8.1. To determine R_T, we use two intuitions: (1) if the AP is malicious, due to random packet loss or various timeouts, the probability of receiving a response for every decoy is not 100% (denoted as $P_m < 1$) and (2) occasionally receiving a response for some decoys from a benign AP is still possible ($P_b \geq 0$), when a random destination happens to be reachable. Thus, lowering R_T or R_S may cause false positives (so more cases need to be scrutinized by the app-layer detection), while increasing them tends to incur false negatives. We next use real-world data-driven statistical modeling to balance this critical tradeoff.

First, to understand how different thresholds affect the percentage of suspicious APs, we conduct an experiment as a beta component (explicitly marked as "for experimental use only" in the UI) of WiFiManager for a month in September 2018. For an opt-in user, its client sends out S_T decoys for TCP hijacking detection and S_D decoys for DNS hijacking detection and then records the number of received responses (R). In total, ∼10,000 APs were tested and ∼20,000 records were

Table 8.1 Notations and their definitions

Notation	Definition
S_T	Amount of TCP decoys sent to the AP
S_D	Amount of DNS decoys sent to the AP
R_T	Threshold for the amount of TCP decoys' responses
R_D	Threshold for the amount of DNS decoys' responses
P_m	Probability of receiving responses from a malicious AP
P_b	Probability of receiving responses from a benign AP
R	Amount of received responses
$\mathbb{P}(R \geq k)$	Probability of an AP's requiring app-layer scrutinizing
$\mathbb{P}(R = k \mid \oplus)$	Probability of receiving k responses for a *malicious* AP
$\mathbb{P}(R = k \mid \ominus)$	Probability of receiving k responses for a *benign* AP

(Reprinted with permission from [13])

Fig. 8.6 Percentage of APs that need app-layer scrutinizing and estimated recall for different TCP thresholds (Reprinted with permission from [13])

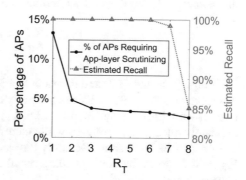

collected. Fig. 8.6 shows the percentage of APs that need scrutinizing (i.e., when the client received at least $R_T = k$ responses) for different k values, which we denote as $\mathbb{P}(R \geq k)$, whose conditional probabilities (given that the AP is malicious ($\oplus$) or benign ($\ominus$)) are modeled by the binomial distribution:

$$\begin{cases} \mathbb{P}(R=k|\oplus)=\mathbb{P}_B(k; S_T, P_m) = \binom{S_T}{k} P_m^k (1-P_m)^{(S_T-k)}, \\ \mathbb{P}(R=k|\ominus)=\mathbb{P}_B(k; S_T, P_b) = \binom{S_T}{k} P_b^k (1-P_b)^{(S_T-k)}. \end{cases} \tag{8.1}$$

Given $R = k$, the recall equals the probability of a malicious AP receiving $R \geq k$ responses:

$$recall = \mathbb{P}(R \geq k \mid \oplus) = \sum_{i=k}^{S_T} \mathbb{P}(R = i \mid \oplus). \tag{8.2}$$

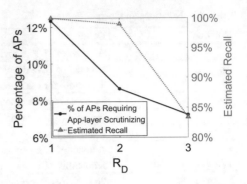

From Eqs. (8.1) and (8.2), we know that to calculate the recall, we need to obtain
the unknown P_m. To this end, according to Bayes' theorem, we have

$$\mathbb{P}(R = k) = \sum_{S \in \{\ominus, \oplus\}} \mathbb{P}(R = k \mid S)\mathbb{P}(S). \qquad (8.3)$$

With Eqs. (8.1) and (8.3) and the values of $\mathbb{P}(R = k)$ from our empirical data, we
can solve that $P_m = 98\%$. This is generally consistent with the measurement result
in prior work [24]. As shown in Fig. 8.6, $R_T = 5$ is empirically a "sweet spot" as it
efficiently filters out 96.6% APs while incurring little loss of recall.

For R_D (the DNS case), we apply the same mechanism and find $P_m = 94.12\%$.
Figure 8.7 shows the corresponding recall and $R_D = 2$ is found to be a proper
balance for our tradeoff.

8.2.3.3 Application-Layer Detection

After the transport-layer detection, the set of suspicious APs for TCP/DNS hijacking
behaviors may have false positives, for example, possible *benign interceptions* of
APs that intercept and respond to users' packets in a similar way as that in adversaries' attacks. Besides, ISPs may implement DNS interceptions [25] for routing
optimizations. To rule out these possibilities, we further employ two scrutinizing
strategies at the application layer for confirming TCP and DNS hijacking behaviors,
respectively. Note that the tradeoff here is that we conservatively determine an AP
as benign as long as we do not detect application-layer attacks, which is thus able to
avoid false positives but can introduce some false negatives.

For DNS hijacking, we examine the received resolution results of our DNS
decoys (if any). Recall that the decoys' carried domain names are randomly selected
from a list of popular websites. Thus, for the suspicious Aps, we determine them as
malicious if the resolved IP addresses conform to any of the following 3 criteria: (1)
these IP addresses have been publicly reported as malicious, (2) they are private IP

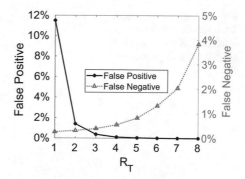

Fig. 8.8 False positive and false negative rates for different TCP thresholds (Reprinted with permission from [13])

addresses, and (3) they are identical, all of which should not be observed in benign DNS interceptions.

For TCP hijacking, we perform detection at the web page level. We host an instrumented decoy web page on WiSC's server, and let the client query for it. To detect attacks, a direct method is to compare the received web page at the client with the original one. However, this can have false positives when legitimate log-in web portal exists. To rule out these cases, we insert 256-bit random strings into the HTML of our web page as its "fingerprints." By checking the fingerprints, we can have high precision in detecting the attacks that do not completely replace web pages but only modify them, e.g., inserting new content. In the design of our web page, we also insert HTTPS links to capture HTTPS-targeted attacks like SSLStrip, which undermines HTTPS by replacing HTTPS links in web pages with HTTP links.

8.2.4   Evaluation

Setup To evaluate WiSC's performance (in terms of false positive and false negative rates), we conduct controlled experiments by, respectively, replaying the targeted attacks (i.e., ARP/DHCP spoofing and TCP/DNS hijacking) on 10 APs of different brands (as listed in Fig. 8.10) and detecting them with WiSC. For environment settings, we setup our experiments in a campus area where 5 WiFi signals simultaneously exist (a common scenario in public places according to WiFiManager's user data); all the signals lie in different channels so that they do not pose direct interference to each other.

LAN Attack Detection In the evaluation of LAN-side attack detection, we replay ARP and DHCP spoofing attacks without introducing the tradeoff scenarios as discussed in Sect. 8.2.2, in which we would always conservatively determine the AP as benign in pursuit of an extremely low false positive rate. As a result, evaluations show that all the replayed ARP and DHCP spoofing attacks can be correctly detected by WiSC, mostly attributed to our careful examinations of cross-connection and historic data.

Fig. 8.9 False positive and
false negative rates for
different DNS thresholds
(Reprinted with permission
from [13])

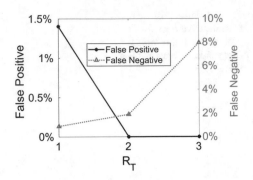

WAN Attack Detection For WAN attack detection, we focus on evaluating the
effectiveness of our crucial parameter settings in the transport-layer detection, as
well as the overall performance. In detail, we first diagnose the APs using solely the
transport-layer detection when the APs are benign and under TCP/DNS hijacking
attacks, respectively. Figure 8.8 shows the false positive and false negative rates
for different parameter settings (R_T) in the TCP case. As shown, our determined
threshold $R_T = 5$ is still a practical balance for the tradeoff between false positive
and false negative, as it effectively reduces false positive (thereby requiring less
unnecessary app-layer scrutinizing) to 0.048% while incurring only 0.82% false
negative. For the DNS case, Fig. 8.9 illustrates the corresponding false positive/false
negative for different R_D values, and $R_D = 2$ is also shown to be the proper choice.

Furthermore, we include the app-layer scrutinizing to evaluate the overall
performance of our WAN attack detection component. The results show that due
to the rigorous rules applied in the app-layer detection, the identified attacks contain
no false positive, while there is a slight increase of false negative from 0.82% (1.9%)
to 1.3% (2.2%) for the TCP (DNS) case.

8.2.5   Large-Scale Deployment and Field Survey

We collaborated with WiFiManager and implemented WiSC as an optional function
for all its users. During the six-month measurement from 10/22/2018 to 04/03/2019,
we recorded a total of 14M opt-in users and 19M WiFi APs, distributed in 178
countries; the vast majority are located in China where WiFiManager's major users
come from. To further confirm the validity of our dataset, with the WiFiManager
team, we carry out a field survey of 100 randomly selected public APs that are
determined to be malicious by WiSC. We choose public APs given that they can
be easily located (using the location data provided by users), accessed, and tested.
Also, we ensure that all the concerned attacks are included in this survey. Field
results show that all the sampled APs indeed manifest malicious behaviors upon
close examinations, indicating that our dataset is able to provide a valid basis for
our analyses.

8.3 Measurement Results

Among all the 19M APs examined by WiSC, we record 445 AP brands, 2660 AP models, and ~750,000 APs bearing WiFi attacks, corresponding to ~1,413,000 attack event traces. To our knowledge, this is so far the largest study regarding WiFi APs and related security events in the wild. By analyzing this, we have multifold findings on WiFi threats as follows.

8.3.1 Prevalence of WiFi Attacks

Previous reports with small-scale measurements suggest that WiFi attacks occur to only 0.21%–1.5% of their examined WiFi APs [7, 8]. Unfortunately, our large-scale, in-the-wild measurement refutes this, revealing that WiFi attacks have been detected on at least 3.92% of all the 19M APs. Worse still, as our detection scheme cannot cover every possible form of attack such as signal monitoring and deauth [26, 27] occurring at the PHY or MAC layer, the prevalence (~4%) in fact only represents a *lower bound* of the reality, indicating a pressing demand for the community's attention today.

In detail, we wonder whether the AP brand impacts the prevalence of attacks, since different AP manufacturers may have distinct security considerations. We plot the top 10 AP brands in Figs. 8.10 and 8.11 in terms of the number of examined and malicious APs, respectively. Among all malicious APs, top 10 brands account for 98.48%. Most notably, nearly half (49%) of them belong to a single brand—Phicomm, whose market share is merely 4.3%. Such a highly skewed distribution can be ascribed to Phicomm APs' specific security vulnerabilities, since we notice that online reports or discussions around Phicomm APs' vulnerabilities are much more common than those of others [28, 29]. Although public vulnerability disclosures can help improve the security of the products, we have not seen

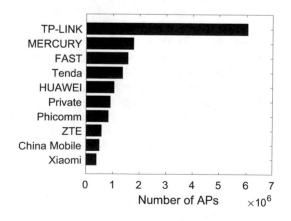

Fig. 8.10 Top 10 WiFi AP brands ordered by the number of examined APs (Reprinted with permission from [13])

Fig. 8.11 Top 10 AP brands ordered by the number of malicious APs detected (Reprinted with permission from [13])

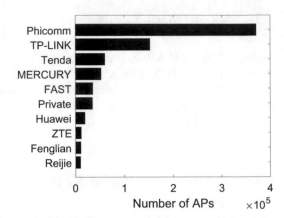

Table 8.2 Top 15 countries ordered by the number of examined WiFi APs

Country	Number of APs	Prevalence	Major attack technique
China	19,119,764	3.92%	TCP hijacking (57.6%)
Burma	7148	4.48%	TCP hijacking (53.1%)
Vietnam	4288	1.8%	DHCP spoofing (40.2%)
Russia	3169	8.93%	DNS hijacking (43.8%)
South Korea	2701	2.07%	ARP spoofing (91.1%)
Cambodia	2213	2.17%	ARP spoofing (47.9%)
Laos	1530	1.05%	DHCP spoofing (43.7%)
Thailand	1350	4.15%	DNS hijacking (53.5%)
Malaysia	1317	2.89%	DNS hijacking (44.7%)
Japan	1315	2.59%	ARP spoofing (67.6%)
Singapore	1133	1.5%	ARP spoofing (50%)
Philippines	840	2.86%	DNS hijacking (45.8%)
Indonesia	796	22.36%	TCP hijacking (91%)
United States	608	1.01%	ARP spoofing (66.6%)
Pakistan	523	1.53%	ARP Spoofing (62.5%)

(Reprinted with permission from [13])

Phicomm act effectively in response. Thus, before the patches for these public vulnerabilities are developed and applied, it would be beneficial for the concerned APs to deploy short-term mitigation strategies such as the novel *MAC address randomization* technique that can help hide vulnerable APs' device fingerprints.

For geographical distribution, we list in Table 8.2 the top 15 countries with the largest number of examined APs among all the involved 178 countries. As shown, some countries like Burma, Russia, and Thailand exhibit even higher prevalence (>4%) of WiFi attacks than China. We note that our results may not be applicable to some of the countries due to limited data scale and the lack of similarity between their manifested behaviors and those of China. However, for countries exhibiting a similar WiFi threat landscape as in China (in terms of prevalence, major types of attacks, and essential behaviors), such as Burma, we propose that our results may be valuable for them as well. Furthermore, by analyzing the geographical distribution of the detected WiFi attacks in China, we confirm that WiFi attacks pervasively exist in almost all areas across the country, without being confined to specific areas or ISPs. Also, the density of attacks is basically proportional to the population density.

8.3.2 WiFi-Based Attack Techniques

The WiFi-based attack techniques used in the wild are found to be heterogeneous and somewhat unexpected. The ratios of the four attack techniques WiSC can detect are TCP hijacking (57%), DNS hijacking (17%), ARP spoofing (16%), and DHCP spoofing (12%). Multiple attack techniques can happen to one AP, so their percentages add up to more than 100%. Although the techniques themselves have all been studied in prior work [25, 30–32], we have several findings that are unknown or significantly different.

First, TCP hijacking accounts for over a half of the detected attacks. This can be attributed to TCP's dominating use today for Internet applications and the attackers' strong capability in undermining TCP connections or even encryptions. In principle, the increasingly wide deployment of HTTPS across the globe should be able to provide protection against TCP hijacking. However, our results clearly indicate that such attacks are still rampant.

To deeply understand the situation, we measure the HTTPS adoption in the wild and reveal a staggering lack of *effective* HTTPS deployment in many countries. Figure 8.12 shows the case of top 100 and top 10,000 websites in China and the USA according to Alexa Traffic Ranking. Although HTTPS is widely *supported* in both countries, quite a few websites do not use HTTPS as default. Besides, more websites (60% in China and 36% in the USA for the top 100 websites) do not enable HSTS (HTTP Strict Transport Security), leaving themselves vulnerable to HTTPS downgrade attacks such as SSLStrip.

Worse still, even for those websites who have enabled HSTS, we notice that the vast majority of them (92.5% in China and 78.1% in the USA for the top 100 websites) fail to properly configure HSTS parameters (e.g., timeout threshold and preload list), rendering HSTS ineffective in practice. For example, TMall, a major online shopping platform in China, configures its HSTS timeout threshold as zero, resulting in an immediate expiration of HSTS upon accesses, thereby letting HSTS be completely bypassed.

In terms of LAN attacks, recall that WiFiManager helps user devices examine their connectivity (LAN connectivity) with APs. Specifically, it measures the con-

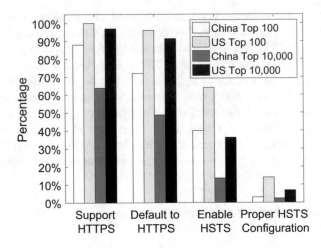

Fig. 8.12 Status quo of top websites' HTTPS/HSTS adoption in China and the USA (Reprinted with permission from [13])

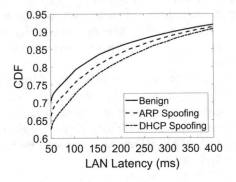

Fig. 8.13 Connectivity for benign APs and APs under spoofing attacks (Reprinted with permission from [13])

nection latency on a user device by periodically pinging the gateway. Figures 8.13 and 8.14 depict the distributions of connectivity for benign APs and the APs under different attacks. As shown in Fig. 8.13, both spoofing attacks are more detected on the APs with poorer LAN connectivity, because they can succeed more easily under worse LAN environments, which allow spoofed responses to reach user devices faster than the legitimate ones. Interestingly, Fig. 8.14 makes an opposite observation: DNS and TCP hijacking attacks are more likely to occur on good network conditions. We will elaborate this in Sect. 8.3.3.

In previous studies, DHCP spoofing was mostly a hypothetical attack under WiFi networks, since all DHCP Discovery messages must be first sent to and then broadcast by the AP. Thus, the AP should be able to respond to such messages more quickly than adversaries [11, 12], rendering any spoofed DHCP Offer messages invalid. However, our observation refutes this by revealing that DHCP spoofing is as

Fig. 8.14 Connectivity for
benign APs and APs under
hijacking attacks (Reprinted
with permission from [13])

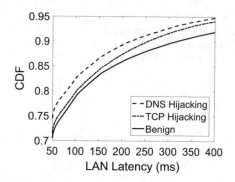

feasible as other popular techniques in practice. We suspect that the attackers adopt
some extreme strategies, such as flooding DHCP Offer messages, to practically
increase the success rate. Such strategies can be especially effective when the LAN
connectivity is poor.

To sum up, the root cause of ARP/DHCP spoofings lies in the AP's uncon-
ditionally forwarding all the broadcasts within the LAN, which conforms to the
design of Ethernet for historical reasons, and can thoroughly address them by
performing packet checking or encryption at the AP, e.g., through *S-ARP* [33] and
DHCP snooping [31]. However, they can also incur non-trivial storage/computation
overhead since they rely on recording all DHCP traffic or asymmetric cryptography,
which may incur additional attack surfaces and are impractical for residential APs
with low-cost hardware.

An alternative may be *MAC-forced forwarding* [34] that enables an AP to
recognize ARP/DHCP messages within the LAN and selectively forward them
instead of simply broadcasting them all. In fact, this technique has been deployed
in some public places (e.g., metro stations) to defend against spoofing [35]. In our
data, we find that 3208 APs are using this technique, and the MAC addresses for all
the connected user devices within the LAN obtained by ARP requests are exactly
the gateway's MAC address, indicating that all ARP traffic within the LAN has been
explicitly directed to and managed by the AP (gateway). It is encouraging to see that
no spoofing attack was detected on any of these 3208 APs.

8.3.3 Malicious Behaviors and Objectives

Our measurement collects 1.4M attack event traces, including both transport-
and application-layer responses for detailed analysis. We make several interesting
observations regarding the "semantics" of such attacks.

- First, we analyze the collected web pages, and notice that 55% of the attack
  events involve web pages being injected with advertisements (ad injection)
  mainly through TCP hijacking.

Fig. 8.15 Physical
movement of benign APs and
malicious APs (Reprinted
with permission from [13])

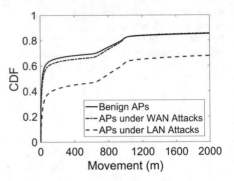

- Second, 26% are typical DoS and passive traffic monitoring through ARP/DHCP spoofing, where attackers manage to trick user devices into recognizing their devices as the network gateway, thereby dropping packets or peeping at users' network traces.
- Third, we observe DNS hijacking where users' DNS queries receive false resolution results, leading to potential phishing attacks, i.e., redirection to malicious websites elaborately disguised as the originally requested ones.
- Fourth, HTTPS-targeted attacks such as SSLStrip are also identified, where HTTPS links have been surreptitiously replaced with HTTP links to compromise users' encryption.

The last two account for <8% of all attacks, which is much smaller than the percentages reported in prior studies [36, 37].

Delving deep, as shown in Fig. 8.15, we notice that APs under LAN attacks exhibit much longer physical movements (median of 724 m, average of 47.3 km) than APs under WAN attacks and benign APs (median of 31 m and 21 m, average of 20.4 km and 20.5 km, respectively). Here the average is much larger than the median due to the existence of mobile APs such as smartphone-based hotspots, and small movements (<50 m) are mostly due to user-side localization errors. We attribute this phenomenon to our observation that ARP/DHCP spoofing attacks are more likely to succeed under poor LAN environments (see Fig. 8.13), which can be more easily noticed by network administrators and then get fixed, compared to the finer networks of WAN-based attacks. Thus, attackers need to strategically relocate (similar events have been noticed in other attacks [38]) to better success and evade detection. Notably, we find that 10% of the APs under LAN attacks even manifest a clear pattern of shifting around several locations, forming one or multiple loops.

Next, we go deeper into the most detected events—ad injections, and make several intriguing findings. We discover that the injected ads are not deliberately hidden through techniques like impression fraud [39], although in this way adversaries can better cover themselves up to avoid being directly captured by users. This is probably because advertisers require ads to be explicitly displayed for achieving real advertising effect. This suggests that there might exist an ecosystem behind

Fig. 8.16 Internet
connectivity for APs with
strong and weak/no
encryption (Reprinted with
permission from [13])

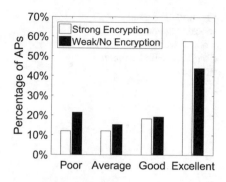

these widespread AP-based ad injection activities, thus motivating us to dig deeper in the next section.

More surprisingly, ad injection is detected on 2.33% of the APs using strong encryption (WPA/WPA2) while on 1% of the APs using no or weak encryption (WEP). Our investigation sheds light on this counter-intuitive observation. WiFi-Manager measures the Internet connectivity of an AP when checking its LAN connectivity (Sect. 8.3.2). The result falls into four categories: *Excellent, Good, Average, and Poor*, representing that in monthly examinations, >90%, 70%~90%, 50%~70%, and <50% connections can be established, respectively. Figure 8.16 shows that better protected APs tend to have better Internet connectivity, thereby providing a better network environment for performing ad injection. The above results probably indicate that solely relying on strong link-layer cryptography may be ineffective against complex real-world threats, whose mitigation requires a cross-layer approach spanning multiple dimensions including encryption, authentication, protocol verification, and human factor, to name a few. For example, mitigating the ad injection attack requires the synergy from secure app-layer protocol (e.g., HTTPS) and robust authentication (e.g., dynamic authentication offered by 802.1X [40]).

8.3.4   Fundamental Motives Behind the Attacks

According to our results, ad injection currently accounts for the largest portion of the detected attacks events and thus has the broadest impact on end users. Also, user devices being injected with ads can fall victim of various kinds of frauds and abuses, leading to possible severe outcomes. Therefore, in this section, we leverage our in-situ attack event traces to understand the fundamental motives behind the AP-based ad injections. By analyzing the injection code, we first observe that adversaries adopt various techniques to evade common security checks, such as domain altering that constantly changes ads' domains to prevent security or ad-blocking software from recognizing them, and code obfuscation to hide the attack logic. Clearly, the

Fig. 8.17 Frequency of
attackers injecting ads to
victims' web pages
(Reprinted with permission
from [13])

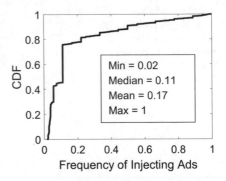

attackers are trying hard to conceal their malicious activities while profiting by
(visible) ad impression.

Meanwhile, we find that a malicious AP only probabilistically injects ads instead
of compromising all intercepted web pages. As shown in Fig. 8.17, for 77% of
the malicious APs, the ad injection probabilities are below the average, 17%. We
believe that qualitatively, this is because excessive ad injection can be easily noticed
by users, henceforth incurring AP reset, firmware upgrade, or even disconnection,
causing the attacker to lose the comprised AP. Nevertheless, we are more interested
in the quantitative explanation: how do attackers choose the injection probability
(frequency) we observe? Is it the result of a mature market's selection or simply the
aggregation of random standalone cases? These are essential to further decoding the
WiFi attack ecosystem (if it exists).

To answer the above questions, we analytically model the economy behind
ad injection attacks. Instead of assuming a fixed number of malicious APs, we
notice that more realistically, malicious APs are only under adversaries' control
for a period of time, before they gradually *recover* to the benign state—a dynamic
process. Intuitively, malicious APs' recovery can be attributed to users' intentional
defense actions triggered by relatively high ad injection probabilities. Moreover, the
APs can also recover through users' unintentional actions, e.g., AP reset or firmware
upgrade. We expect these two factors to independently influence APs' recovery.

To obtain the percentage of APs recovered through unintentional actions (when
ad injection probability is low), we choose to inspect the 35,782 APs that experience
the lowest ad injection probability (0.02) during our measurement to exclude the
influence of high-probability ad injections arousing users' vigilance. We track their
recovery process for 14 weeks and plot the percentage of recovered APs ($\mathbb{P}_F$) for
each week (t) in Fig. 8.18. As an AP's recovery is an independent and random event,
we fit the measurement data using exponential distribution [41]:

$$\mathbb{P}_F(t) = 1 - e^{-0.054t}. \tag{8.4}$$

We find that the *coefficient of determination* (R^2) [42] is as high as 0.89, suggesting
that $\mathbb{P}_F(t)$ can well fit our data.

Fig. 8.18 Percentage of APs
that recover through
reset/upgrade for each week
and our fitting curve
(Reprinted with permission
from [13])

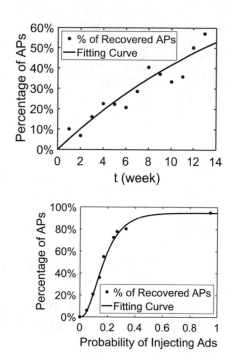

Fig. 8.19 Percentage of
recovered APs influenced by
ad injection probabilities and
our fitting curve (Reprinted
with permission from [13])

Recall that for all recovered APs, we divide them into two parts: (1) the APs recovered due to intentional defense actions and (2) the APs recovered through unintentional actions. Since we know the number of all recovered APs (Parts I and II) for each week, we can estimate the size of Part I by first approximating the size of Part II with Eq. (8.4) and then removing it from the total size. Next, we calculate the average ad injection probability for each week. Figure 8.19 then plots the percentage of recovered APs ($\mathbb{P}_L$) due to intentional defense actions for different ad injection probabilities, which exhibits the curve of an S-function [43]. Among common S-functions, we find that the Bertalanffy function [44] can best fit our data with R^2 being 0.99:

$$\mathbb{P}_L(P_{ad}) = 0.95 * (1 - 1.99e^{-10.12P_{ad}-0.67})^3, \qquad (8.5)$$

for an injection probability P_{ad}. We therefore have the probability for an AP's remaining malicious ($\mathbb{P}_m$) at time t:

$$\mathbb{P}_m(P_{ad}, t) = (1 - \mathbb{P}_L(P_{ad}))(1 - \mathbb{P}_F(t)). \qquad (8.6)$$

Suppose there are a total number of M APs, each AP is injected with an average of N ads, and each ad brings a unit profit of $Profit_{unit}$; then the adversaries' profit

Fig. 8.20 Our inferred profit model that shows how the profit varies for different ad injection probabilities (Reprinted with permission from [13])

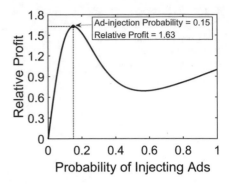

would be

$$Profit(P_{ad}) = \sum_{t=0}^{\infty} M * N * Profit_{unit} * P_{ad} * \mathbb{P}_m(P_{ad}, t) \qquad (8.7)$$

for injection probability P_{ad}. Although the exact values of M, N, and $Profit_{unit}$ are unknown, we can know how $Profit(P_{ad})$ varies relative to $Profit(P_{ad} = 1)$ for different P_{ad} values as

$$Profit_{relative}(P_{ad}) = \frac{Profit(P_{ad})}{Profit(1)} = \frac{P_{ad}(1 - \mathbb{P}_L(P_{ad}))}{1 - \mathbb{P}_L(1)}. \qquad (8.8)$$

We plot $Profit_{relative}(P_{ad})$ for different P_{ad} values in Fig. 8.20 to showcase how different ad injection probabilities impact adversaries' profit. As shown, the maximum profit appears at $P_{ad} = 15\%$, which matches real-world adversaries' choices (averaging at 17%). With this finding, we suspect that most adversaries have carefully tuned their behaviors to achieve maximum profit in the long run.

In summary, we notice that most adversaries carry out ad injection attacks in a rather mature manner through rate throttling, which can not only prevent users from easily noticing them but also maximize their profits. The high consistency between our analytical results and attackers' real-world practices suggests *these attackers are both judicious and rational, revealing a rather mature ecosystem*, which we discuss next.

8.4 Undermining the Attack Ecosystem

In this section, we first describe how we figure out the underground WiFi attack ecosystem. Then, we present the interplay among the various players in the ecosystem. Next, we show how we discover its Achilles' heel that enables our subsequent proactive counterstriking.

8.4.1   Uncovering the Underground Ecosystem

Our analysis in Sect. 8.3.4 implies that an immense, mature ecosystem probably exists behind WiFi attacks. As shown in Fig. 8.21, to fully understand it, we closely examine adversaries' code that is inserted into the web page as external JavaScript resources. We notice that in >99% of the recorded ad injection attacks, the injection code consists of two separate JavaScript files: one serves to inject ads and the other contains code that is inserted through a JavaScript resource link from legitimate domains, most notably hm.baidu.com. Tracing this lead, we find out that this domain name belongs to a web analytics platform named Baidu Analytics. By cross-referencing the code with Baidu Analytics' official documents, we know that the code records various statistics of the advertising effect such as the *click-through rate* and reports them to the web analytics platform. In total, we discover only four such web analytics platforms: Baidu Analytics, UMeng, OeeBee, and 360zlzq.

These platforms provide traffic and user behavior analysis for a registered link/website to help developers better assess the "effectiveness" of their websites, which in our case is the effectiveness of the injected advertising pages. The piece of code we discover is written as the user end of their statistics collection infrastructure, which monitors and records web traffic on the advertising pages and uploads corresponding data to web analytics platforms to generate an analytical report. This is a most intriguing finding that quickly leads us to the primary question: *why do adversaries require such services of web analytics if they simply compromise APs and inject ads for themselves?* Considering the function of these web analytics services, their presence hints that the attackers might be interacting with another entity of the ecosystem.

Leveraging this finding, we can now infer the panorama of the WiFi attack ecosystem, where adversaries are not advertisers that produce and distribute ads for marketing purposes. In fact, they mainly act as a proxy that is only responsible

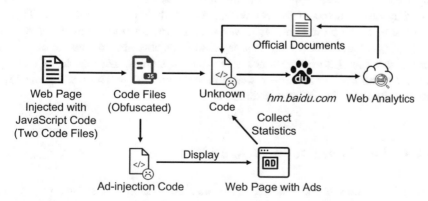

Fig. 8.21 Procedure of uncovering web analytics platforms in the underground ecosystem of WiFi attacks (Reprinted with permission from [13])

for delivering ads to end users for other advertisers. In online advertising, such a role is termed as the *ad-serving platform* [45]. This is the reason why participation of web analytics platforms is required—to provide independent evaluation for the actual advertising effect of the ad-serving platforms. We next detail the interplay among advertisers, adversaries/ad-serving platforms, and web analytics platforms to present how the ecosystem operates, as well as a weak link within.

8.4.2 Interplay and Weakness

Figure 8.1 (early in Sect. 8.1) depicts the interplay within the WiFi attack ecosystem. First, advertisers hire ad-serving platforms (adversaries) to help distribute ads to end users. Then via malicious APs, ads and statistics collection code are injected into users' requested web pages. The ads are later displayed to end users. Meanwhile, the statistics collection code tracks users' interactions with injected ads and uploads collected statistics to web analytics platforms. At the monetization stage, adversaries use ad analytics signed by web analytics platforms as a proof to receive payment from advertisers.

In detail, we extract the resource links of ad injection code from the HTML files of logged web pages and classify them according to the resource links' domain names or IP addresses. As a result, we identify a total number of 25 ad-serving platforms. In addition, we have observed transnational activities of several adversaries. For example, 5myr.cn's activities involve 8 countries, the largest in our data. Also, a major adversary t.7gg.cc (which accounts for 36% of all ads) has been detected in 6 countries across 3 continents.

Furthermore, we notice that two largest among the four analytics platforms, Baidu Analytics and UMeng, are third-party authoritative services that take 87% of the market share and participate in distributing 80.8% of the ads. The massive participation of these major legitimate services is surprising, though we believe that they are involved in the ecosystem due to their public credibility. That is, adversaries might be required by advertisers to provide *credible* evidence of their advertising effect to decide the final payment. This phenomenon, on the other side, reveals Achilles' heel of the attack ecosystem: *it heavily relies on legitimate web analytics platforms for the most essential monetization stage.* This provides a unique opportunity for active defense (detailed next).

8.4.3 Real-World Active Defense Practices

Given that the ecosystem mainly relies on only four web analytics platforms, we take an active defense approach by contacting them and providing our detailed findings regarding their supported adversaries (ad-serving platforms) in August 2019. As of August 2020, we observe that Baidu Analytics stopped serving 67% of the reported

Table 8.3 Attackers that stop serving ads after our action

Adversary	Percentage of all Ads	Entity we report to
t.7gg.cc	35.8%	Baidu analytics
5myr.cn	8.9%	OeeBee
agtsjb.com	8.7%	UMeng/Adblock Plus
103.49.209.27	1.2%	360zlzq/Adblock Plus
withad.com	0.4%	UMeng/Adblock Plus
zfkmw.com	0.3%	UMeng/Adblock Plus
js.union-wifi.com	0.06%	360zlzq/Adblock Plus
172.81.246.180	0.05%	360zlzq/Adblock Plus

(Reprinted with permission from [13])

links, resulting in 49.8% decrease of ad injections. For UMeng, we have managed to establish communications with their teams, who have promised to take actions toward the reported ad links in the near future. Shortly after our complaint, OeeBee seems to be shut down according to its website.

While waiting for responses from 360zlzq, we report our identified illegal ad campaigns to mainstream ad blockers and observe real-world effects as well. For example, a major adversary agtsjb.com, which accounts for 8.7% of all the ads, has been included in the blacklist of Adblock Plus, a popular browser plugin for ad blocking. Later, we find that the related ads have all become inaccessible. Table 8.3 lists major adversaries that have completely stopped serving their ads (i.e., unable to access them) after our actions.

These efforts mark the first success of active defenses against WiFi attacks by breaking the critical chain of monetization. We realize though that fully defeating the massive, well-organized ecosystem requires joint efforts from other entities like browsers, ad blocks, and OSes. We are actively pursuing this research direction.

8.5 Conclusion

In this work, we carry out a nationwide measurement study of WiFi security. We develop a lightweight WiFi threat detection system called WiSC that takes advantage of both active probing and complementary cross-layer information. We then deploy WiSC in the wild to examine 19M WiFi APs connected by 14M real-world users. With the crowdsourced data, we perform a comprehensive analysis on state-of-the-art WiFi attacks, the adversaries' profit-driven motives, and the interactions among multiple entities in the WiFi attack ecosystem. We also discover the critical role played by major web analytics platforms on monetizing the adversaries and leverage it to effectively combat the preponderant ad injection attacks at the national scale.

References

1. Hetting C. New numbers: Wi-Fi share of US mobile data traffic lingers at around 75% in Q2. https://wifinowevents.com/news-and-blog/new-numbers-wi-fi-share-of-us-mobile-traffic-lingers-at-around-75/
2. HACKERNOON. A hacker intercepted your WiFi traffic, stole your contacts, passwords, & financial data. https://hackernoon.com/a-hacker-intercepted-your-wifi-traffic-stole-your-contacts-passwords-financial-data-heres-how-4fc0df9ff152
3. Cimpanu C. Hacker group has been hijacking DNS traffic on D-link routers for three months. https://www.zdnet.com/article/hacker-group-has-been-hijacking-dns-traffic-on-d-link-routers-for-three-months
4. Miley J. Starbucks' free WiFi hijacked computers of customers to mine cryptocurrency. https://interestingengineering.com/starbucks-free-wifi-hijacked-computers-of-customers-to-mine-cryptocurrency
5. Group LNR. Arpwatch, the ethernet monitor program; for keeping track of ethernet/IP address pairings. https://ee.lbl.gov/
6. Ramachandran V, Nandi S (2005) Detecting ARP spoofing: an active technique. In: Proceedings of ICISS, pp 239–250
7. Shijia O. Security report of China public WiFi in 2017. http://www.chinadaily.com.cn/business/tech/2017-03/08/content_28474488.htm
8. Security T. 2018 mobile security report by tencent mobile security lab (in Chinese). https://m.qq.com/security_lab/news_detail_471.html
9. Greenberg A. Researchers found they could hack entire wind farms. https://www.wired.com/story/wind-turbine-hack/
10. Torralba C. Student admitted to ARP spoofing his school network through android device. https://www.androidauthority.com/student-admitted-to-arp-spoofing-his-school-network-through-android-device-49129/
11. Whitewinterwolf.com. DHCP exploitation guide. https://www.whitewinterwolf.com/posts/2017/10/30/dhcp-exploitation-guide/
12. Pritchett WL, De Smet D (2013) Kali Linux cookbook. Packt Publishing
13. Gao D, Lin H, Li Z, Qian F, Chen QA, Qian Z, Liu W, Gong L, Liu Y (2021) A nationwide census on WiFi security threats: prevalence, riskiness, and the economics. In: Proceedings of ACM MobiCom, pp 242–255
14. Plummer DC et al. (1982) An ethernet address resolution protocol: or converting network protocol addresses to 48.bit ethernet address for transmission on ethernet hardware. RFC 826:1–10
15. Stallings W, Brown L, Bauer MD, Bhattacharjee AK (2012) Computer security: principles and practice. Pearson Education, Upper Saddle River
16. Salgueiro P, Diaz D et al. (2011) Using constraints for intrusion detection: the NeMODe system. In: Proceedings of PADL, pp 115–129
17. Group IW et al. (2016) IEEE standard for wireless LAN medium access control (MAC) and physical layer (PHY) specifications. IEEE Std 802.11-2016 (Revision of IEEE Std 802.11-2012) 802(11):1–3534
18. Wustrow, E., et al.: Telex: Anticensorship in the network infrastructure. In: Proceedings of USENIX security, p 45
19. Houmansadr A, Nguyen GT, Caesar M, Borisov N (2011) Cirripede: circumvention infrastructure using router redirection with plausible deniability. In: Proceedings of ACM CCS, pp 187–200
20. IANA Special-use IPv4 addresses, RFC3330. Tech. rep. (2002)
21. Bouch A, Kuchinsky A, Bhatti N (2000) Quality is in the eye of the beholder: meeting users' requirements for internet quality of service. In: Proceedings of ACM CHI, pp 297–304
22. Shneiderman B (1984) Response time and display rate in human performance with computers. ACM Comput Surv 16(3):265–285

23. Padmanabhan R, Owen P, Schulman A, Spring N (2015) Timeouts: beware surprisingly high delay. In: Proceedings of ACM IMC, pp 303–316
24. Korhonen J, Wang Y (2005) Effect of packet size on loss rate and delay in wireless links. In: Proceedings of IEEE WCNC, pp 1608–1613
25. Liu B, Lu C, Duan H, Liu Y, Li Z, Hao S, Yang M (2018) Who is answering my queries: understanding and characterizing interception of the DNS resolution path. In: Proceedings of USENIX security, pp 1113–1128
26. Maxim M, Pollino D (2002) Wireless security. McGraw-Hill/Osborne
27. Bellardo J, Savage S (2003) 802.11 denial-of-service attacks: real vulnerabilities and practical solutions. In: Proceedings of USENIX security, pp 2–2
28. Report C. Phicomm: security vulnerabilities. https://www.cvedetails.com/vulnerability-list/vendor_id-16810/Phicomm.html
29. Report C. Vulnerability of phicomm hotspots: CVE-2019-19117. https://cxsecurity.com/cveshow/CVE-2019-19117/
30. Conti M, Dragoni N, Lesyk V (2016) A survey of man in the middle attacks. IEEE Commun Surv Tutorials 18(3):2027–2051
31. Abad CL, Bonilla RI (2007) An analysis on the schemes for detecting and preventing ARP cache poisoning attacks. In: Proceedings of IEEE ICDCS, pp 60–60
32. Singh A et al. (2008) Vulnerability analysis for DNS and DHCP. In: Vulnerability analysis and defense for the internet, pp 111–124
33. Bruschi D, Ornaghi A, Rosti E (2003) S-ARP: a secure address resolution protocol. In: Proceedings of IEEE ACSAC, pp 66–74
34. Melsen T, Blake S (2006) MAC-forced forwarding: a method for subscriber separation on an ethernet access network. Tech. rep., RFC 4562
35. Wifi8.com. Selective broadcasting in metro station. http://www.wifi8.com/
36. Han H, Sheng B, Tan CC, Li Q, Lu S (2011) A timing-based scheme for rogue AP detection. IEEE Trans Parallel Distrib Syst 22(11):1912–1925
37. Fahl S et al. (2012) Why eve and Mallory love android: an analysis of android SSL (in)security. In: Proceedings of ACM CCS, pp 50–61
38. Li Z, Wang W, Wilson C, Chen J, Qian C, Jung T, Zhang L, Liu K, Li X, Liu Y (2017) FBS-radar: uncovering fake base stations at scale in the wild. In: Proceedings of NDSS
39. Springborn K, Barford P (2013) Impression fraud in on-line advertising via pay-per-view networks. In: Proceedings of USENIX security, pp 211–226
40. Congdon P, Aboba B, Smith A, Zorn G, Roese J (2003) IEEE 802.1X remote authentication dial in user service (RADIUS) usage guidelines. RFC 3580:1–30
41. Balakrishnan K (2018) Exponential distribution: theory, methods and applications. Routledge
42. Nagelkerke NJ et al. (1991) A note on a general definition of the coefficient of determination. Biometrika 78(3):691–692
43. Dmitry K, Roland D (2011) Application of S-shaped curves. Proc Eng 9:559–572
44. Von Bertalanffy L (1968) General system theory. New York 41973(1968):40
45. Goldfarb A, Tucker C (2011) Online display advertising: targeting and obtrusiveness. INFORMS Market Sci 30(3):389–404

Chapter 9
Understanding IoT Security with HoneyCloud

Abstract With the wide adoption, Linux-based IoT devices have emerged as one primary target of today's cyber-attacks. Traditional malware-based attacks can quickly spread across these devices, but they are well-understood threats with effective defense techniques such as malware fingerprinting and community-based fingerprint sharing. Recently, *fileless attacks*—attacks that do not rely on malware files—have been increasing on Linux-based IoT devices and posing significant threats to the security and privacy of IoT systems. Little has been known in terms of their characteristics and attack vectors, which hinders research and development efforts to defend against them. In this chapter, we present our endeavor in understanding fileless attacks on Linux-based IoT devices in the wild. Over a span of twelve months, we deploy 4 hardware IoT honeypots and 108 specially designed software IoT honeypots and successfully attract a wide variety of real-world IoT attacks. We present our measurement study on these attacks, with a focus on fileless attacks, including the prevalence, exploits, environments, and impacts. Our study further leads to multifold insights toward actionable defense strategies that can be adopted by IoT vendors and end users.

Keywords IoT security · Honeypot · Public cloud

9.1 Introduction

Internet of Things (IoT) has quickly gained popularity across a wide range of areas like industrial sensing and control [1], home automation [2], etc. In particular, the majority of today's IoT devices have employed Linux (e.g., OpenWrt and Raspbian) for its prevalence and programmability, and such a trend has been growing continuously [3]; meanwhile, the number of cyber-attacks against Linux-based IoT devices is also increasing rapidly [4]. In this work, we, therefore, focus on Linux-based IoT devices and the attacks targeting them. The Linux-based IoT attacks generally fall into two categories: *malware-based attacks* and *fileless attacks*.

Threats from malware-based attacks (e.g., Mirai, PNScan, and Mayday) have been widely known in IoT networks. For example, global websites like GitHub and

Twitter became inaccessible for hours in October 2016, since their DNS provider, Dyn, was under DDoS attack by Mirai, which infected over 1.2 million (= 1.2M) IoT devices [5]. These incidents raised high awareness of malware-based attacks on IoT systems; throughout the past few years, their characteristics have been extensively studied and effective defense solutions have been developed. For instance, the hash (e.g., MD5 or SHA-n) of a malware's binary file can be computed to fingerprint these IoT malware, and such fingerprints are then shared with the community, e.g., through VirusTotal. For a malware that has not been fingerprinted, static and dynamic analysis can be applied to determine their malice [6].

Fileless attacks (also known as non-malware attacks or zero-footprint attacks) on IoT devices differ from malware-based attacks in that they do not need to download and execute malware files to infect the victim IoT devices; instead, they take advantage of existing vulnerabilities on the victim devices. In the past few years, increasingly more fileless attacks have been reported [7, 8], e.g., McAfee Labs reports that fileless attacks surged by 432% over 2017 [9]. Traditional servers and PCs defend against fileless attacks using sophisticated firewalls and antivirus tools [10]; however, these solutions are not suitable for the vast majority of IoT devices due to the limited computing and storage resources. As a result, fileless attacks pose significant threats to the IoT ecosystem, given that IoT devices are often deployed in private and sensitive environments, such as private residences and healthcare centers. At the moment, there is limited visibility into their characteristics and attack vectors, which hinders research and development efforts to innovate new defense to combat fileless attacks.

Study Methodology To understand Linux-based IoT attacks in the wild, we use *honeypots* [11], which are known to be an effective method for capturing unknown network attacks. We, therefore, first set up several common Linux-based IoT devices in different places as hardware honeypots. Each honeypot is coupled with a Remote Control Power Adapter which can reset the honeypot when it is compromised. These offer us valuable insights into the specialties of IoT attacks. However, we notice that this first endeavor incurs unaffordable infrastructure and maintenance costs when deployed at scale. We, therefore, attempt to explore a *cheap* and *scalable* approach to effectively capture and analyze real-world IoT attacks.

Intuitively, such an attempt can be empowered by public clouds spread across the world. This seems to be a possible host for our quickly deploying numerous software honeypots. Nevertheless, this approach is subject to several practical issues. *First,* the honeypots should behave similarly to actual IoT devices, so as not to miss the relatively rare fileless attacks. *Second,* they should expose in-depth information of the interaction processes, to facilitate our characterizing the usually hard-to-track fileless attacks. *Finally,* they have to conform with diverse policies imposed by different cloud providers, so that one cloud's limitations would not essentially influence the coverage of our study results. To this end, we heavily customize the design of software honeypots by leveraging the insights collected from hardware honeypots, such as kernel information masking, encrypted command disclosure, and data-flow symmetry monitoring. We carefully select eight public clouds to disperse

108 abovementioned software honeypots, and the system is called HoneyCloud. These software honeypots employ OpenWrt, which is one of the most popular Linux distributions for IoT devices [3] and also suitable for customization.

Compared to a hardware honeypot as we show in Sect. 9.2.2, a software honeypot attracts 37% fewer suspicious connections and 39% fewer attacks on average. On the other hand, the average monthly maintenance fee of a software honeypot (∼6 US dollars) is 12.5× less than that of a hardware honeypot (∼75 US dollars). More importantly, all the types of attacks captured by our hardware honeypots have also been captured by HoneyCloud (but not vice versa). This shows the effectiveness of our design in practice.

Findings and Implications During one year's measurement (06/15/2017–06/14/2018), we observed 264M suspicious connections to our honeypots, of which 28M successfully logged in and enabled attacks.[1] Among these successful attacks, 1.5M are identified as fileless attacks,[2] by investigating which we acquire the following key insights:

- **We introduce the first taxonomy for fileless IoT attacks by correlating multi-source information.** For lack of malware files and fingerprints, it is not an easy task to identify and classify fileless attacks: by comprehensively correlating the disclosed shell commands, monitored filesystem change, recorded data-flow traffic, and third parties' online reports, we identify the numerous fileless attacks and empirically classify them into eight different types in terms of behaviors and intents (Sect. 9.3.3). To our knowledge, this is the first taxonomy for fileless attacks in the IoT area.
- **Fileless attacks aggravate the threats to IoT devices by introducing stealthy reconnaissance methods and unique types of IoT attacks**. On the one side, we notice that 39.4% of the captured fileless attacks are collecting system information or performing de-immunization operations (e.g., shut down the firewall and kill the watchdog) in order to allow more targeted and efficient follow-up attacks. We suspect this is because fileless attacks are harder to fingerprint and thus are highly suitable for stealthy attack reconnaissance or preparations. On the other side, we find that fileless attacks can also be powerful attack vectors on their own while maintaining high stealthiness. Specifically, we capture a fileless attack in the wild that launched a targeted DDoS attack. The attack neither modifies the filesystem nor executes any shell commands but can manipulate a swarm of IoT devices and make the attacker(s) invisible to victims. Since the only indication of such an attack is anomalous patterns of

---

[1] The rest of connections (i.e., 89.4% of the observed suspicious connections) cannot intrude into our honeypots, since they failed to crack the passwords of our honeypots.

[2] Different from previous studies on IoT attacks where fileless attacks were scarcely reported, our honeypots captured substantially more fileless attacks with diverse features. Also, we find that a root cause lies in the weak authentication issue of today's IoT devices, which makes it unprecedentedly easy for attackers to obtain remote control and then perform malicious actions without using malware.

outbound network traffic, it is highly challenging for existing host-based defense mechanisms to detect it effectively.

- **IoT attacks in the wild are using various types of information to determine device authenticity**. According to our measurements on hardware honeypots, 9132 attacks executed commands like `lscpu` to acquire sensitive system information. In addition, with HoneyCloud, we find an average of 6.7% fewer attacks captured by a honeypot hosted on AWS than one hosted on other public clouds, probably because AWS has disclosed all its VM instances' IP ranges and some malware like Mirai does not infect (in fact intentionally bypasses) specific IP ranges [5]. These insights are then leveraged to improve the design and deployment of HoneyCloud in fidelity and effectiveness.

- **We discover new security challenges posed by fileless attacks and propose new defense directions.** While leaving zero footprint on the filesystem, almost all the captured fileless attacks are using shell commands and thus are detectable by auditing the shell command history of IoT devices. Unfortunately, we notice that many IoT devices use a read-only filesystem to mitigate malware-based attacks but unexpectedly increase the difficulty (in persisting the shell command history) of detecting fileless attacks. This is a fundamental tradeoff between the auditability of fileless attacks and the security against malware-based attacks, which presents a new IoT security challenge posed by fileless attacks. Moreover, we observe that the majority (65.7%) of fileless attacks are launched through a small set of commands: `rm`, `kill`, `ps`, and `passwd`, which are enabled by default in our honeypots (and almost all real-world Linux-based IoT devices). For these commands, in fact not all of them are necessary for a special-purpose IoT device, which thus creates opportunities to effectively reduce the attack surface by disabling them.

The insights above provide us with actionable defense strategies against fileless attacks, and we integrate and embody them into a practical workflow we call IoTCheck. For a Linux-based IoT device, the IoTCheck workflow can guide the manufacturers and administrators how to check its security and what to check, along with giving the corresponding defense suggestions that are easy to follow. We also release our data collected in the study at https://honeycloud.github.io, as well as the customization code for building the honeypots.

9.2 Honeypot Deployment

As an effective tool for understanding known and unknown attacks, honeypots have been widely used and deployed on the Internet [11]. Conceptually, a honeypot is a system connected to a network and monitored, when we *expect* it to be broken into and even compromised [12]. Given the fact that a honeypot is not a production system that aims to provide services, nobody has really decent reasons to access it.

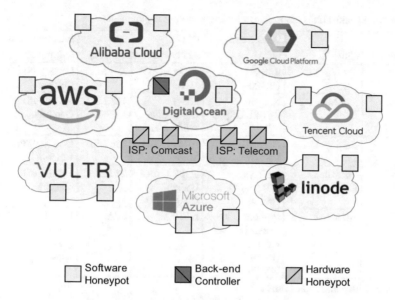

Fig. 9.1 Deployment overview of HoneyCloud (Reprinted with permission from [13])

Thus, we believe that communication packets going to and coming from a honeypot should be typically *suspicious*.[3]

9.2.1 Overview

Figure 9.1 gives an overview of our IoT honeypot deployments, termed Honey-Cloud. It consists of both hardware IoT honeypots (Sect. 9.2.2) and cloud-based software IoT honeypots (Sect. 9.2.3). The hardware IoT honeypots are deployed at four different geographical locations as shown in Table 9.1. The software IoT honeypots are deployed on 108 VM instances (whose geo-distribution is depicted in Fig. 9.2) from eight public clouds across the globe, including AWS, Microsoft Azure, Google Cloud, DigitalOcean, Linode, Vultr, Alibaba Cloud, and Tencent Cloud.

Hardware IoT Honeypots Our first endeavor is to build and deploy hardware IoT honeypots. Section 9.2.2 describes our design, implementation, and operation experiences. We deployed four hardware honeypots on Raspberry Pi, Netgear R6100, BeagleBone, and Linksys WRT54GS placed in residences of the team

---

[3] For honeypots deployed in public clouds, the situation can be slightly different since VM instances can report diagnostic data (which are of course legitimate) to cloud providers. Fortunately, such traffic can be easily recognized and we do not consider it in our analysis.

Table 9.1 Specifications of our hardware IoT honeypot deployment

Honeypot	City	Device and price	CPU architecture	Memory	Internet access (per month)
1	New York, US	Raspberry Pi, US$20	ARM @700 MHz	256 MiB	US$80, ISP: Comcast
2	San Jose, US	Netgear R6100, US$55	MIPS Big-Endian @560 MHz	128 MiB	US$80, ISP: Comcast
3	Beijing, CN	BeagleBone, US$45	ARM @720 MHz	256 MiB	US$20, ISP: Unicom
4	Shenzhen, CN	Linksys WRT54GS, US$40	MIPS Little-Endian @200 MHz	32 MiB	US$20, ISP: Telecom
*	All above	Remote Control Power Adapter (RCPA), US$30	N/A	N/A	US$30 (US), ISP: Comcast US$10 (CN), ISP: Unicom/Telecom

Reprinted with permission from [13]

Fig. 9.2 Geo-distribution of our deployed software honeypots (Reprinted with permission from [13])

members from different cities. Table 9.1 lists the location, hardware configurations, and the monetary cost of the deployment.

From June 2017 to June 2018, the hardware IoT honeypots attracted 14.5M suspicious connections. 1.6M among the suspicious connections successfully logged in and were taken as effective attacks. Among these attacks, 0.75M are malware-based attacks, and 0.08M are fileless attacks. Note that the remaining 0.79M cannot be classified into malware-based or fileless attacks because they did nothing after logging in.

Despite their effectiveness, hardware IoT honeypots are expensive and require high maintenance overhead. The deployment of four hardware honeypots costs 280 US dollars for devices and 280 US dollars *per month* for Internet connections.

Given that the lifespan of an IoT device is typically a couple of years, the monthly infrastructure fee is around 300 US dollars. Moreover, although the deployment and maintenance schemes of the other three honeypots are almost identical to that of the first honeypot, the (manual) labor of maintenance to check low-level infrastructure dependencies cannot be avoided for the other three honeypots.

Software IoT Honeypots The insights and experiences collected by running hardware IoT honeypots drive us to build software-based IoT honeypots that can be deployed in the cloud at scale. Since June 2017, we have deployed 108 software IoT honeypots at eight public clouds across the globe. As of June 2018, we had observed 249M suspicious connections to our software honeypots, of which 10.6% successfully logged in and became effective attacks. Among these attacks, 14.6M are malware-based attacks, and 1.4M are fileless attacks. The remaining 10.4M cannot be classified into malware-based or fileless attacks because nothing happened after successfully logging in.

Since an IoT device typically possesses quite low-end hardware, we only need to rent entry-level VM instances to accommodate software honeypots (i.e., one VM instance hosts one software honeypot). The typical configuration of a VM instance comprises a single-core CPU @2.2GHz, 512 MB of memory, 10–40 GB of storage, and 100 Mbps of network bandwidth.

9.2.2   Hardware IoT Honeypots

Design and Implementation Figure 9.3 shows our hardware honeypot implementation, which consists of three parts: (a) basic hardware including Network Interface Card (NIC), RAM, and CPU/GPU, (b) the OpenWrt operating system, and (c) the honeypot services for attracting attackers.

Our hardware honeypot records all actions of the attackers (including the commands typed or programs executed by the attackers) and reports these actions to the Data Collector (see Fig. 9.3). We expose *ash*—a shell provided by BusyBox—to attackers, so as to record their operations when they execute shell commands. The password of the `root` user is set to `root` by modifying the `shadow` file. The SSH service is provided by Dropbear on port 22 and the Telnet service is provided by BusyBox on port 23.

When we identify an attack that intrudes a hardware honeypot, we capture threat information of this attack and then *reset* the honeypot. Our implementation utilizes *initramfs* to achieve an in-memory filesystem, where the filesystem is first loaded from the flash memory or the SD card and then unpacked into a RAM disk, and all modifications to the system state will be lost after the reset.

If our hardware honeypot is unavailable (i.e., it does not report data to the Data Collector, or we cannot log in to it), we *reboot* the honeypot. While Linux has a built-in watchdog for automatically rebooting, we observed that attackers typically use malware (e.g., Mirai) to disable the watchdog. Therefore, we build a Remote

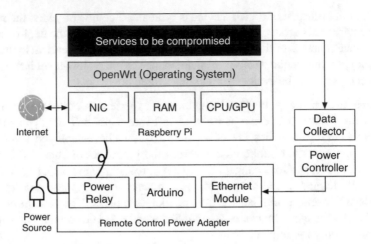

Fig. 9.3 System architecture of our developed hardware IoT honeypot based on Raspberry Pi (Reprinted with permission from [13])

Control Power Adapter (RCPA), as shown in Fig. 9.3, to physically reboot the honeypot.

The RCPA is made up of an Arduino, a power relay, and an Ethernet module. The RCPA uses the Message Queuing Telemetry Transport (MQTT) protocol [14] to subscribe the reboot topic from the Power Controller. Once the RCPA receives a reboot command, it triggers the power relay to power off and on the honeypot.

Experiences Deploying and maintaining hardware IoT honeypots are non-trivial. As shown in Table 9.1, while building a hardware IoT honeypot only costs 20 and 30 US dollars for purchasing a Raspberry Pi and the RCPA (which are quite cheap), the Internet access fee for the two devices reaches 80 and 30 US dollars *per month*, respectively (which are relatively expensive). Note that the two devices cannot share an Internet connection (e.g., through NAT), because the honeypot has to be directly exposed to the Internet without NAT (otherwise, many attacks cannot reach the honeypot).

Moreover, maintaining hardware IoT honeypots incurs high overhead. In particular, the attempts to reset hardware honeypots are not guaranteed to be successful. Oftentimes, we have to manually check low-level infrastructure dependencies, such as the underlying Internet connections, the power supply, and the hardware devices. Glitches of any involved entity would increase the maintenance overhead.

Implications to Software IoT Honeypots Our experiences show that hardware IoT honeypots are hard to scale due to the excessive deployment cost and maintenance overhead. To deploy IoT honeypots at scale would require software-based solutions. Our experiences reveal that the main obstacles of hardware deployments lie in the examination of low-level infrastructure dependencies. Therefore, if we can guarantee the reliability and scalability of low-level infrastructures, the issues would be effectively avoided or alleviated. This drives our efforts to build cloud-based software IoT honeypots, as cloud platforms offer probably the most reliable, scalable, and cost-efficient solution to a global-scale deployment of virtual computing infrastructure.

Meanwhile, we require the cloud-based software honeypots to possess a similar level of fidelity to the hardware IoT honeypots. Our collected measurement data from the hardware honeypots offers us useful implications for ensuring the fidelity of software honeypots. First, we find that 9132 attacks attempted to acquire sensitive system information via commands like `lscpu` and `cat/proc/cpuinfo`, which enables attackers to detect software honeypots running on VM instances; thus, our software honeypots should be able to forge real system information (e.g., CPU information), making the software honeypots look like real IoT devices (detailed in Sect. 9.2.3.1). Second, we notice that 187 attacks used commands like `lsusb` (listing connected USB devices) to detect potential honeypots; thus, we should enable common buses to ensure the fidelity (detailed in Sect. 9.2.3.1).

9.2.3   Software IoT Honeypots

Figure 9.4 illustrates our software-based IoT honeypot design. We extend the Data Collector and the Power Controller described in Sect. 9.2.2 to integrate our hardware IoT honeypots. This includes implementing the reset capability for software IoT honeypots in the Power Controller.

The internal structure of a software IoT honeypot consists of three modules: High Fidelity Maintainer (Sect. 9.2.3.1), Shell Interceptor and Inference Terminal (Sect. 9.2.3.2), and Access Controller (Sect. 9.2.3.3). The software IoT honeypot can emulate the following typical IoT devices featured by their heterogeneous architectures and compositions:

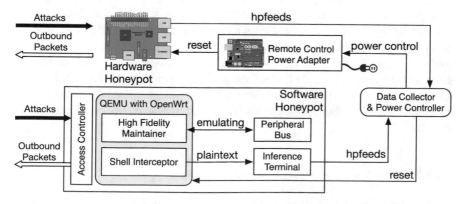

Fig. 9.4 Architectural overview of our system, as well as the internal structure of a software IoT honeypot (Reprinted with permission from [13])

Intel Galileo Gen 1 with x86; Dreambox 600 PVR with PowerPC; BeagleBoard with ARM Cortex-A8; Orange Pi Zero with ARM Cortex-A7; Omega2 with MIPS 24K; RouterBOARD RB953GS with MIPS 74Kc.

9.2.3.1   High Fidelity Maintainer

The High Fidelity Maintainer implements a set of strategies to prevent attackers from identifying our honeypots.

Customizing QEMU Configurations   To enhance the fidelity of software honeypots, we tune the hardware configurations of QEMU in each software honeypot so that it can resemble its emulated IoT device in capability. As QEMU provides a series of CPU profiles, we select the CPU profile that best matches the CPU metrics of the emulated IoT device. We set its memory capacity as equal to that of the emulated IoT device. As we use *initramfs* to achieve an in-memory filesystem (Sect. 9.2.2), there is no need to emulate disks (most IoT devices do not own disks).

Masking Sensitive System Information   Since attackers can probe whether an IoT device is emulated by a VM based on system and kernel information (e.g., by checking /proc) [15], we mask the VM system and kernel information. For each software honeypot, we forge /proc/cpuinfo in OpenWrt and make it look like a commercial CPU used by real IoT devices.

VM Instances Rearrangement Among Public Clouds   Since we deploy our software IoT honeypots in public clouds, it is possible for attackers to infer our deployment based on IP addresses, because the IP ranges of public clouds can be fully or partially retrieved. For example, AWS fully releases its IP address ranges through public web APIs, and the IP address ranges of some public clouds can be partially acquired by examining their ASes.

We built twofold approaches to mitigate the possibility of identifying VM-based honeypots based on IP addresses. First, when we rent a VM instance from the eight public clouds, we fragmentize the IP address selection for our honeypots by fragmentizing the selection of VMs' regions, zones, and in-zone IP ranges. Second, we notice that all the eight public clouds offer the option of *elastic* IP addresses (without extra charges). Hence, we periodically change the IP address of each software honeypot. During the first six months' deployment, we noticed that 6.7% of fewer attacks are captured by an average honeypot hosted on AWS than an average honeypot hosted on other public clouds. Thus, we move some honeypots from AWS to Vultr.

9.2.3.2   Shell Interceptor and Inference Terminal

We build two modules, Shell Interceptor and Inference Terminal, inside and outside QEMU, respectively (see Fig. 9.4), in order to capture the actions the attackers

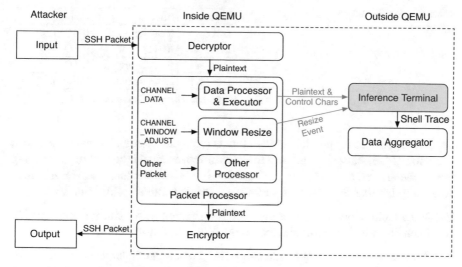

Fig. 9.5 Workflow of the Shell Interceptor (Reprinted with permission from [13])

conduct as well as the context of these actions such as operation ordering. We modified Dropbear to recover the whole interaction process of SSH sessions. Specifically, we track the following events: connecting, logging in, resizing the window, exchanging data, and logging out.

Shell Interceptor Figure 9.5 details how we extract and parse the plaintext data from the interaction traffic flows in an SSH session. When a data packet arrives at the server (using our modified Dropbear), it is first decrypted to plaintext. Next, the packet processor detects the packet type, among which we focus on CHANNEL_DATA (the actual terminal data) and CHANNEL_WINDOW_ADJUST (the resize event coming from the terminal emulator). The plaintext terminal data (including both ordinary and control characters) and the resize event are then sent to the Inference Terminal for further analysis. Here we omit the description of Telnet data interception since it is much simpler than SSH data interception.

Inference Terminal Although the Shell Interceptor has acquired plaintext data, there are still control characters and escape sequences to be handled in the data. For example, the input sequence {"a," "b," "←," "c"} should result in "acb." If we simply ignore the control characters and escape sequences, we will get the wrong result "abc." Thereby, we need to recover the *context* of interactions. To fulfill this, we feed the shell and terminal data into *pyte*, a VTxxx (the video terminal standard for terminal emulators)-compatible terminal emulator. Since the terminal is screen-based (new content flushes old content), we modify the program of *pyte* to recover the full history of interactions instead of getting the interactions screen by screen.

We convert special control characters and escape sequences listed in Table 9.2 to plaintext so that we can know what has exactly happened. Also, we store a separate

Table 9.2 Special escape sequences

Sequence	Effect	Converted text
1Bh c	Reset terminal	[ESC c]
1Bh [H	Reset cursor	[ESC [H]
1Bh [n J	Erase in display	[ESC [n J]
1Bh [n K	Erase in line	[ESC [n K]

Reprinted with permission from [13]

copy of keystrokes for possible hidden inputs (e.g., passwords). We track the resize event for two reasons. First, the window size of the terminal is crucial for recovering the characters that may cross lines. Second, it is a bellwether that indicates a human attacker rather than an automatic script (i.e., the authenticity of the attacker).

Evidence Collection To collect as much information as we can for investigation and forensics, we also report and record the following information:

- *CPU usage* as an important indicator of the execution of complex computations. For example, new types of cyber-attacks, such as crypto-currency mining and ransomware, can be identified based on this information.
- *Process list* that can track any unintentional suspicious process that indicates potential threats.
- *Network packets.* We first use *libpcap* to capture almost the full trace of network activities. Then, to filter out irrelevant packets, we ignore (1) the packets sent to the Inference Terminal and (2) the SSH packets between attackers and honeypots since these packets will eventually be handled by the Shell Interceptor.

9.2.3.3   Access Controller

Once a software honeypot is compromised by attackers, we should ensure that the attackers cannot utilize it to attack more IoT devices. Otherwise, HoneyCloud would become a new malware incubator. An intuitive defense is to use access control. However, the access control policy is difficult to specify in our scenario, because we do not know which outbound packets should be allowed or denied. Too restrictive policies could block benign requests (e.g., DNS packets), while relaxed policies would be of high risk.

We adopt a data-driven approach that leverages the continuously observed data to dynamically infer what packets are likely to be malicious and then only block those dangerous outbound accesses. Our implementation employs Snort (running on the host VM instance rather than the emulated IoT device) to monitor ingoing and outgoing packet traffic. By analyzing the reports generated by Snort, we can easily figure out the symmetry of data flows—asymmetry of data flows is taken as the indicator of potential attacks blocked by public clouds.

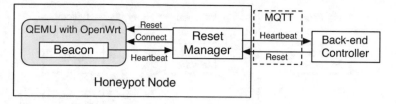

Fig. 9.6 Heartbeat-based failure recovery (Reprinted with permission from [13])

9.2.3.4 Reset Manager

We built *heartbeat-based reset* to periodically send heartbeat messages to the back-end controller. Once the back-end controller finds three consecutively missed heartbeats, it would send a reset command to the QEMU. We also notice that some malware (e.g., Mirai) can kill the process of the SSH/Telnet server; therefore, the Reset Manager also periodically tries to connect to the QEMU via SSH/Telnet. Once the Reset Manager finds that the connection fails, it also resets the QEMU. Figure 9.6 demonstrates how the Reset Manager interacts with our backend controller.

9.3 Findings and Implications

This section analyzes the collected results of our deployed honeypots in a whole year (06/2017–06/2018). We first introduce the working flows and general statistics of our captured attacks (Sect. 9.3.1). Then, we present the detailed study on fileless attacks (Sects. 9.3.3 and 9.3.4) and suggest defense strategies against fileless attacks (Sect. 9.3.5).

9.3.1 General Characteristics and Statistics

As mentioned in Sect. 9.1, attacks on IoT devices are either malware-based or do not involve malware (fileless). The former must download certain malware files from the Internet to launch the attacks, while the latter do not need to download any malware file. Based on the attacks captured by us, their general working flows are depicted in Fig. 9.7. For malware-based attacks, there are generally three steps to go through (1) intrusion, (2) infection, and (3) monetization. In the intrusion phase, most malware uses brute-force methods (e.g., common usernames and weak passwords) to attempt to log in to IoT devices. After the attackers successfully log in, they enter the infection phase where *wget* and *tftp* are typically used to download the required malware. The downloaded malware usually connects to the command and control

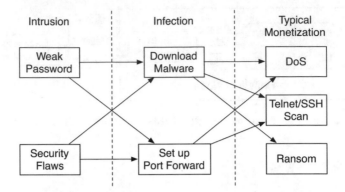

Fig. 9.7 General workflows of our captured attacks (Reprinted with permission from [13])

(a.k.a., C&C) server to wait for the command. Once receiving the command, the malware can perform various kinds of attacks, such as DoS attacks and Telnet/SSH scans. Note that the malware-based attack flows we captured are basically consistent with those found in previous work [16].

For fileless attacks, the attack behaviors we captured differ from those for malware-based attacks in the second and third phases. In the infection phase, no malware is downloaded; therefore, traditional detection techniques based on malware fingerprinting cannot be applied. Instead, attackers modify certain system-level files and/or set up port forwarding and backdoors for later use. In the monetization phase, apart from DoS and Telnet/SSH scan, some other goals are achieved as detailed in Sect. 9.3.3 and Fig. 9.8.

Quantitatively, from June 2017 to June 2018 our hardware IoT honeypots attracted more than 14.5M suspicious connections. Among these connections, 85.8% are SSH/Telnet (ports 22, 23, 2222, and 2323) connections, 6.2% are SMB (port 445) connections, and 2.5% are HTTP(S) (ports 80, 443, and 8080) connections. As mentioned in Sect. 9.2, these connections led to 1.6M effective attacks,[4] where 0.75M are malware-based attacks, and 0.08M are fileless attacks. In other words, each hardware honeypot receives 9930 suspicious connections and 1100 effective attacks per day on average, showing that *attacks on IoT devices are actually frequent at present*.

Besides the four hardware honeypots, we have deployed 108 software honeypots in eight public clouds since June 2017. They are geo-distributed across Europe, Asia, North America, South America, and Australia. As of June 2018, we had observed 249M suspicious connections to them, among which 78.3% are SSH/Telnet connections, 8.9% are SMB connections, and 3.2% are HTTP(S) connections. Other connections use ports 3389 (RDP), 3306 (MySQL), 1433 (SQL

---

[4] A successful login is counted as an effective attack. If any file is downloaded (via wget), it is counted as a malware-based attack. If no file is downloaded but any command is executed, it is counted as a fileless attack.

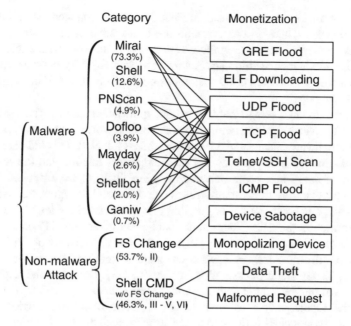

(a) Attacks captured by hardware honeypots.

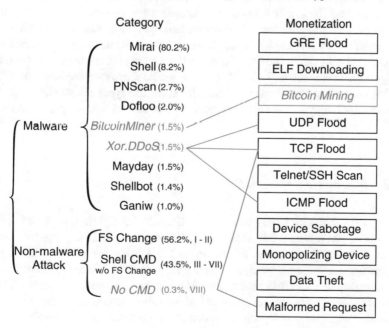

(b) Attacks captured by software honeypots.

Fig. 9.8 Attacks captured by our hardware and software honeypots in HoneyCloud. FS is short for filesystem and CMD is short for command. Note that in (**b**) we only plot the new connection lines relative to those in (**a**) (Reprinted with permission from [13])

Server), and so on. As mentioned in Sect. 9.2, these connections led to 26.4M effective attacks, where 14.6M are malware-based attacks, and 1.4M are fileless attacks. Meanwhile, only 37 window resize events are captured, indicating that most attacks are launched automatically (refer to Sect. 9.2.3.2). In other words, each software honeypot receives 6300 suspicious connections and 670 effective attacks per day on average.

Compared to an average hardware honeypot, an average software honeypot attracts 37% fewer suspicious connections and 39% fewer attacks (more specifically, 28% fewer malware attacks and 37% fewer fileless attacks). This indicates that our developed software honeypots do not possess perfect fidelity, and the reasons are mainly two folds. First, some public clouds are likely to have prevented certain types of attacks before these attacks reach our software honeypots. Second, even if attacks reach our honeypots, it is possible that some attackers leveraged more in-depth information (e.g., CPU bugs and model-specific registers [17]) and advanced techniques (e.g., execution analysis [18]) to infer the VM identity of our honeypots, although multifold endeavors have been made to mitigate the exposure of VM identity in HoneyCloud (as specified in Sect. 9.2.3.1). Both reasons might reduce the amount of our detectable malware and fileless attacks.

In order to understand to what extent a public cloud has carried out such prevention, we launched various common attacks (such as port scanning and brute-force authentication cracking) against our honeypots in the eight public clouds from universities and the public clouds. The attacks were launched once per hour and lasted for a whole day. The results show that all our attacks can reach our honeypots in the public clouds except Alibaba Cloud.[5] This indicates that attack filtering in public clouds may indeed be one of the possible causes, but the impact to our study is not significant since the majority (7) of the 8 public clouds we used are not affected. Besides, according to the results shown later, all the types of attacks captured by our hardware honeypots are also captured by our software honeypots (but not vice versa).

9.3.2   Malware-Based Attacks

In total, our hardware honeypots have collected 426 different types of malware (in terms of fingerprints) downloaded by the attackers, and they can be classified into seven general categories as shown in Fig. 9.8a according to VirusTotal. In comparison, our software honeypots have collected 598 different types of malware, fully covering the 426 different types captured by hardware honeypots. The 598 different types of malware can be classified into nine general categories as shown in Fig. 9.8b. Among these categories, Mirai takes a significant portion—when malware

---

[5] After performing port scanning using *nmap*, Alibaba Cloud blocked our SSH connection from the same machine.

binaries successfully intrude into our honeypots, 73.3% and 80.2% of them are Mirai as for hardware honeypots and software honeypots, respectively.

In addition, we find that the vast majority ($\sim$92.1%) of malware-based attacks are targeting multiple architectures of IoT devices. This characteristic is observed before by previous work [16], and we are able to confirm and further quantify it. Specifically, our collected malware (e.g., Mirai, Dofloo, and Ganiw) is usually capable of running upon various architectures with various versions of binaries, including 32/64-bit x86 (28.9%), ARM (v7 & v8, 27.3% in total), MIPS[6] (Big & Little Endian, 25.7% in total), PowerPC[7] (9.2%), and SPARC[8] (8.9%). This highlights the pressing need for a flexible, software IoT honeypot solution, as a software honeypot can be easily configured to support the above architectures.

9.3.3 Fileless Attack Taxonomy

Besides malware-based attacks, our software honeypots have captured eight different types of fileless attacks (in terms of behaviors and intents). In comparison, our hardware honeypots have captured only five types (II–V and VII) among the abovementioned eight types, probably because the number of hardware honeypots is much smaller. Without the malware files, we find that it is more difficult to identify and classify fileless attacks. To the best of our knowledge, we are the first to systematically characterize fileless attacks on IoT systems in the wild. Specifically, by comprehensively correlating the disclosed shell commands, the monitored filesystem change, the recorded data-flow traffic, and third parties' online reports, we identify 1.5M fileless attacks and empirically infer their behaviors/intents as follows (the value in the parentheses denotes the percentage of the corresponding fileless attacks):

- Type I: Occupying end systems (1.8%), e.g., by altering the password of an IoT device (via `passwd`). Once the password is changed, the attacker is able to access the device later and prevent other people from logging in.
- Type II: Damaging system data (54.4%), e.g., by removing or altering certain configuration files or programs (via `rm` and `dd`). The typical scenario is to remove the watchdog daemon, which opens the watchdog device (`/dev/watchdog`) and makes several tests to check the system status. Once the daemon is removed, the watchdog device will not be opened. Then, the device will not reboot when it malfunctions. Thereby, the attacker may occupy and utilize the system for a longer time.

---

[6] Broadcom and Atheros have made lots of MIPS SoCs for WiFi routers. Ingenic also provides various MIPS solutions.

[7] There are a number of PowerPC-based set-top boxes and game consoles like Wii and PlayStation.

[8] SPARC-based SoCs have been produced over years, such as LEON.

- Type III: Preventing system monitoring/auditing services (8.5%), e.g., by killing the watchdog processes or stopping certain services (via `kill` and `service`). For instance, after stopping the firewall service, attackers can better exploit known vulnerabilities to launch attacks.
- Type IV: Retrieving system information (7.4%), e.g., by getting the hardware information (via `lscpu`) and the system information (via `uname`, `netstat`, `ps`, and `free`). Such information may be useful for launching further attacks for specific purposes, e.g., downloading and executing platform-specific malware binaries.
- Type V: Stealing valuable data (23.5%), e.g., by reading passwords and/or certain configuration files (via `cat`). Note that although passwords stored in `/etc/shadow` are salted and hashed, the attackers may still be able to analyze user behaviors or recover the passwords using tools like "John the Ripper" password cracker.
- Type VI: Launching network attacks (0.3%), e.g., by sending malformed HTTP requests to exploit the vulnerabilities of targeted web servers (via `wget` and `curl`) to launch DoS attacks [19]. Other typical attacks include OpenSSL Heartbleed and SQL injections.
- Type VII: Issuing other shell commands for unclear reasons (3.8%). There are other shell commands issued in our observed fileless attacks, whose purposes are currently not entirely clear to us, including `who`, `help`, `lastlog`, `sleep`, and so on. For some commands like `who` and `lastlog`, we speculate that the attacker may be collecting and analyzing other system users atop the same device.
- Type VIII: Conducting attacks where no shell command is involved (0.3%). A typical example, referred to as *SSH Tunneling Attack*, is demonstrated in Fig. 9.9, where the attacker has compromised an IoT device when launching this attack. Once he gets the correct credentials of the SSH service (usually via brute force) on another IoT device, he converts this (another) IoT device into a proxy server by setting up SSH port forwarding on the compromised device (i.e., our honeypots, see the SSH Tunnel in Fig. 9.9). Usually, he binds the SSH port forwarding service (on the compromised device) to a loopback address to prevent other machines from connecting to the service. Then, the attacker launches the attack from the compromised device. Because the network flows are all proxied to the other IoT devices, the real IP address of the attacker is hidden and it is rather difficult to track such attacks.

The last type of fileless attacks is actually quite challenging to detect since there is no shell command issued and typically no filesystem change noticed. In order to pinpoint such attacks, we usually have to make cross-community explorations.

Fig. 9.9 Details of the SSH
Tunneling Attack (Reprinted
with permission from [13])

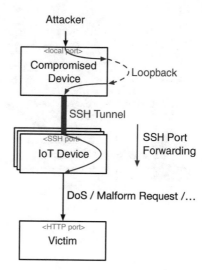

Figure 9.10 illustrates how we identify the SSH tunneling attack. First, by examining
the recorded data-flow traffic, we found that the outbound network traffic in one of
our deployed software honeypots suddenly exceeded a reasonable limit at 16:08,
October 25, 2017 (UTC).

Also, the anomalous pattern of outbound traffic lasted for a couple of minutes,
continuously sending HTTPS requests to a Bitcoin lottery website https://freebitco.
in. Then, we searched the domain name of the website together with the keyword
"attack" via Google, and fortunately, we discovered a message posted on Twitter
by the website's operators, reporting that they are under DDoS attacks on the same
day.[9]

Furthermore, we searched for the attack in several antivirus communities (including EXETOOLS, MalwareMustDie, and IET Cyber Security Community) and
found that a newly reported kind of pivoting attacks [7] well matched the behaviors
of the attack we observed.[10] Also, we learned that this attack is not only stealthy but
also powerful and scalable—it can easily amplify its effect by manipulating a swarm
of IoT devices and establishing multiple layers of SSH tunnels (as demonstrated in
Fig. 9.11).

---

[9] https://twitter.com/freebitco/status/923298533972652032.

[10] Since the collected data were encrypted, we did not have direct, ideal evidence but actually
noticed that the patterns well matched. Note that the SSH tunnel is used for forwarding data and
does not involve shell interactions, so we cannot decrypt the data using the Shell Interceptor and
Inference Terminal (Sect. 9.2.3.2).

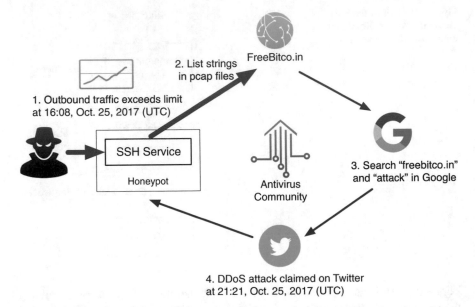

Fig. 9.10 Analysis procedure of the SSH Tunneling Attack (Reprinted with permission from [13])

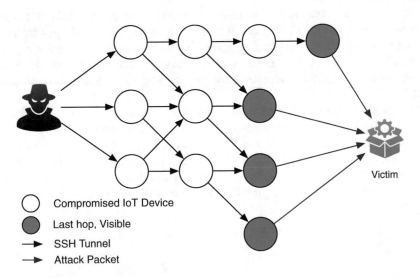

Fig. 9.11 Network flow of the SSH Tunneling Attack (Reprinted with permission from [13])

9.3.4   Key Insights for Fileless Attacks

Aggregating the detailed study results in Sect. 9.3.3, we acquire several valuable insights with respect to fileless IoT attacks. First, almost all the previous studies on IoT attacks are focused on malware-based attacks, while fileless attacks have been scarcely reported. This may well mislead people to take fileless attacks as marginal and insignificant. On the contrary, our study reveals that fileless attacks are not only substantially more than expected—the number of fileless attacks is as large as 9.7% of that of malware-based attacks—but also capable of fulfilling a variety of functions and goals, some of which are pretty powerful and stealthy (e.g., the SSH Tunneling Attack). Additionally, we find that a root cause of this lies in the weak authentication issue of today's IoT devices, i.e., many widely used IoT devices are using a weak password at present [20]. The issue makes it unprecedentedly easy for attackers to obtain remote control of IoT devices and then perform malicious actions without using malware.

Also, we observe that some system components (embodied by specific shell commands) are "favored" by fileless attacks. Figure 9.12 lists the top-10 frequently used shell commands by fileless attacks. Solely rm is used by 48% of the fileless attacks, while all the other commands (excluding top 10) are used by only 2.7% of the fileless attacks. In particular, the majority (65.7%) of our captured fileless attacks are launched through a small set of commands: rm, kill, ps, and passwd, which are enabled by default in our honeypots (and almost all real-world Linux-based IoT devices). For these commands, actually not all of them are necessary for a special-purpose IoT device. Thus, for a certain IoT device, if some of these frequently exploited shell commands are indeed unnecessary, the manufacturers can disable them by customizing the device system so that the attack surface can be reduced.

In addition, we notice that fileless attacks can also help malware-based attacks or subsequent fileless attacks both stealthily and effectively. Although it is not always necessary for adversaries to acquire system information before attacking the system (e.g., they may first download the malware binaries of various architectures together

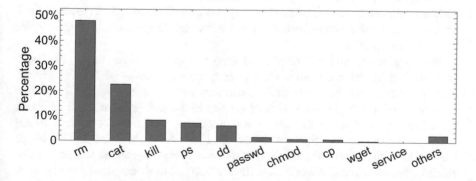

Fig. 9.12 Usage frequency of the shell commands (Reprinted with permission from [13])

and then run them one by one [21]), to our observations, 39.4% of the fileless attacks are collecting system information or performing de-immunization operations (e.g., shut down the firewall and kill the watchdog) to allow more targeted and efficient follow-up attacks.

Although the attack vectors discussed in this section are also applied to general-purpose computers, the attack effects are totally different. PCs and servers are usually highly protected with enhanced credentials, and thus they are significantly less impacted by the attacks studied in this work.

9.3.5   New Security Challenges and Defense Directions

Based on the insights from our study, we are able to identify both new security challenges introduced by fileless attacks and new defense solution directions. First, 56.2% of fileless attacks (Type I and Type II) modify the filesystem of the compromised IoT devices. To resist such attacks, the device manufacturers should use a non-root user as the default system user.

Second, we find that 99.7% of fileless attacks (Type I–VII) are using shell commands, making these attacks detectable by auditing the shell command history of IoT devices. Unfortunately, in practice, many IoT devices use a read-only filesystem (e.g., SquashFS) with the hope of enhancing security. This mitigates malware-based attacks but unexpectedly increases the difficulty (in persisting the shell command history) of detecting fileless attacks. However, if we make certain parts of the file system writable to enable shell commend logging, e.g., using a hybrid filesystem (e.g., OverlayFS) or a versioning filesystem (e.g., Elephant [22]), this inevitability makes it possible for malware-based attacks to download malware files. Thus, this is a fundamental tradeoff between the auditability of fileless attacks and the security against malware-based attacks, which we think is a new IoT security challenge introduced by fileless attacks.

Third, we notice that 0.3% of fileless attacks (Type VIII) neither modify the filesystem nor execute any shell commands. Take the aforementioned SSH Tunneling Attack as an example, which exploits the SSH service in a number of IoT devices with weak passwords to construct a "tunnel" for launching attacks while hiding the real sources.

We suggest that any IoT device unsuited to using a *unique* strong password (e.g., limited by the production and assembly process—low-end IoT devices are usually programmed before assembly, and thus the firmware of multiple devices is often identical) stop providing SSH service to the public Internet. In case that users have to manipulate the device remotely, they could utilize a VPN to get access to the device; in other words, the SSH service is always restrained to the local area network (LAN). The above defense strategies can be integrated and embodied in an actionable workflow called IoTCheck, as demonstrated in Fig. 9.13. To assist manufacturers and administrators to validate and harden the security of their IoT devices effectively (with regard to fileless attacks), the IoTCheck workflow

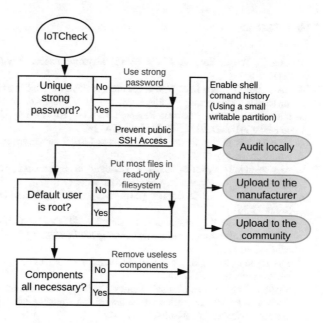

Fig. 9.13 The IoTCheck workflow. Red texts denote that essential actions should be taken. Blue boxes represent the possible auditing schemes (Reprinted with permission from [13])

comprehensively examines their multifold information including the password strength, root privilege, filesystem type, shell environment, SSH access, unnecessary components, and so forth. Based on the checking results, defense suggestions are then provided.

9.4 Conclusion

IoT attacks are pervasive and becoming severe security threats. Existing researches in addressing IoT attacks mainly focus on malware-based IoT attacks. While malware-based attacks (e.g., Mirai) can quickly spread across IoT devices, they can be effectively resisted by malware fingerprinting or static/dynamic malware analyses. In the past few years, fileless attacks have been increasingly observed and reported, in particular on Linux-based IoT devices. Such attacks pose significant threats to the widely deployed IoT devices across the world but have not been systematically studied or comprehensively analyzed. To understand Linux-based IoT attacks with a focus on fileless attacks, we build and deploy several IoT devices as hardware honeypots, and a large number of specially designed software honeypots in multiple public clouds, to capture and analyze such attacks at scale in the wild. We collect the data of a variety of real-world fileless attacks, profile their characteristics and influences, and propose actionable defense strategies. We believe that traditional threat models of IoT security, which have been focusing on malware, need to take fileless attacks into serious consideration, and a global unified defense framework for fileless attacks is in dire need.

References

1. Zhou Z, Wu C, Yang Z, Liu Y (2015) Sensorless sensing with WiFi. Tsinghua Sci Tech 20(1):1–6
2. Han J, Pan S, Sinha MK, Noh HY, Zhang P, et al. (2018) Smart home occupant identification via sensor fusion across on-object devices. ACM Trans Sensor Netw 14(3–4):23:1–23:22
3. Internet of Things Security Research Report (2017) http://www.nsfocus.com.cn/upload/contents/2017/12/20171205171653_35944.pdf
4. New Trends in the World of IoT Threats (2019) https://securelist.com/new-trends-in-the-world-of-iot-threats/87991/
5. Antonakakis M, April T, Bailey M, Bernhard M, Bursztein E, et al. (2017) Understanding the Mirai botnet. In: Proceedings of USENIX security
6. Gandotra E, Bansal D, Sofat S (2014) Malware analysis and classification: A survey. J Inf Secur 05:56–64
7. MMD-0062-2017 - Credential Harvesting by SSH Direct TCP Forward Attack via IoT Botnet (2017). http://blog.malwaremustdie.org/2017/02/mmd-0062-2017-ssh-direct-tcp-forward-attack.html
8. Zhu T, Ma Q, Zhang S, Liu Y (2014) Context-free attacks using keyboard acoustic emanations. In: Proceedings of ACM CCS
9. McAfee Labs: Cybercriminal Tactics Shifting From External Malware Threats to 'fileless' Attacks (1982) https://www.dqindia.com/mcafee-labs-cybercriminal-tactics-shifting-external-malware-threats-fileless-attacks/
10. Now You See Me: Exposing Fileless Malware – Microsoft Secure. https://cloudblogs.microsoft.com/microsoftsecure/2018/01/24/now-you-see-me-exposing-fileless-malware/
11. Spitzner L (2003) Honeypots: Tracking hackers, vol 1. Addison-Wesley Reading
12. Provos N (2004) A virtual honeypot framework. In: Proceedings of USENIX security
13. Dang F, Li Z, Liu Y, Zhai E, Chen QA, Xu T, Chen Y, Yang J (2019) Understanding fileless attacks on Linux-based IoT devices with HoneyCloud. In: Proceedings of ACM MobiSys, pp 482–493
14. International Organisation for Standardization (ISO) (2016) ISO/IEC 20922:2016 Information technology – Message Queuing Telemetry Transport (MQTT) v3.1.1. http://www.iso.org
15. Linux - easy way to determine virtualization technology - Unix & Linux stack exchange. https://unix.stackexchange.com/questions/89714/easy-way-to-determine-virtualization-technology
16. Pa YMP, Suzuki S, Yoshioka K, Matsumoto T, Kasama T, et al. (2015) IoTPOT: Analysing the rise of IoT compromises. In: Proceedings of USENIX WOOT
17. Raffetseder T, Kruegel C, Kirda E (2007) Detecting system emulators. In: Proceedings of ISC
18. QEMU emulation detection. https://wiki.koeln.ccc.de/images/d/d5/Openchaos_qemudetect.pdf
19. NVD - CVE-2018-7262. https://nvd.nist.gov/vuln/detail/CVE-2018-7262
20. Loi F, Sivanathan A, Gharakheili HH, Radford A, Sivaraman V (2017) Systematically evaluating security and privacy for consumer IoT devices. In: Proceedings of ACM IoT S&P
21. Donno MD, Dragoni N, Giaretta A, Spognardi A (2018) DDoS-capable IoT malwares: Comparative analysis and Mirai investigation. Secur Commun Networks 7178164:1–7178164:30
22. Santry DJ, Feeley MJ, Hutchinson NC, Veitch AC (1999) Elephant: The file system that never forgets. In: Proceedings of ACM HotOS

Part VI
Last Thoughts

Chapter 10
Concluding Remarks

Abstract This chapter discusses important emerging techniques and the possible future work on Internet content distribution.

Keywords CCN · ICN · NDN · SDN · RDMA · DPDK · Network emulation

10.1 Emerging Techniques

Internet content distribution has long existed for decades and substantially influenced the everyday life of human beings, e.g., online videos are substituting TV broadcasts, voice on IP (VoIP) is supplementing traditional phone calls, and cloud-based Internet meeting is changing the way of our routine work, especially during the pandemic of COVID-19. Meanwhile, it is a frontier research area that has constantly benefited from the innovations in other areas, e.g., the invention of optical fibers, the upgrade of network switchers and routers, the emergence of new architecture/OS paradigms (e.g., Remote DMA and user-space IO), the prosperity of novel wireless communication techniques (e.g., 5G/6G, WiFi 6/7, and satellite communication), and even the development of quantum communications. Below we introduce in brief a few important emerging techniques.

Cloud-Based CDN (CCDN) In the past decade, numerous Internet content providers have rented the CDN service to accelerate their content distribution. Some websites (e.g., Hulu and Netflix) even rent the services of multiple CDNs and utilize their own clouds to schedule the resources from multiple CDNs [1, 2]. On the contrary, in recent years, we have noted that some CDNs start to rent cloud resources to provide better CDN services [3], which is referred to as *cloud-based CDN* or CCDN for short. This is because CDN service providers also need the high scalability, resilience, and geographical availability of cloud computing to help them adaptively adjust their infrastructure costs and quality of service.

Edge-Based CDN (ECDN) Traditionally, CDN accelerates content distribution by strategically deploying a number of edge servers across the Internet. Recently, we have seen the idea and practice of leveraging edge end-user devices (e.g.,

Z. Li et al., *Content Distribution for Mobile Internet: A Cloud-based Approach*,
https://doi.org/10.1007/978-981-19-6982-9_10

home routers) to construct or assist a CDN. Of course, the owners of participated edge devices will get paid according to their contributed bandwidth and storage resources. Typical examples include the XY-CDN [4] based on Xunlei Red home routers [5]. It is worth noting that the edge-based CDN is distinct from P2P content distribution, since both its underlying protocols and delivered content are transparent to participated users.

Remote Direct Memory Access (RDMA) The vast majority of undergraduates majoring in computer science and engineering should have learnt the notion of Direct Memory Access (DMA), a method that enables an I/O device to directly send or receive data to or from the main memory, thereby bypassing the CPU's control (and limitation) to speed up data access operations. Traditionally, DMA is only used in a standalone computer or a mainframe (with a specialized communication infrastructure named InfiniBand) for reliability and security concerns, which is quite understandable due to the lack of CPU's management and surveillance. Around ten years ago, RDMA was adopted to build computer storage, key-value store, and distributed transaction systems over the commercial Ethernet [6–9], usually with tens of servers. Nearly five years ago, RDMA came into large-scale data center networks to support some highly reliable and latency-sensitive services over the advanced commercial Ethernet [10, 11]. At the moment, we are looking forward to the application of RDMA in common networks, particularly the WiFi and cellular networks.

UIO, SPDK, and DPDK The user-space I/O framework (UIO) [12] was introduced in Linux 2.6.23 in October 2007, which enables I/O device drivers to be written *almost entirely* in user-space (i.e., there is still a small kernel module to write and maintain). Naturally, this implies that before the 2.6.23 version of Linux, I/O device drivers can only be written in kernel space, which might be difficult for the development, inconvenient for the maintenance, and inflexible for the distribution of I/O device drivers. Of course, for those standard I/O devices well supported by the existing kernel subsystems, UIO is unnecessary or not a must. In other words, UIO is particularly suited to non-standard I/O devices that desire special functions or advanced performance.

A representative application of UIO is Storage Performance Development Kit (SPDK), which moves as many necessary drivers as possible from kernel space into user-space, thus averting system calls and enabling zero-copy access from the upper-layer application. Besides this, the performance gains from SPDK are also owing to the poll mode rather than the original interrupt mode, for learning the completion of storage hardware operations. In addition, SPDK strives to eliminate all resource locks along the I/O path by means of message passing. According to its developers in Intel, SPDK can remarkably increase the throughput of NVMe devices by 6–10 times [13].

Similar to SPDK, Data Plane Development Kit (DPDK) offloads the processing task of TCP packets (which can be very heavy for high-speed networks) from the kernel space into the user-space, and it also provides the poll mode for the Network Interface Controller (NIC) to replace the original interrupt mode. Letting upper-layer programs directly interact with the NIC (bypassing CPU), DPDK effectively empowers the development of network applications (e.g., online AR/VR) dealing with high-speed data packets.

CCN/ICN/NDN/SDN-Driven Content Distribution In the past few years, several metaphysical networking terms, CCN, ICN, NDN, and SDN, have quickly become eye-catching. Here CCN denotes Content Centric Networking, ICN denotes Information Centric Networking, NDN represents Named Data Networking [14], and SDN means Software-Defined Networking. Among them, the most promising seems to be the OpenFlow SDN project [15] initiated in Stanford University. Presently, Openflow has been adopted by not only large networking device manufacturers such as Cisco, Huawei, and NEC, but also a wide variety of network-related researchers and practitioners.

As the underlying facilities of Internet content distribution, network switchers and routers have long been regarded as hardware—once they are shipped by the manufacturers, their functions are generally fixed and the users can only make very simple configurations. The emergence of SDN renovated this situation by enabling network switchers and routers to support various user-customized software applications, like what personal computers and smartphones do. With SDN, programmers can run complex logic on network hardware, realize advanced software functions, and eventually reshape the paradigm of Internet content distribution.

10.2 Future Work

In the near future, we feel that the promising topics worth to explore with respect to Internet content distribution are at least as follows.

OS Impact on Internet Content Distribution Generally speaking, the performance of Internet content distribution relies on network conditions and protocols. Nevertheless, we have lately noticed that content distribution in some systems is also heavily determined by the operating system (OS), particularly the kernel and I/O system. For example, handling the same data updates with the same user device under the same network environment, Dropbox exhibits diverse performance when running on top of Linux, Windows, and macOS [16, 17]. The situation becomes more complicated when other cloud storage services (e.g., Google Drive, Microsoft OneDrive, and iCloud Drive) and mobile OSes (like iOS and Android) are taken into consideration [18]. Consequently, the profound impact of OSes on Internet content distribution deserves further and deeper investigation.

Mobile Virtual Network Operator Driven by the growing market demands, Mobile Virtual Network Operators (MVNOs) or mobile carriers for short have gained enormous popularity in recent years, exemplified by Google Fi in the USA and Xiaomi Mobile in China. They operate over existing cellular infrastructures of base carriers (such as AT&T and China Mobile) but usually provide cheaper or more flexible mobile data plans. As a consequence, MVNOs are able to improve the utilization of base carriers' infrastructures and gear up benign competition within the telecommunication market [19].

On the other hand, MVNOs have been confronted with multifold technical and non-technical issues that may restrict or impair their development. Technically, some base carriers may deliver MVNO customers' data packets with lower priorities ("MVNO discrimination"), so MVNO customers would suffer from inferior QoS. Non-technically, since MVNOs typically do not have physical service halls for reliable user identity authentication, many cyber fraud gangs purchase MVNO phone cards with fake identities, severely undermining the reputation of MVNOs [20]. At the moment, considerable opportunities and challenges co-exist in this promising yet immature area.

Full-Fledged Emulation of Network Devices Networking research is oftentimes considered more difficult to conduct than AI/DB/theory research because new network paradigms, architectures, and algorithms are usually very hard to implement and evaluate convincingly in practice, especially for those small, independent academic groups or individuals. Even when the source code and workloads have been entirely released with regard to a network research, other researchers can still feel incompetent to repeat the experiments or reproduce the results because they do not have the required devices, environments, or platforms.

To address the deficiency, several approaches have been proposed and implemented. The earliest effort can date back to 1989, when Lawrence Berkeley National Laboratory developed the Network Simulator (NS-1) to help analyze the performance of a network in an abstract manner. The simulation focuses on the network topology, mathematical models of network devices, and node/link property configurations; obviously, it is highly simplistic and sometimes deviates greatly from real-world situations. Although quite a few features were added in the subsequent versions (NS-2 and NS-3), NS-x remains an attribute-based, mostly theoretical system.

Seeking for a more realistic approach, Larry Peterson and David Culler initiated the PlanetLab project in 2002, which manages 1000+ geo-distributed computers contributed by 500+ participants to form a global, shared testbed for network research. Each research project was allocated with a "slice" of PlanetLab, i.e., virtual machine (VM) access to a subset of the 1000+ nodes. However, the VM functionality in PlanetLab is rather weak and implicit. Hence, when powerful and versatile VMs became available in public clouds, the significance of PlanetLab became trivial and was shut down in May 2020.

Although cloud computing can help researchers emulate many aspects of realistic networks (in particular the wired networks), mobile network emulation is rarely and poorly supported at present since cloud platforms are all made up of stationary servers. To this end, full-fledged emulation of mobile devices is worth paying special attention to. Apart from the QEMU-based HoneyCloud system described in the previous chapter, we have recently built the VirtualBox-based APIChecker [21] and OverlayChecker [22] systems for mobile malware analysis, as well as devised the Direct Android Emulation [23] technique to enable smooth mobile gaming on x86 Windows PCs. As a matter of fact, we are integrating a variety of advanced virtualization technologies into full-fledged mobile emulation, so as to make it efficient, compatible, and secure at the same time.

References

1. Adhikari V, Guo Y, Hao F, Hilt V, Zhang ZL (2012) A tale of three CDNs: an active measurement study of Hulu and its CDNs. In: Proceedings of the 15th IEEE global internet symposium, pp 7–12
2. Adhikari V, Guo Y, Hao F, Varvello M, Hilt V, Steiner M, Zhang ZL (2012) Unreeling Netflix: understanding and improving multi-CDN movie delivery. In: Proceedings of the 31st IEEE international conference on computer communications (INFOCOM), pp 1620–1628
3. Wang M, Jayaraman PP, Ranjan R, Mitra K, Zhang M, Li E, et al. (2015) An overview of cloud based content delivery networks: research dimensions and state-of-the-art. Trans Large Scale Data Knowledge Centered Syst, 131–158
4. XY-CDN http://xycdn.com
5. Xunlei Red home router. http://red.xunlei.com
6. Ongaro D, Rumble SM, Stutsman R, Ousterhout J, Rosenblum M (2011) Fast crash recovery in RAMCloud. In: Proceedings of the 23rd ACM symposium on operating systems principles (SOSP), pp 29–41
7. Mitchell C, Geng Y, Li J (2013) Using one-sided RDMA reads to build a fast, CPU-efficient key-value store. In: Proceedings of the USENIX annual technical conference (ATC), pp 103–114
8. Dragojević A, Narayanan D, Nightingale EB, Renzelmann M, Shamis A, Badam A, Castro M (2015) No compromises: distributed transactions with consistency, availability, and performance. In: Proceedings of the 25th ACM symposium on operating systems principles (SOSP), pp 54–70
9. Kalia A, Kaminsky M, Andersen DG (2016) FaSST: Fast, scalable and simple distributed transactions with two-sided RDMA datagram RPCs. In: Proceedings of the 12th USENIX symposium on operating systems design and implementation (OSDI), pp 185–201
10. Guo C, Wu H, Deng Z, Soni G, Ye J, Padhye J, Lipshteyn M (2016) RDMA over commodity Ethernet at scale. In: Proceedings of the ACM SIGCOMM conference, pp. 202–215
11. Zhu Y, Eran H, Firestone D, Guo C, Lipshteyn M, Liron Y, et al. (2015) Congestion control for large-scale RDMA deployments. In: Proceedings of the ACM SIGCOMM conference, pp 523–536
12. Koch HJ, Gmb HL (2011) Userspace I/O drivers in a realtime context. In: Proceedings of the 13th realtime Linux workshop
13. Yang Z, Harris JR, Walker B, Verkamp D, Liu C, Chang C, et al. (2017) SPDK: A development kit to build high performance storage applications. In: Proceedings of the IEEE international conference on cloud computing technology and science (CloudCom), pp 154–161
14. Jacobson V, Smetters DK, Thornton JD, Plass MF, Briggs NH, Braynard RL (2009) Networking named content. In: Proceedings of the 5th ACM international conference on emerging networking experiments and technologies (CoNEXT), pp 1–12

15. McKeown N, Anderson T, Balakrishnan H, Parulkar G, Peterson L, Rexford J, Shenker S, Turner J (2008) OpenFlow: enabling innovation in campus networks. ACM SIGCOMM Comput Commun Rev (CCR) 38(2):69–74

16. Li Z, Jin C, Xu T, Wilson C, Liu Y, Cheng L, Liu Y, Dai Y, Zhang ZL (2014) Towards network-level efficiency for cloud storage services. In: Proceedings of the 14th ACM internet measurement conference (IMC), pp 115–128

17. Li Z, Wilson C, Jiang Z, Liu Y, Zhao B, Jin C, Zhang ZL, Dai Y (2013) Efficient batched synchronization in dropbox-like cloud storage services. In: Proceedings of the 14th ACM/IFIP/USENIX international middleware conference (Middleware), pp 307–327. Springer

18. Li Z, Zhang Y, Liu Y, Xu T, Zhai E, Liu Y, Ma X, Li Z (2019) A quantitative and comparative study of network-level efficiency for cloud storage services. ACM Trans Model Perform Eval Comput Syst (TOMPECS) 4(1):1–32

19. Xiao A, Liu Y, Li Y, Qian F, Li Z, Bai S, Liu Y, Xu T, Xin X (2019) An in-depth study of commercial MVNO: measurement and optimization. In: Proceedings of the 17th ACM annual international conference on mobile systems, applications, and services (MobiSys), pp 457–468

20. Li Y, Zheng J, Li Z, Liu Y, Qian F, Bai S, Liu Y, Xin X (2020) Understanding the ecosystem and addressing the fundamental concerns of commercial MVNO. IEEE/ACM Trans Networking 28(3):1364–1377

21. Gong L, Li Z, Qian F, Zhang Z, Chen QA, Qian Z, Lin H, Liu Y (2020) Experiences of landing machine learning onto market-scale mobile malware detection. In: Proceedings of the 15th European conference on computer systems (EuroSys), pp 1–14

22. Yan Y, Li Z, Chen QA, Wilson C, Xu T, Zhai E, Li Y, Liu Y (2019) Understanding and detecting overlay-based Android malware at market scales. In: Proceedings of the 17th ACM annual international conference on mobile systems, applications, and services (MobiSys), pp 168–179

23. Yang Q, Li Z, Liu Y, Long H, Huang Y, He J, Xu T, Zhai E (2019) Mobile gaming on personal computers with direct Android emulation. In: Proceedings of the 25th ACM annual international conference on mobile computing and networking (MobiCom), pp 1–15

Printed in the United States
by Baker & Taylor Publisher Services